Generative AI for Sign Language Recognition and Translation

Other related titles:

You may also like

- PBPC084 | Kolekar | Generative AI for Video Surveillance Applications (Multimedia book series) | 2025
- PBPC082 | Dalal | Generative AI in Multimedia Content Processing: Security and privacy perspectives (Multimedia book series) | 2024
- PBPC080 | Karna | Prompt Engineering Techniques for Optimizing Generative AI | 2024
- PBPC0762 | Ramamurthy | Generative AI Unleashed: Advancements, transformative applications, and future frontiers | 2025

We also publish a wide range of books on the following topics:
Computing and Networks
Control, Robotics, and Sensors
Electrical Regulations
Electromagnetics and Radar
Energy Engineering
Healthcare Technologies
History and Management of Technology
IET Codes and Guidance
Materials, Circuits, and Devices
Model Forms
Nanomaterials and Nanotechnologies
Optics, Photonics, and Lasers
Production, Design, and Manufacturing
Security
Telecommunications
Transportation

All books are available in print via https://shop.theiet.org or as eBooks via our Digital Library https://digital-library.theiet.org.

IET COMPUTING 078

Generative AI for Sign Language Recognition and Translation

Elakkiya Rajasekar

The Institution of Engineering and Technology

About the IET

This book is published by the Institution of Engineering and Technology (The IET).

We inspire, inform, and influence the global engineering community to engineer a better world. As a diverse home across engineering and technology, we share knowledge that helps make better sense of the world, to accelerate innovation and solve the global challenges that matter.

The IET is a not-for-profit organization. The surplus we make from our books is used to support activities and products for the engineering community and promote the positive role of science, engineering, and technology in the world. This includes education resources and outreach, scholarships and awards, events and courses, publications, professional development and mentoring, and advocacy to governments.

To discover more about the IET, please visit https://www.theiet.org/

About IET books

The IET publishes books across many engineering and technology disciplines. Our authors and editors offer fresh perspectives from universities and industry. Within our subject areas, we have several book series steered by editorial boards made up of leading subject experts.

We peer review each book at the proposal stage to ensure the quality and relevance of our publications.

Get involved

If you are interested in becoming an author, editor, series advisor, or peer reviewer, please visit https://www.theiet.org/publishing/publishing-with-iet-books/ or contact author_support@theiet.org.

Discovering our electronic content

All of our books are available online via the IET's Digital Library. Our Digital Library is the home of technical documents, eBooks, conference publications, real-life case studies, and journal articles. To find out more, please visit https://digital-library.theiet.org.

In collaboration with the United Nations and the International Publishers Association, the IET is a Signatory member of the SDG Publishers Compact. The Compact aims to accelerate progress to achieve the Sustainable Development Goals (SDGs) by 2030. Signatories aspire to develop sustainable practices and act as champions of the SDGs during the Decade of Action (2020–2030), publishing books and journals that will help inform, develop, and inspire action in that direction.

In line with our sustainable goals, our UK printing partner has FSC accreditation, which is reducing our environmental impact on the planet. We use a print-on-demand model to further reduce our carbon footprint.

British Library Cataloguing in Publication Data

A catalogue record for this product is available from the British Library

ISBN 978-1-83724-142-2 (hardback)
ISBN 978-1-83724-143-9 (PDF)

Typeset in India by MPS Limited

Cover image credit: Yuichiro Chino/Moment via Getty Images

Contents

About the author

Elakkiya Rajasekar is an accomplished researcher, educator, and innovator, currently serving as an Assistant Professor in the Department of Computer Science at the Birla Institute of Technology and Science (BITS), Pilani, Dubai Campus. She earned all her academic degrees from Anna University, Chennai, consistently demonstrating academic excellence. She secured the University First Rank and was awarded a Gold Medal for her exceptional performance during her graduation studies. She completed her bachelor's degree in Computer Science and Engineering (2010), master's degree in Software Engineering (2012), and PhD (2018), with her doctoral research specializing in sign language recognition.

Dr Rajasekar has been recognized among the Top 2% World Scientists by the Stanford-Elsevier global rankings for her significant contributions to artificial intelligence and image processing. Her research has resulted in the publication of over 75 research articles, 6 patents, 6 authored books, and 8 book chapters, with her work cited extensively.

Over her career, Dr Rajasekar has secured 16 extramural-funded projects as principal investigator and co-principal investigator, with grants awarded by prestigious agencies including DST-RFBR (Indo-Russian Joint Collaboration), SERB-SRG, DRDO-iDEX, AICTE-RPS, Royal Society UK-IES, TVS Motors, TVS Credits, and Trajectorie Business Solutions. She has also led bilateral research projects under Indo-Russian and Indo-UK programs, fostering global partnerships in artificial intelligence-driven healthcare and assistive innovations. In addition to her research engagements, Dr Rajasekar actively serves as an AI/ML consultant for industries, delivering several cutting-edge technology projects across diverse sectors.

Dr Rajasekar is the chair of the ACM-W Professional Dubai Chapter and vice president of the ACM Dubai Professional Chapter, both of which are the UAE's first ACM Professional Chapters convened under her leadership. She also serves as the associate head of the Anuradha and Prashanth Palakurthi Centre for Artificial Intelligence Research (APPCAIR) and the chairperson of the Staff Welfare Committee at BITS Pilani Dubai Campus. She has successfully organized and coordinated several international conferences and workshops, including CINS 2023 and 2024 and InterSys 2023, 2024, and 2025.

Her excellence has been acknowledged through numerous accolades, such as the Young Achiever Award (INSc, 2019), the iDEX Challenge Winner Award (DIO-DRDO, 2021), the Rising Star Educator Award (AIMER Society), and recognition as an Intel OneAPI Innovator. She has also been an invited speaker and panellist at over 40 prestigious national and international events.

Dr Rajasekar is a professional member of ACM, ACM-W, IEEE, IEEE Young Professionals, IEEE Women in Engineering, and a lifetime member of the International Association of Engineers. Her research aims to bridge the critical gaps across multidisciplinary fields, integrating computer science, mathematics, engineering, and application domains, with a focus on advancing artificial intelligence and machine learning solutions for real-world impact.

Chapter 1

Introduction: Background and history of sign language translation

Sign languages hold a deep significance for the speech- and hearing-impaired community: a lively culture-bearing language that affords users a rich collection for conveying ideas, emotions, and cultural stories. Sign languages, in contrast to spoken languages, which use auditory modality (sound signal), convey meanings through visual-manual modalities such as hand gestures, facial expressions, and body movements. Consequently, sign language users and those who primarily use spoken languages need to be connected through a specialized sign language translation (SLT) system.

SLT is the process of interpreting spoken or written language into sign language, or vice versa. Human interpreters and automated systems can perform this translation procedure. As more speech- and hearing-impaired people integrate into mainstream education, employment, and social activities, the provision of effective SLT systems has become increasingly important. Automated systems can help overcome the limitations of human interpreters by providing continuous, real-time translation, eliminating the need for an interpreter.

1.1 Historical context

SLT evolved from many forms of communication aids for the deaf that historically served as predecessors. Supporting the efforts of deaf learners and deaf litigants and making the deaf more socially accessible, the earliest forms of SLT relied heavily on human interpreters who relied faithfully on their hands. Even today, SLT and interpreting still require each other. Interpreters, authentically bilingual in spoken languages and signed languages, help deaf and hearing people connect linguistically; without interpreters, our society would be far less accessible to the deaf. Long before the development of SLT, the practice of manually hand-signed interpreting existed. It was also, inevitably, a reason why SLT had to wait, sometimes for centuries, before finding its own voice. Historians document many reasons why relying on human interpreters would, indeed, make signing hard to materialize.

The twentieth century marked the symbolic beginnings of modern efforts at mechanized SLT. While the idea of mechanical recording of sign language was probably around much earlier (such as in the Phonographe Disque Phonographe et

Phonoscope invented by Charles De La Fontaine, first exhibited in 1881), the first modern systems of SLT according to modern understandings of translation emerged after 1900. By today's standards, the first techniques tended to be very crude, employing feeble motion capture systems to analyze sign language or video recordings to capture and play back sign language for later analysis. Hardware limitations, including low-resolution video, quantization errors, and limited processing power, often constrained these early techniques, as did the relative inexperience of the researchers utilizing these new systems. The designs of the first systems were often, no doubt, quite inventive, but they were also frequently clumsy. They exhibited all of the hallmarks of the early days of a new technological age. Early mechanized takeovers of complex and challenging human skills faced a series of reductions and accuracy trade-offs, offering only a slight improvement over what the human eye could perceive. In many ways, they lacked the level of sophistication and dynamism seen in the spontaneous performances of signers that accompanied them.

For example, during the 1960s and 1970s, researchers began to investigate using motion capture technologies to collect and process sign language gestures. Such systems typically use mechanical sensors placed on the body to track movement, but these arrangements are unwieldy and uncomfortable for users. Video-based approaches arose later, providing a less intrusive way to collect data on sign language. Early systems presented a low resolution and lacked corresponding processing capabilities, making it difficult to recognize and analyze signs.

In the late twentieth and early twenty-first centuries, computer vision and machine learning techniques emerged, leading to the development of more sophisticated systems capable of handling complex gestures. Computer vision efforts specifically focused on the technical aspects of extracting and analysing minute aspects of SLT, such as hand movements, facial expressions, and body postures, making automatic SLT achievable.

One such study, for instance, dates back to the early 2000s. In this study, researchers trained machine learning algorithms to identify patterns in data collected from sign language video recordings. Learned on a large database of existing data, the models could make predictions about the relative meaning of different gestures based on patterns they automatically detected. Later in the decade, the subfield of machine learning known as deep learning began making significant strides in enabling much greater accuracy and performance. Deep learning systems, such as the class of models known as convolutional neural networks (CNNs), are ideally suited to recognition problems involving images or video.

The integration of artificial intelligence (AI) has also accelerated the pace of development in this area, with real-time, automatic SLT systems potentially becoming a reality. AI could use large datasets and complicated algorithms to learn patterns in sign language data. They could then identify specific signs and generate their translations. The potential for a more effective and efficient translation system is significant, as AI systems can handle numerous signs per second and accurately translate each one. Figure 1.1 illustrates the main milestones in the history of SLT from the nineteenth century to the twenty-first century, when interpreters and AI technology were successfully used.

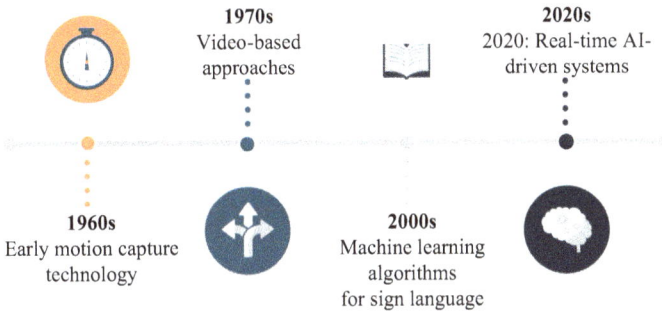

Figure 1.1 Historical timeline of sign language translation

1.2 Modern advances

Modern systems make use of improved AI and machine learning, making it possible to use a wider range of advanced techniques such as deep neural networks and reinforcement learning to enhance accuracy and speed. For example, SLT systems are being designed to work with video input from ordinary webcams or mobile phones that can be held close to a signer's hands and arms. These systems use computer-vision algorithms to track hands, body movements, and facial expressions in real time and generate synthesized spoken or written outputs matching the sign-language input.

For one, very large, annotated sign language datasets became available, and second, researchers began pulling together datasets of sign languages and sharing them with each other. Currently, researchers have access to annotated data sets, including millions of signs produced by hundreds of signers across years of fieldwork. Many efforts to share sign data are collaborative projects between researchers, universities, and sign language communities. Some have even been built by teams documenting sign languages that are used by Indigenous communities. This implies that the datasets include not only a variety of signing styles but also the contexts and regional dialectal variations necessary for training models to effectively cater to numerous users across various scenarios.

1.3 Terminology in sign language and artificial intelligence

1.3.1 Sign language terminology

I'm a fan of sign language, which raises an important question for those who don't know the lingo: how would you translate it? Here are some fundamental terms to get you started and the same is illustrated in Figure 1.2:

- **Signs:** The smallest units of sign language – the signs have the same role that words play in spoken languages (thus, the name sign language). The signs are

Signs
Handshapes
Movements
Locations

Non-Manual Signals
Facial Expressions
Head Movements
Body Postures

Sign Language Terminology

Finger Spelling
Handshapes for Letters
Alphabets
Numbers

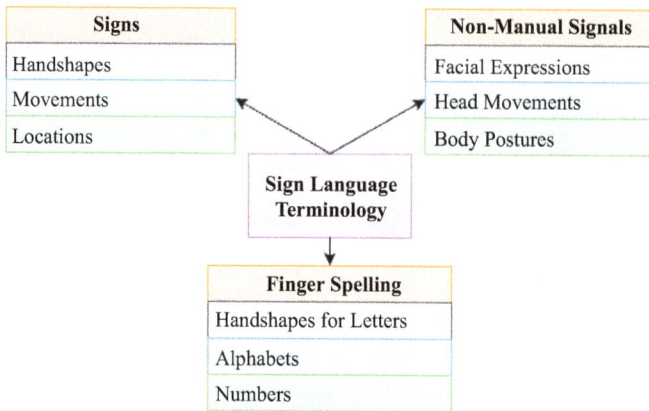

Figure 1.2   Basic terminology in sign language translation

made up of discrete handshapes, locations, and movements. Each sign language has its own set of signs, which can be quite different from each other.

- **Non-manual signs:** Facial expression, head movements, body movements that accompany manual 'words' to provide additional meaning. Non-manual signs are as important to sign language as words are to spoken languages. Without them, the meaning becomes contextless and irrelevant.
- **Fingerspelling:** Using handshapes representing words one letter at a time that correspond to individual letters of the alphabet. This is often used to spell out names, technical terms, and otherwise unknown/uncommon words that do not have established signs.
- **Grammar and syntax**: The rules about the order and structuring of signs within a sentence. All languages have the same grammatical categories; however, it's crucial to understand that the grammatical rules in sign languages can differ significantly from those in spoken languages, necessitating a comprehensive understanding for accurate translation.

1.3.2   AI terminology

Gain a fundamental understanding of the technological aspects by familiarizing yourself with some key terms in the field of AI.

- **AI:** refers to the capacity of machines, particularly computers, to replicate human cognitive processes. AI is generally the umbrella term for multiple subfields, especially machine learning and deep learning. We design an AI system to perform tasks typically associated with the human mind, such as data analysis, visual perception, speech recognition, decision-making, self-teaching, learning, and reasoning.
- **Machine learning (ML):** a part of AI that develops predictions or decisions based on data. Exposure to more data over time enhances the performance of

ML algorithms. We can train ML algorithms to interpret a video input as a sign.

- **Deep learning (DL):** A subfield of machine learning that makes use of multi-layer neural networks (hence 'deep') to analyze high-dimensional data, especially sequences of images and videos. DL algorithms can automatically learn relevant features from unstructured raw data. This makes them particularly well-suited for problems such as gesture recognition.

- **Generative models:** a class of AI models that can produce new data based on the data with which they have been trained. A generative model for sign-language translation, for example, could synthesize realistic sign-language gestures from spoken or written language inputs, recreating the signs that the model has learned but in new combinations tailored to a particular input. The more adaptable a system becomes, the less we may be able to predict its behaviour. The goal of explicitly modelling human sign languages goes beyond aesthetics. It drives the system to model the inputs more precisely.

- **Computer vision (CV):** the branch of AI that lets computers analyze and interpret visual information in the world. Using CV techniques, an AI app for SLT can identify handshapes and facial expressions from a video input, subsequently classifying each one into a specific category (object detection). We use techniques like image segmentation or motion tracking to determine when to segment the input into an independent entity, such as a new word.

- **Natural language processing (NLP):** A branch of AI concerned with the relationships between computers and human language. NLP is concerned with analysing human language as well as methods for helping computers simulate natural human speech. This field holds particular importance in converting text or voice to sign and vice versa, utilizing techniques such as tokenization, syntactic parsing, and sentiment analysis.

- **Reinforcement learning (RL):** A machine learning paradigm where an agent acts in an environment to maximize cumulative reward in order to learn how to make decisions. In a robot, RL may improve reading and translating sign language for real-time performance and user satisfaction.

1.4 Country-wise sign languages and their differences

1.4.1 Overview of different sign languages

Although they are not mutually intelligible, sign languages are just like spoken languages: they vary by country and in very different ways worldwide. There can actually be a tremendous deal of variation from one country to another, or even a region within a country. Here are several examples of different sign languages and it is shown in Figure 1.3:

- **American sign language (ASL):** primarily used in the United States and parts of Canada, utilizing signals that have their own unique grammar and syntax. There is quite a bit of expression, as well as non-manual signals.

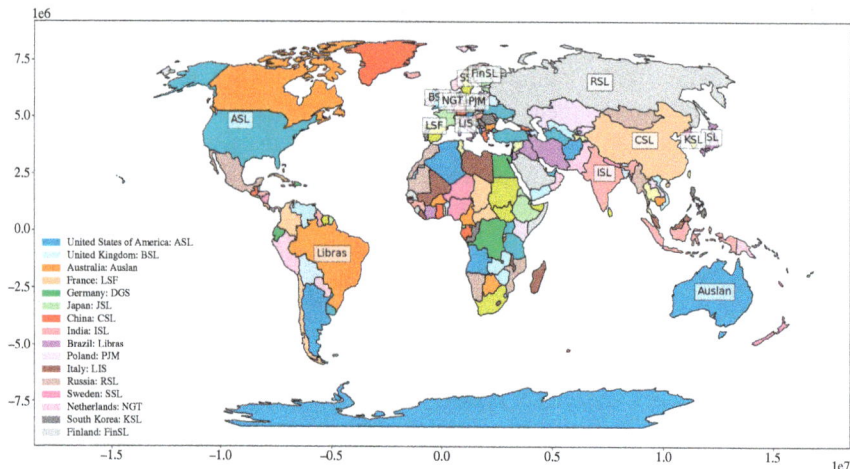

Figure 1.3   Sign language distribution: country-wise illustration

- **British sign language (BSL):** the language that is predominantly used in the southeastern half of Britain. The differences between BSL and ASL are enormous: BSL uses a two-handed fingerspelling system, whereas ASL uses only one hand.
- **Australian sign language (Auslan):** is a widely used language throughout Australia. It incorporates unique features derived from BSL, as well as those specific to the language and its lexicon.
- **French sign language (LSF – Langue des Signes Française):** one of the world's oldest sign languages, it served as the model for many other sign languages, including ASL.
- **German sign language (DGS – Deutsche Gebärdensprache):** DGS is used in Germany. Unlike other sign languages, DGS has its own grammar and vocabulary.
- **Japanese sign language (JSL 日本Preferences 占拝):** this is found in Japan, and which differs from both ASL and BSL in its unique signing and grammatical styles.
- **Chinese sign language (CSL):** used in China, CSL contains local differences and is influenced by Chinese culture and topology.
- **Indian sign language (ISL):** used in India, it varies regionally and includes signs from the linguistic diversity of the country.
- **Arabic sign language (ArSL):** used by deaf signers in all the Arab countries, ArSL has regional variations that reflect the spoken dialects of the Arab world.
- **Spanish sign language (LSE – Lengua de Signos Española):** This is the sign language used in Spain and has a grammar of its own, not related to the Latin ASLs.

- **Brazilian sign language (Libras):** used in Brazil, also with a grammar and vocabulary specific to the language (it is based on Portuguese).
- **Polish sign language (PJM – Polski Język Migowy):** PJM is used in Poland and has its own grammar and vocabulary.
- **Italian sign language (LIS – Lingua dei Segni Italiana):** used in Italy, with its own vocabulary and grammar.
- **Russian sign language (RSL):** uses signs that are unique to Russia, rather than relying on signs from another language. The grammar reflects the Russian language and culture.
- **Swedish sign language (SSL – Svenskt Teckenspråk):** used in Sweden, it is a language distinctly different from the other Scandinavian sign languages.
- **Nederlandse Gebarentaal, or Dutch sign language (NGT):** is an independent language, complete with its own grammar, expletives, and vocabulary used in the Netherlands.
- **Korean sign language (KSL):** used widely in South Korea. The order of signs varies among signed languages.
- **Finnish sign language (FinSl):** Finland's natively developed sign language.
- **Other Nordic sign languages:** a catch-all category for the independently developed, native sign languages of Denmark, Norway, and Sweden. It's important to note that Danish, Norwegian, and Swedish are related languages, so the corresponding sign languages also share a lot of similarities.

1.4.2   Differences between sign languages

There are several ways in which sign languages can differ from each other, including:

- **Grammar and syntax:** the internal organization of all languages involves the arrangement of sentences, word order, and grammatical markers, such as the topic-comment structure in ASL or the subject-object-verb order in BSL.
- **Lexicon:** the vocabulary of signs can vary tremendously. The sign for 'duck' in one language might have nothing to do with the concept in another, and it might not even mean 'duck' at all; it might instead mean 'elbow' or 'hammer'.
- **Fingerspelling:** the fingerspelling alphabet [just like the manual alphabets used in BSL] is not universal; ASL uses a one-handed fingerspelling system, while BSL uses two hands.
- **Non-manual signals:** different people can employ facial expressions, head movements, and body posture in different ways. Some sign languages use more non-manual signals to convey meaning.
- **Cultural influences:** the culture of the signing community has a marked impact on the sign language. Nearby spoken languages cross-contaminate this, impacting everything from local customs to social norms.

For example, while British and American sign language (BSL and ASL, respectively) both rely on gestural systems used by deaf communities in medieval Great Britain, they diverged over time because British and American signers

Table 1.1   Difference between country-wise sign language

Feature	ASL	BSL	DGS	JSL	ISL	Libras	PJM
Grammar	Topic-comment	Subject-object-verb	Subject-object-verb	Topic-comment	Subject-object-verb	Subject-verb-object	Subject-object-verb
Syntax	Subject-verb-object	Different structure	Different structure	Different structure	Subject-verb-object	Subject-object-verb	Different structure
Finger-spelling	One-handed	Two-handed	One-handed	One-handed	Two-handed	One-handed	One-handed
Lexicon	Large, influenced by English	Large, influenced by English	Diverse, unique signs	Rich, unique signs	Diverse, influenced by regional languages	Large, unique signs	Rich, unique signs

evolved apart, unlike speakers of English or French and some of the differences are shown in Table 1.1. Moreover, not all varieties of ASL are mutually intelligible. For example, a fluent user of ASL would have no difficulty communicating with people from other countries using sign language, whereas someone fluent in ASL would likely not understand BSL without formal instruction. These basic principles of language evolution have also been applied to other signed languages. In a single country, sign languages can even develop dialects in line with spoken native languages. Regional dialects of ISL, for example, can vary considerably from one region of India to the next, reflecting regional spoken tongues and cultures.

1.4.3   Sign language families

Some sign languages, such as the French sign language family, which encompasses ASL, LSF, and several other sign languages across Europe and the United States, share a common history due to their close intertwining. As they were (eventually) separated, they evolved in different directions. Other quasi-families include the BSL family, which includes Auslan and New Zealand sign language (NZSL).

1.5   Processes in SLT

The translation pipeline of the SLT involves several processes to accurately and effectively translate sign language to spoken language, or vice versa. The main processes include sign language recognition (SLR), sign language generation or synthesis, and related technologies. Here is an overview of each of them.

1.5.1   Sign language recognition

SLR includes recognizing or capturing signs from an image or video stream, tracking hand location from non-rigid deformable 2D contours, and retrieving words from linguistic resources. This process comprised several discrete steps.

- **Data acquisition:** obtaining video or motion capture recordings of sign language: huge, annotated datasets are needed for training models.
- **Noise handling:** separating sign language from distracting background noise is complex, given how close signs often are to the body.
- **Preprocessing:** improving the accuracy of the collected data by increasing contrast and/or normalizing and augmenting the size of data (e.g., resizing video frames from their native resolution to 256×256 and removing background noise from speech recordings).
- **Feature extraction:** identifying and extracting salient features from the raw data, for example, the position and shape of hands, the movements of eyes – techniques such as CNNs are often used to achieve this.
- **Classification:** transforming the features into rules (i.e., classifying them according to certain signs); models for classification include deep neural networks (DNNs), RNNs, and so on.
- **Post-processing:** tweaking back the recognized signs to generally remove the error and make them more foolproof and accurate. This would involve smoothing out some recognition errors and incorporating context.

1.5.2   *Sign language synthesis or production*

Sign language synthesis (SLS) can be broken down into four expert system modules: text analysis, sign generation, animation and rendering, and synchronization. A verbal or written text serves as the initial input for SLS, and you must decide which of four conversation types to use based on the original text and any additional information you have. Specific utterances trigger actions involving particular gestures and marks that build up into sentences. By creating a large database of gestures, marks, and utterances, SLS can produce a custom sign language that matches an input of text.

- **Text analysis:** signs are appropriate; these days, we might use NLP to analyze syntax, context, and pragmatic meaning.
- **Sign generation:** creating visual samples of the signs, for example, with the avatar and/or with video synthesis. We can generate the signs either serially, by playing a collection of pre-recorded video segments, or synchronically, as a shifting visual texture or tapestry of computer graphics, to prevent brittle copying.
- **Animation and rendering:** making the signs come alive. Animated motion gives the generated signs a fluidity and movement that make them seem authentic. Keyframe animation techniques and motion capture (in which a physical actor's movements are captured as data for a digital avatar) can create realistic sign-language animations.
- ***Synchronization***: so that the generated signs move in time with whatever audio or text is given to them, including timing the signs down to the nearest word with the given speech or text.

1.5.3   Related processes

Besides recognition and synthesis, several related processes are also vital for SLT:

- **Gesture recognition:** discriminating between the same signs that are pointed to, nude or shaken at, or inclined, shaken at, or rotated to indicate negation or affirmation (e.g., using a nod or shake of the head).
- **Facial expression analysis:** processing non-manual signals that communicate emotion, stress, irony, and so forth. This entails detecting and interpreting changes in facial features such as eyebrow curvature, eye size and configuration, and mouth openings and closures.
- **Context:** try to understand the context; this will help you refine the translation. This applies to both situations-conversations and texts-where context is relevant. Context is the larger picture of the interaction or text surrounding the word you translate.
- **User feedback and adaptation:** obtaining user feedback to improve the translation system adaptively on the fly by adapting to the user's signing style and preferences.

1.6   Challenges in SLT

1.6.1   Linguistic diversity

The linguistic diversity of sign languages presents many of the greatest challenges to developing translation systems. Due to a lack of written, phonetic forms and often only sketchy documentation, sign languages, largely oral traditions with no aural component, are typically less well-documented than spoken languages. Each of the thousands of sign languages worldwide – ASL, BSL, and its many dialects, as well as more than 200 other first-language sign languages across the United States, the United Kingdom, Europe, India, sub-Saharan Africa, and many other locations – has its own unique grammar and syntax, sometimes with stark differences within the same language and country.

While there are some similarities between ASL and BSL, and skilled signers of one can reasonably understand those of the other, there are many more differences. Common words and phrases have different signs, and grammar is often very different. Without major adjustments, a translation system for ASL would not work well for BSL. Any universal translation system must also account for the numerous regional dialects in each language.

1.6.2   Gesture recognition

The huge variety of gestures in sign language constitutes a key technical challenge. As with speech, the word-like formations of signs, along with synchronic and diachronic variants and expressive poses, represent a challenge for any recognition system. The user and reference model exhibit joint, cone, and cylinder similarity. Gesture recognition is a modality-specific issue that arises in the automatic processing of sign languages. We must track gestures using multiple coordinates on the hands and body, considering the temporal patterning and speed of gestures, and distinguishing between lexically ambiguous signs. According to Tim Woods of the University of Maryland, automatic gesture recognition technology would facilitate the retrieval of video documents in sign language, saving time for many deaf people.

Modern gesture-recognition systems use advanced computer vision techniques such as CNNs and recurrent neural networks (RNNs), which process a video input to identify gesture content. Large-scale annotated databases of videos from sign language corpora train the models, teaching them to feature the properties of various signs. However, achieving high, robust recognition performance under real-life conditions remains a challenge.

1.6.3   Real-time processing

Real-time processing is critical for successful SLT, particularly conversational translation. The algorithms must be highly efficient, and the hardware must be fast enough to limit latency and enable high accuracy over the long durations or variable rates that frequently occur in conversational sign language. Optimal real-time processing requires system design considerations for both the recognition and generation platforms. Real-time processing is particularly interesting because it requires speed and consistency in processing inputs at the same time.

Real-time SLT systems must cope with video at a high frame rate, track a number of points on the hands and face, and produce translations within tight latency constraints. Achieving this requires many optimized algorithms and hardware accelerators (e.g., Graphics processing units (GPUs), Tensor processing units (TPUs)).

1.6.4   Data scarcity

They begin with a shortage of high-quality, annotated sign language datasets; it is very expensive and time-consuming to collect and annotate data in sign languages, which requires being fluent in sign language as well as in data annotation. Due to the lack of representative datasets, it is not guaranteed that translated systems will work for sign languages that are not represented in their training corpora. So, there is a need to tackle this lack of data by building large, quality-controlled datasets that represent the entire range of signing variants and contexts.

Building these datasets requires collaboration between researchers, universities, and sign language communities. For example, at Gallaudet University in Washington, DC, the Sign Language Linguistics Laboratory has built and released multiple sign language corpora annotated at different linguistic levels, which can be useful to train and test translation models in sign language. Other approaches involve crowdsourcing to collect and annotate data in sign language from a variety of population groups.

1.6.5   Variability in signing styles

Different signers have different styles, which depend on factors such as where they learned sign language, how old they are, or which signing classmate they hang out with. If translation systems aren't flexible enough to work with this diversity, then they will only convert a limited range of varieties of sign language. With sign languages' broad expression and endless variation, it's important that translation systems can handle different signing speeds, styles, and accents. Only with this versatility will translation systems be easy to use and actually adopted.

Approaches include transfer learning, where a pre-trained model is tweaked on a smaller, task-specific dataset to accommodate new signing styles (without having to re-train on the original dataset from scratch), as well as data-augmentation techniques, such as applying transformations to the input videos (such as rotation, scaling, and noise).

1.7   Introduction to AI-driven SLT

1.7.1   The role of AI in SLT

Artificial intelligence, specifically machine learning and deep learning, drives this forward. Machine learning and deep learning systems utilize large sets of data tied to complex algorithms that learn to find patterns in sign language data – if there is data. These systems can analyze video data input for signs, interpret the language, and translate out into speech or text.

For example, an ASL sign typically involves a particular configuration of the hand (e.g., the four fingers extended, and the thumb distended), a specific movement path (e.g., jumping or flourishing outward on a diagonal, and back in), and often some facial expressions (e.g., a tongue gesture). A deep learning model trained on a large dataset of video of ASL signs would come to emit the correct translation of an ASL signature in real-time if presented with a video of the signs being performed For an ASL-to-text sign-language translation system to work, the AI must be capable of quickly recognizing specific handshapes, movement paths and expressive facial movements; understanding how they interact and cluster to form signs; and converting that information into text. But here's the twist: exposed to more data, these systems can steadily improve.

1.7.2   Key components of AI-driven translation systems

AI-driven SLT systems typically consist of several key components:

- **Data collection and preprocessing:** data collection and preprocessing refer to collecting and preparing the datasets (i.e., sign language) required for training the model. That is, finding video recordings of sign language that are to be used for training, manually annotating the data with labels (see below), and preprocessing the data so that it is of good quality, uniform and can be easily processed. Examples of preprocessing are shrinking and normalizing the frames of the video to a standard size, deleting background noise and enhancing the contrast and brightness of the image.
- **Feature labelling:** this involves extracting features from sign language data. The goal here is to identify the different sign language movements to be used

as input for the classifiers. To do this, we need algorithms that can learn and recognize features within the data. For example, to convert language into letters using speech recognition, the speech recognition model needs to be trained with thousands of different speech features.

- **Model training:** training a machine learning model to identify (classify) sign language gestures from images as well as training a machine learning model to generate the gestures. It would involve training a neural network (a specific class of machine learning models) on an annotated dataset while optimizing the parameters of the model and evaluating the model's performance. Deep learning models, in particular, take a very long time to train and require a lot of computational power, and even more time to tune the hyperparameters of the model (the learning rate, size of the minibatch, network architecture, and so on).
- **Real-time processing:** the system keeps up with real-time processing where latency and accuracy are important. In addition to low latency, real-time processing requires low power but high throughput, and should include learning in order to adapt to new data. Efficient algorithms combined with suitable hardware can help handle continuous input and near-instantaneous response. Techniques such as model compression, quantization, and hardware acceleration can all help lead to a system with lower memory requirements.
- **User interface:** designing the interface where human users interact with the translation system. This interface should be usable, accessible, and provide users with feedback regarding what is going on when they use it. For example, this should accurately depict what signs the system visualizes, or provide real-time translations accompanied by options to alter settings and preferences.

1.7.3   Current state of AI-driven SLT

Although research and development are moving forward at a brisk pace, it is still too early to say that AI-based computer systems for SLT have arrived. What we can say is that there are several systems out there that are making good progress in a very challenging area – an area that remains in its infancy both in terms of technology and progress, and potentially even ethics. There is a long way to go, but it is clear that continued research and dedicated effort will further improve the capacity of these systems, making them more robust, accurate and useful for many individuals and communities. Not least, advancements in the broader field of AI – such as transfer learning, domain adaptation and multimodal learning – promise to make this work even more effective in the future.

For example, multimodal learning is tested, which trains models to process multiple modalities, including video, audio and text, simultaneously; this supports more robust behaviour of the translation system by exploiting complementary cues. We can also use domain adaptation to adapt models trained on an input language, such as ASL, to another sign language with less supervised data, thus avoiding retaining modellers.

1.8   Future directions

There are promising research avenues open on the automated translation of sign language to speech through AI, and some of the adventures in research and development in this area are as follows:

- **Improved gesture recognition:** making gesture recognition algorithms more accurate and fault-tolerant when facing a larger variation in signing styles and circumstances as well as differing cultural and language backgrounds. This involves developing new architectures and techniques, such as better handling the temporal dynamics of gestures and adaptive context models, for example.
- **Customized translation systems:** developing procedures for creating personalized translation systems, essentially for each user, while taking into account variations in their signing styles, and – if possible – their own personal preferences. An obvious goal would be to create more personalized (and therefore more accurate) translations. Achieving this could potentially involve the use of user-specific models or learning systems that (automatically) adapt to the user in real time – making data-driven improvements that account for quality feedback provided by the user.
- **Integration with other technologies:** consider how each such system has the potential to communicate in conjunction with other assistive technologies, such as hearing aids and cochlear implants, as well as augmented reality devices that superimpose the moving mouths of signers on real-world scenes. This could ultimately improve communication for deaf and hard-of-hearing individuals.
- **Multi-linguistic/cross-linguistic models:** building models capable of operating on several sign languages and switching back and forth between them – a key step toward universal SLT systems that can be used by sign language communities worldwide.
- **Ethical and inclusive AI:** making sure that systems for AI-powered SLT are properly and inclusively developed in ways that take into account privacy, possible bias and cultural context to provide services in the best way possible. This will require engagement with sign language users and communities in the co-design process, as well as an examination of the possible ethical problems associated with these implementations.

Exercises

(I) Multiple choice questions
  1. Which of the following is NOT a part of the sign language recognition process?
     (A) Data acquisition
     (B) Preprocessing

(C) Text generation

(D) Feature extraction

2. Which sign language is used primarily in the United States and parts of Canada?

   (A) British sign language (BSL)

   (B) Australian sign language (Auslan)

   (C) American sign language (ASL)

   (D) French sign language (LSF)

3. What is the role of computer vision (CV) in sign language translation?

   (A) To analyze and understand spoken language

   (B) To generate new signs from text input

   (C) To recognize hand shapes, movements, and facial expressions from video input

   (D) To train machine learning models

4. Which of the following is a challenge specific to sign language translation systems?

   (A) Lack of internet access

   (B) Variability in signing styles

   (C) High electricity consumption

   (D) Limited spoken language vocabulary

5. Reinforcement learning (RL) in the context of sign language translation is used to:

   (A) Simulate human facial expressions

   (B) Maximize cumulative reward by making decisions in an environment

   (C) Translate written text into speech

   (D) Collect sign language data from users

(II) **Short answer questions**

   1. What is the primary purpose of sign language translation?

   2. List three key components of AI-driven sign language translation systems.

   3. Explain the term 'non-manual signals' in the context of sign language.

   4. What are the challenges associated with real-time sign language processing?

   5. How does cultural influence shape sign languages?

(III) **Discussion Questions**

   1. Discuss the evolution of sign language translation over time by emphasizing key technologies with which this has become more and more possible. Why has technology made sign-language translation a viable option? What are the implications of this for the speech and hearing-impaired populations?

   2. Compare and contrast the use of American sign language (ASL) and British sign language (BSL). What are the main differences between their grammar, syntax, and non-manual features?

3. Perhaps you are familiar with 'sign language'. In the absence of a spoken system, how will translation occur?
4. Identify and describe possible challenges of creating automated real-time sign language translation. What are the current limits of this technology and how could it be improved in the future?
5. Think about the design choices and ethical implications of the use of AI in sign-language translation systems. How can users be involved sensitively and inclusively in design?

(IV) **Practical Exercise**
1. Sign language recognition simulation: choose a short video of someone uttering a simple sentence in a sign language such as American sign language (ASL). Manually annotate the signs and non-manual signals that you can see in the video. If you have had time, compare those annotations against any that were produced by an AI-based sign language recognition system. Discuss the discrepancies and reasons for these differences.

Further readings

[1] Yule G. *The Study of Language*. Cambridge University Press; 2022.
[2] Müller AC, Guido S. *Introduction to Machine Learning with Python: A Guide for Data Scientists*. O'Reilly Media, Inc.; 2016.
[3] Goodfellow I, Bengio Y, Courville A. *Deep Learning*. MIT Press; 2016.
[4] Núñez-Marcos A, Perez-de-Viñaspre O, Labaka G. "A survey on sign language machine translation". *Expert Systems with Applications*. 2023; 213:118993.
[5] Tursyn MS. "Role of artificial intelligence in sign language recognition". *Вестник науки*. 2024;4(5 (74)):1329–41.

Chapter 2
Fundamentals of sign language linguistics

2.1   Introduction to sign language linguistics

Sign language linguistics is the scientific study of the structure, function, and use of sign languages. Sign languages are natural languages that are based on visual-manual modalities (rather than on the auditory-vocal modalities of spoken languages). Sign languages combine hand movements, facial expressions, and body postures in order to convey meaning. Every sign language, just like spoken languages, has its own grammar, syntax, and lexicon. Sign language linguistics includes a number of sub-disciplines, including phonology (the study of the smallest units of meaning), morphology (the structure and formation of signs), syntax (the organization of signs into sentences), semantics (the meaning of signs), and pragmatics (the real-world use of signs).

Sign languages are not universal; each deaf community has had to invent its own language, often virtually from scratch. The sign language used in the United States and parts of Canada is called American sign language (ASL), while in the United Kingdom, the sign language is British sign language (BSL). Of course, these languages are not mutually intelligible, while sign languages elsewhere are equally diverse. We can understand the structure, function, and evolution of sign languages by studying sign language linguistics. Beyond being an interesting academic pursuit, the knowledge of sign languages is essential for educational, interpretive, and increasingly technological applications.

2.1.1   Importance in AI translation

The use of AI in sign language translation has enormous potential to increase communication accessibility for deaf people. However, the development of AI models that can perform effectively relies heavily on sign languages. Without a clear understanding of what those are and how they can be designed into algorithms, AI and machine learning models will be unable to accurately recognize and interpret the visual and gestural aspects of sign languages.

Handshapes, movements, and locations in space, and non-manual signals like facial expressions or body posture, are all part of the meaning of a sign and have grammatical functions. For instance, raising your eyebrows can turn a statement into a question in many sign languages. AI models for sign-language translation that fail to take these aspects of grammar into account will not be able to generate accurate translations.

For example, sign languages often use the space around the signer in three dimensions to encode grammatical information, such as subject, object, and even verb agreement. AI systems must model this grammatical information to produce fluent translations. This means using sophisticated computer vision and machine learning techniques, guided by linguistic research.

Bringing knowledge from sign language linguistics to AI development could make translation systems more robust and effective, thereby opening up the world to deaf people in ways that can make it easier for them to communicate with hearing people and access information and services that were previously inaccessible.

2.1.2   Brief history of sign language research

The formal study of sign languages started only quite recently, in the 1960s and 1970s. Prior to this, people frequently misunderstood sign language. They were considered inferior, or perhaps even primitive, to spoken languages. William Stokoe, among other researchers, began rehabilitating sign languages.

Inspired by this, in the early 1960s, Stokoe, then a professor of anthropology at Gallaudet University, a small liberal arts college for deaf students in Washington, DC, began work on ASL, showing that it was as complete and natural a language as any spoken one, just with its own grammar (morphology) and syntax. He identified the basic units of ASL (which he called cheremes) and analyzed their structure, in much the same way that phonemes are analyzed in spoken languages. His paper on his findings was called sign language structure, and it is in many ways the founding paper of modern sign language linguistics.

Stokoe's work also led to an interest in the documentation and empirical analysis of other sign languages. Researchers began to study the phonological, morphological, syntactic, and semantic structures of sign languages. This work documented a large body of highly innovative linguistic features in sign languages. Like spoken languages, sign languages have dialects and regional variations, with historical changes.

Their recognition as bona fide natural languages had dramatic consequences: it led to the development of education programs for deaf children that teach sign languages and to the fighting for the rights of deaf people to receive services and information in their native sign languages.

New technologies are also creating new opportunities for sign language research and application. Recent advances in AI and machine learning technologies provide the basis for the development of automated sign language recognition and translation systems. With access to the extensive body of linguistic research that has been conducted in the past decades, AI developers can help to create more accurate, reliable, and linguistically sensitive systems.

The emerging field of sign language linguistics, then, represents an important area of research at the intersection of AI and communication accessibility that could, in the future, make a big difference in deaf people's lives. Indeed, the story of sign language linguistics demonstrates the importance of sustained research between linguists, technologists, and deaf communities to ensure that future technological solutions are guided by a rich understanding of the linguistic and cultural context of sign languages.

2.2   Phonology

2.2.1   Basic units of sign language (cheremes)

Cheremes are the smallest semantically relevant units in sign languages. They are to sign language what phonemes are to spoken language: the visual features that distinguish signs. Cheremes have several aspects or features. Signers use their hands to make a variety of handshapes in different locations and directions, with different movements and speeds. These features combine to create the cheremes of sign languages. Just as phonemes can be manipulated to produce different sounds and thus different words, these features of signs can be manipulated to form different signs.

An understanding of cheremes is necessary for the interpretation as well as the production of accurate signs. With a single change in one or two of these features, a sign can become an entirely different sign and thus a different word. If you sign with a shifted location, you go from 'mother' to 'father' in ASL [1] and the same is illustrated in Figure 2.1.

2.2.2   Parameters of signs

(a)   **Handshape**
Handshape is the positioning of the hand(s) used in signs. Sign languages use a variety of hand shapes to convey different meanings. Some of these are the

Figure 2.1   Illustration of the change of hand location from 'mother' (left one) to 'father' (right one) in ASL

flat hand, fist, and claw shapes. For example, in ASL, we use the flat hand to sign 'book', and the fist shape to sign 'school'.

The International SignWriting Alphabet (ISWA) is a standardized system to transcribe handshapes and other features of signs. It allows for the standardization of the representation of handshapes across different sign languages and helps researchers and students learn sign languages. Handshapes (the shapes made by the hand) are what distinguish signs from one another and are often the first feature a student of sign language will learn.

(b) **Location**

Location specifies the position of the hand(s) relative to the signer's torso in producing the sign. Common locations include near the face, chest, and the neutral space in front of the signer. The location of a sign can convey grammatical and semantic information. In ASL, to specify a sign about thinking or intelligence, for instance, the sign will often be produced near the signer's forehead, whereas to specify a sign about feelings or emotions, it will often be produced near the chest. Locations are divided into different regions on and around the body. These include:

- Head region: Signs made near the face and head.
- Torso region: Signs made near the upper body, including the chest and shoulders.
- Neutral space: Signs produced in the space in front of the signer, but not touching the body.

It is necessary to know precisely in what position in the sentence a certain sign occurs to interpret it correctly; for there are cases where the sign is moved to another place in the sentence, and yet has the same function and grammatical meaning.

(c) **Movement**

Movement refers to the movement of the hand(s) during the production of a sign. Movements can be up, down, straight, circular, zigzag, outwards, or inwards, and so on. Movements vary along different dimensions, such as direction, speed, and repetition. For example, while the sign for 'help' in ASL requires an upward movement, the sign for 'drive' requires a back-and-forth movement.

Incorporating movement into signs makes them more expressive; it also contributes to the grammar of sign languages. It can be used to indicate tense, aspect, and mood, for example, as shown in Figure 2.2 by repeating a movement to indicate a habitual action ('reading') [2], or a sharp single movement to indicate a completed action ('read').

Gestures can also encode information about the relationships between signs in the sentence. For instance, verbs that describe movement in ASL use motion to indicate who is doing what to whom. The direction of movement can index the subject and the object of the verb.

(d) **Orientation**

Orientation refers to the orientation of the palm and fingers as they are produced. If we flip the orientation, it can create a different meaning. For example, as shown in Figure 2.3, the sign for 'paper' [2] in ASL is when the

Figure 2.2   Hand movement to represent 'Read' (top) and reading (bottom) in ASL

Figure 2.3   Palm orientation of ASL signs 'Table' (top) and 'Paper' (bottom)

palm faces up. The sign for 'table' is the exact same handshape but with the palm facing downwards.

Orientation is a covert parameter, one that can flip the meaning of a sign. For example, the difference between palm-up and palm-down orientation can convert a directional verb from 'I give you' to 'you give me'. It is a critical parameter for production and perception.

(e) **Non-manual signals**

Non-manual signs are signs that are used in combination with manual signs, such as facial expressions, head movements, or body postures that accompany a sign and that modify the grammatical or emotional information conveyed by the sign. For example, a question in sign language might be expressed by signing with raised eyebrows, whereas a head shake would express negation.

Non-manual signals are integral to sign language grammar. For example, they might signal that the sentence is a question, that it is a relative clause, or that it is a conditional. The facial expression might communicate happiness, surprise, or sadness. Non-manual signals are also commonly used alongside manual signs to create a full linguistic expression, such as the use of a manual sign for alongside a headshake to form a complete linguistic expression for 'not understand' and it is shown in Figure 2.4.

Figure 2.4 Linguistic expression of 'understand' and 'not understand' in ASL

2.3   Morphology

2.3.1   Formation of signs

Signs in sign languages are composed of multiple parameters: handshapes, locations, movements, and orientations. All of these components are equally important
in the construction of the sign. In spoken languages, such as English, sounds are
combined to form words. In sign languages, different visual-gestural units called
cheremes are combined to form signs. This is a 'holistic' unit that is more than the
sum of its parts.

For example, as shown in Figure 2.5, the sign for the tree in ASL consists of a
particular handshape (a flat open hand with fingers spread far apart), a location (to
the side of the head), a movement (a small twisting motion), and an orientation (a
palm facing outward). Each of these features is necessary to produce and recognize
the sign.

This complexity and richness of signs are demonstrated in the infinite ways
that a single parameter can be manipulated to produce different signs: shifting one's
palm orientation a little to the side, or adding a twist to it, can create a completely
different sign with a different meaning, and so on. This is why sign languages can
represent so many different concepts and ideas.

2.3.2   Derivation and inflection

(a)   **Derivation**

In derivation, a new sign is formed from an existing one by adding a prefix or
a suffix, or by modifying part of an existing one to get 'unhappy' or 'teach' to
get 'teacher'. In sign languages, derivation can produce a meaning shift or a
new sign related to the concept of the original sign.

For instance, in ASL, the sign 'teach' consists of a certain handshape and
movement. Modifying the handshape, or adding movement, can produce a
new sign. Changing the movement of the sign 'teach' to repetitive motion can
derive the sign 'teacher'. We can apply this kind of derivation to verbs, nouns,
adjectives, and other parts of speech.

Figure 2.5   Formation of signs using cheremes

Derivation includes compounding, the combination of two or more signs to form a new one: the ASL sign for 'home' is a compounding of the signs for 'eat' and 'sleep' because it represents the place where people eat and sleep.

(b) **Inflection**

What is known as inflection changes the form of signs to convey grammatical meanings such as tense, number, and aspect, to specify further information about the event or concept expressed by the sign. For example, inflectional changes might include repetition, speeding up or slowing down a sign, or increasing or decreasing its intensity.

For example, repeating a sign can be used for pluralization in ASL. Signing a book twice means books. Changing the rate or vigor of a sign can also be used to communicate different parts of an action. A slow, smooth movement might signal an action that is ongoing, while a quick, sharp movement might signal an action that has been completed.

Inflection can also signal tense. In ASL, you can add a backward movement to the sign for 'go' to indicate that it was done in the past or a forward movement to indicate that it will be done in the future. These inflectional changes are essential to signal grammatical information. In sign languages, these elements are used to express complex temporal relations.

2.3.3   Use of space

Sign languages use the three-dimensional space around the signer to encode grammatical relations. Spatial grammar is one of the defining features of sign languages and can be used to show who is the subject of the verb, who is the object, and the type of verb agreement, by placing signs at different locations in space.

For example, in ASL, the space in front of the signer can be divided into an infinite number of regions, enough to indicate how many people or objects are in a sentence. The signer can establish a referent by pointing to a location, and then use that location to indicate actions related to that referent (sometimes called 'deictic pointing' or 'space as a representational medium'). These gestures facilitate the representation of complex sentences.

Directional verbs in sign languages are one of the clearest examples of spatial grammar. The movement direction of a verb changes in different constructions to indicate the subject and object of the action. The sign for 'give', for example, involves hand movement from the giver to the receiver. By changing the direction of the movement, the signer can also indicate different subjects and objects: I give you/you give me.

Spatial grammar is also present for non-manual signals, such as facial expressions and body orientation. A signer might lean slightly in the direction of a referent, or use eye gaze to highlight the relationship between signs. Spatial and non-manual elements work together to create a three-dimensional sign language.

2.4 Syntax

2.4.1 Sentence structure

In sign languages, the order of the elements in a sentence can take different shapes when compared with spoken languages. Spoken languages tend to show a certain word order – for example, subject-verb-object (SVO) for English sentences such as 'Janet plays football'. By contrast, sign languages tend to allow for more flexibility in syntactic constructions, which can be determined by context, emphasis, and space.

In many sign languages – for instance, in ASL – the SVO order is the norm. But it is not always the same. It depends on what you want to focus on, or where you want to put the stress. A simple SVO sentence in ASL could be: I eat an apple. The first part – I – is the subject, the verb is eat, and the object is apple. But this might shift depending on what you want to stress.

2.4.2 Word order

(a) **Subject-verb-object**
    SVO word order is the norm in many sign languages, including ASL. The SVO word order in ASL is the same as you'd expect it to be: subject, then verb, then object: I see you. I (subject) see (verb) you (object).

(b) **Topicalization**
    Topicalization is a syntactic process where the topic of the sentence is placed at the beginning of the utterance regardless of its grammatical role. This type of structure is used in many sign languages and is also used to emphasize the topic or to give context. Raised eyebrows and a slight pause are common non-manual signals in ASL that indicate the topic.

    For example, in the sentence The book, I read it, the book is the topic placed at the start of the sentence and is paired with the non-manual signal of raised eyebrows over this word, indicating that this is the topic of the sentence. After the eyebrows come down, the comment follows.

    Topicalization enables a signer to foreground semantic information, making the sentence more vivid or transparent, especially when introducing a new subject to a conversation or shifting emphasis within an ongoing exchange.

2.4.3 Role of non-manual signals

Non-manual signals are an integral part of the syntax of signed languages. They include facial expressions, head movements, and body postures that provide additional grammatical information and emotional colorings (e.g., questions, negations, conditionals, etc.).

(a) **Questions**
    ASL questions are marked by raising the eyebrows and leaning slightly forward – a non-manual signal that signals the difference between a statement

and a question. For example, the sentence You go can be converted into the question Are you going? by raising the eyebrows and leaning forward over the sign.

(b) **Negations**

Negations, for instance, are often indicated by special non-manual markers such as a headshake when signing. A negative headshake is a strong marker of negation in ASL. You can add a 'not' or a negative headshake to a verb to make it negative – 'I go' can become 'I am not going' by adding a headshake.

(c) **Conditionals**

Non-manual signals also feature in the production of conditional sentences, or 'if-then' statements. In ASL, raising the eyebrows during the 'if' clause and then lowering them to a neutral or different facial expression during the 'then' clause is a common feature. If you go, I stay would feature raised eyebrows while signing if you go, then lowering them during I stay.

(d) **Non-manual signals in complex sentences**

Importantly, non-manual signals can also be used with more complex sentences, such as those containing clauses or more nuanced information. For example, in relative clauses – clauses that provide extra information about another noun – non-manual signals can be used to emphasize the relative clause more than the main clause, helping to signal the clause and keep the flow of information regular and clear. Raised eyebrows and a slight head tilt, for instance, can indicate that the part of the sentence following 'who' is the relative clause and can play a role in conveying the meaning.

2.5   Semantics

2.5.1   Meaning of signs

The semantics of sign languages concern how individual signs function to communicate meaning. A sign in sign language represents a wide range of concepts and denotata, including concrete entities, actions, abstract ideas, and emotions. Each sign is a visual-gestural form unit that has a certain meaning by virtue of its manifestation as a combination of handshapes, movements, locations, orientations, and nonmanual signals.

There is a distinction between merely recognizing a sign's visual form (perceiving it as the sign that it is) and interpreting its use in context (perceiving its meaning, or how it is used to signify something). For instance, in ASL, a sign for 'tree' is formed by extending the fingers and slightly rotating the hand near the head – a design that visually resembles the shape of a tree. In this way, it has an iconic relationship to the object it represents (it looks like a tree, so it can, in part, signify 'tree'). Not all signs are iconic, though. Many are arbitrary and must be learned through exposure and practice.

A single, clear-cut meaning is not necessarily the only meaning of a sign, and the context might allow it to have an extended semantic scope. The sign for 'book', for example, is made by opening the hands like opening a book. It can, of course, represent the noun book. However, in different contexts, the same sign might be used in metaphoric or idiomatic expressions, allowing it to refer to other concepts in an extended semantic scope.

2.5.2   Classifiers

Classifiers are a semantic device unique to sign languages: they help specify an action or characteristic of the noun further. For example, the noun 'car' might be made more specific by adding a classifier, which would help specify the size, shape, movement, or other qualities of the car. Classifiers are like pronouns in spoken languages, but more descriptive.

For example, the flat handshape (called B-hand) is used in ASL as a classifier for a surface or flat object, such as a table or a piece of paper, while a claw handshape (5-hand with fingers spread and slightly curved) might be used to represent a round or irregular object, such as a rock or a cluster of objects.

This feature is particularly important because classifiers can indicate their actions and interactions as well as static properties of objects. For example, the same claw handshape as in the example above can be moved in a rolling manner, or with the palm flat and motionless, to indicate a stationary rock as shown in Figure 2.6, and can even be thrown, or another hand moved toward it to indicate picking it up. In this way, signers can convey rich semantic information with just one handshape, moving it dynamically.

Classifiers can also be used to encode scenes and actions; for instance, a signer might use one handshape to index the person and another to index the table, placing the two in visual–spatial relation to one another. This type of representation provides additional meaning that is visually driven and con-textually grounded.

Figure 2.6   Use of classifiers with ASL signs 'Rock' (top) and 'Mountain' (bottom)

2.5.3   Context

Context – both situational (e.g., a picture of a vase lying on the table), linguistic (e.g., a word coming before or after a relevant sign), and cultural (e.g., a frequently mentioned occurrence or person) – plays an essential role in the interpretation of the meaning of signs in sign languages. In fact, the same sign can also mean different things in different contexts (that is, it is ambiguous), and context helps disambiguate otherwise ambiguous signs.

For instance, as shown in Figure 2.7, you can use the ASL sign for 'book' to signify 'to book' (as in 'to book a ticket') [3]. The distinction is made through the signs placed around it, and through the context of the conversation itself. When someone is talking about travel plans, then you're more likely to interpret the given sign as 'to book a ticket'. In an academic context, you're more likely to interpret it as 'the physical object called a book'.

Context is also important, especially the cultural context in which signs are used. For instance, there might be a conventional use of a sign that is culturally specific to a particular language and that is hard to recognize by non-native signers.

2.5.4   Ambiguity and polysemy

Ambiguity is present in sign languages in that a single sign referent can relate to more than one sign. This is referred to as polysemy. Polysemy is also a common phenomenon in natural languages, and sign languages are no exception. The most common tool to resolve ambiguity is context, providing the means to discern the exact sign referent.

For example, the sign for 'fly' can refer to the act of flying (as in a bird flying), the insect fly, or the zipper on pants; context disambiguates. If someone is talking about a trip, the sign for 'fly' means air travel. If they're talking about insects, it means the bug.

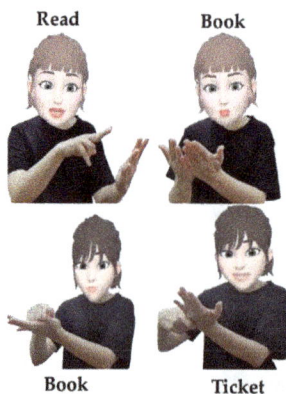

Figure 2.7   Contextual use of signs 'Read a book' and 'Book Ticket'

This means that polysemy requires flexibility on the part of signers and interpreters – the ability to read context and adjust. This concerns AI systems for sign language translation, too, since they will need to be programmed to read context and to disambiguate based on it.

2.6   Pragmatics

2.6.1   Contextual use

Pragmatics studies how context conditions the use and interpretation of signs. Unlike semantics, which is concerned with the inner meaning of signs, pragmatics is concerned with how meanings are made through context. Pragmatics covers what is known as contextual meaning, that is, how meaning is influenced by the context in which the communication takes place, including the social context, the relationship between the interlocutors, and the communicative intention.

(a)   **Social setting**
   The social context in which a conversation is held can also affect the signs that are used or the use of certain signs. Signers might use more formal signs and structures in formal settings, such as in a classroom or a business meeting, compared to using colloquial expressions, slang, and relaxed signing styles in more informal settings, such as chatting with friends.

(b)   **Relationship between interlocutors**
   The relationship between those who are communicating is also significant in pragmatics: a conversation between friends can have a lot more informal and playful signs, while between a student and a teacher, it can be more formal and respectful. Shared experiences between the interlocutors can create inside jokes, shortcuts, and signs that have a certain meaning only for those involved.

(c)   **Communicative intent**
   A sender's intent also impacts sign use and interpretation: whether the signer is requesting, commanding, asserting a fact, or asking a question will influence the signs they choose, as well as their non-manual signals. For example, the same sign can be produced with different facial expressions or body language to indicate politeness, urgency, sarcasm, or emphasis.

2.6.2   Conversational norms

Sign language conversations operate in accordance with certain norms and rules, just like spoken languages do. Those norms help to make the conversation flow smoothly.

(a)   **Turn-taking**
   Unlike turn-taking in spoken language, which relies on auditory cues, sign language turn-taking employs visual cues such as pauses, changes in eye gaze, and slight body shifts that signal the end of the turn and invitation for the

other participant to respond. Interruptions are usually initiated with more forceful gestures or with a hand held up to take the floor.

(b) **Eye contact**

Eye contact is also very important in sign language communication. It is a way of maintaining the conversation – when you look at your interlocutor, you show that you are waiting for them to convey more information. It also shows that you are receiving the visual information and that you are interested and attentive – when you look away, the other person may think that you are bored.

(c) **Use of space**

The space around the signers is part of the conversation. Signers place spatial references for people, objects, and actions, and they track those references as they talk. This spatial use saves time and reduces ambiguity in complex or extended conversations.

(d) **Politeness and social cues**

Sign language politeness can also be conveyed through non-manual signals and the choice of signs. For example, we see that signers in spoken languages often use specific strategies to show respect, deference, or friendliness, such as a softer facial expression, a less abrupt movement, and a proper spatial distance.

2.6.3   Code-switching and bilingualism

Most sign language users are bilingual, speaking both a sign language and a spoken/written language. We code-switch by toggling between them during a conversation – sometimes to better express an idea, sometimes to accommodate the language preferences of other speakers, or sometimes because some concepts are better expressed in one than the other.

(a) **Code-switching**

Code-switching can occur at various levels:

- Intersentential: Switching languages between sentences. A signer could sign a full ASL sentence and then follow it with a spoken English sentence.
- Intrasentential: Changing between languages in the middle of a sentence. In some cases, this might involve embedding a spoken word in a sentence in a signed language, or conversely, embedding a signed word in a sentence in a spoken language.
- Tag-switching: Using a tag – that is, an additional phrase at the end of the sentence – from the source language in a sentence of the target language, such as signing a sentence and then voicing a spoken 'you know?'

(b) **Reasons for code-switching**

The reasons for code-switching are varied and include:

- Identity expression: Bilingual signers might switch to a different language to express their cultural identity or group membership.

- Contextual fit: Some notions are better or more appropriately expressed in one language as opposed to another.
- Audience consideration: Signers may code-switch in order to accommodate the language preference or proficiency of their conversation partners.

(c) **Challenges for AI systems**

As a language feature, code-switching presents particular problems for AI translation systems since the same utterance contains switches between the two languages as well as single phrases in one of the languages: the system has to identify both the languages and the switches and translate them context-sensitively. This requires very elaborate algorithms able to handle bilingual data and context-sensitive translation.

2.7 Variation and change

2.7.1 Dialects and regional variations

Just like spoken languages, sign languages have regional varieties and dialects that emerge from geographical and cultural influences, as well as social factors. Signs for the same idea are quite different in different parts of the world.

(a) **Regional variations**

Much like in spoken languages, there are regional differences in signs that vary by country. For example, signers in the northern United States might use a different sign for 'broken' than signers in the southern United States. Some varieties of signs are more like regional accents, with differences that might be more or less common in one region or another. For example, the sign for 'birthday' in ASL can vary in many different ways, and individuals might use one variety or another depending on where they grew up and it is illustrated in Figure 2.8.

(b) **Community-specific variations**

Dialectal differences can also arise between communities in a region, due to local culture and customs. Deaf schools and institutions can become centers of these dialects. For instance, a group of students at one deaf school might develop signs that are used internally but not understood externally. This is like slang in spoken languages, where words or phrases are used by a group.

(c) **Cultural influences**

Regional variation is also driven, at least in part, by cultural influences. Signs can reflect different cultural practices, values, and norms depending on the cultural context in which they are used. There might be a sign for a holiday, food, or custom that is quite different depending on the cultural background of the region. The sign for 'Christmas' in ASL [2] could differ from the sign for 'Christmas' in BSL [4] shown in Figure 2.9, because the cultural practices surrounding the holiday might differ between the United States and the United Kingdom.

Figure 2.8   Standard variant (top) and Pennsylvania variant of 'Birthday' (bottom)

Figure 2.9   Sign 'Christmas' in ASL and BSL

2.7.2   Historical changes

Because sign languages are living languages, not static collections of words, they change over time. Historical changes in sign languages can be caused by a variety of factors, including language contact, technological innovation, and changes in social attitudes.

(a) **Language contact**

Like any other language, contact with other sign languages or spoken languages sometimes leads to borrowing and the creation of new signs. For example, international gatherings of deaf people, such as the Deaflympics or World Federation of the deaf conferences, often lead to the exchange of signs and their adoption. When a sign of one language is adopted into another, this is an example of language borrowing. While it often enriches the vocabulary of sign language, it sometimes leads to the creation of hybrid signs.

(b) **Technological advancements**

New technologies influence the world of sign languages, and the sign lexicon undergoes constant change. Every new technology often requires the creation of new signs to describe it. There are new signs for terms such as email, texting, and Wi-Fi, which entered the world of sign languages because of the incredible rise of the internet and the arrival of smartphones. The lexical innovations for terms related to technology often spread very fast and become part of the shared sign lexicon within the deaf community.

(c) **Social attitudes and trends**

Social attitudes and fashions also impact changes in sign language. For instance, changes in how society views disability, identity, and inclusivity may cause variations in sign languages – for instance, as deaf culture and identity have become more widespread, along has come an increased push to develop more signs that reflect deaf pride and identity. Changes in education policies and the learning of sign language in mainstream school curricula can also cause changes in the spread and standardization of signs, sometimes leading to the demise of others.

2.7.3   Influence of other languages

Sign languages are not immune to the influences of other languages. Extensive contact with spoken languages can lead to entire lexicons and grammatical systems being overhauled, as can contact with other sign languages.

(a) **Borrowing from spoken languages**

Another way for differing signed languages to become similar is through contact with each other; sign languages often contain signs that represent words from the dominant spoken language. This happens when sign and spoken languages are both taught in educational settings, where bilingualism is encouraged. For instance, ASL has many signs that are basically from English, often technical terms and proper nouns. The ASL sign for 'computer' comes from typing on a keyboard.

(b) **Influence of other sign languages**

Interaction with other sign languages may also lead to the incorporation of foreign signs. This is especially true in communities with significant deaf migration or international collaboration. ASL, for instance, has spread to many other sign languages around the world via the global influence of American deaf education and media. However, the influence goes both ways. ASL has been shaped by the French sign language (FSL), with which it shares a deep historical relationship.

(c) **Creation of hybrid signs**
While fluent signers of multiple sign languages might create hybrid signs that combine elements from each language, they can be born in multilingual deaf communities or through happenstance when signers of different languages come together to interact, such as during international events. Many of these hybrid signs meld the handshapes, movements, or locations of more than one language into an entirely new – and mutually understandable – sign.

2.8 Non-manual signals

The non-manual signals are as important as the manual signs themselves, combining facial expressions, head movements, and body postures to complement the manual signs when conveying emotional information, grammatical functions, and emphasis.

2.8.1 Facial expressions

Facial expressions also form a significant part of sign language communication, often conveying information that is essential for the correct interpretation of a sign or sentence.

(a) **Emotions**
Facial expressions are also important emotional markers in sign languages. For example, they can convey happiness, sadness, surprise, anger, and confusion. A smile, for instance, can signal happiness or friendliness, while a frown can signal displeasure or confusion. The intensity and duration of facial expressions can also modify the emotional tone of a sign.

(b) **Grammatical information**
Besides conveying emotion, facial expressions also carry grammatical information. They can signal syntactic and morphological properties of a sentence, or the question, negative, conditional, or topicalized nature of a sentence. In ASL, for example, raising one's brows marks the yes/no question. Raising the brows distinguishes 'Do you want a donut?' (question) from 'You want a donut' (statement), and thus adds a layer of grammatical meaning.

(c) **Emphasis**
Facial expression can even be deployed to highlight particular parts of a sentence (for instance, raising the brows to emphasize a word or phrase) or to highlight the utterance itself (for instance, widening the eyes to mark it as particularly important). By enhancing what is communicated with expression,

the mode of expression adds a nuanced and detailed layer to the communication.

2.8.2   Head movements

Head movements are also crucial non-manual signals in sign languages and serve as important supplementary components to manual signs; they enrich the meaning of the signed utterance.

(a) **Affirmation and negation**
Nodding and shaking the head are very common head movements that signal 'yes' and 'no', respectively. A nod indicates affirmation or agreement, while a head shake indicates disagreement or negation. A nod to the sign for 'yes' indicates affirmation or agreement; a shake to the sign for 'no' indicates disagreement or negation.

(b) **Syntactic constructions**
Head movements are also used to mark syntactic constructions such as clausal boundaries, constituency, and syntactic dependency. A nod might delimit a relative clause while a head bob marks a particular noun or verb as the center of attention. These head movements contribute to the conversational structure and parsing effort.

(c) **Emphasis and focus**
Similar to the use of head movements to enhance facial expressions, head movements can also enhance the core meaning of a sign. For instance, when telling a story or describing something in detail, an abrupt, sharply articulated head movement can highlight an important aspect of the message, thus making that part of the message pop out of the overall scene for the receiver.

2.8.3   Body posture

Similar to speech, the meaning and effectiveness of sign language are also expressed through body posture and movements, which give context, add emphasis, and help with turn-taking.

(a) **Indicating interest and engagement**
A shift in body orientation may also signal interest or engagement in an exchange. For example, a signer may ask a question while leaning slightly forward, which can communicate interest or emphasis like facial expressions. Likewise, when a signer becomes more attuned to the exchange, they may switch from a sideways profile toward their partner to a front-facing position.

(b) **Marking subjects and objects**
Second, body orientation can be used to reference different subjects or objects in discourse. By tilting the body or pointing, a signer can establish spatial references that stand for different participants, objects, or discourse items to keep track of what is being talked about in complex narratives or discourse involving multiple entities.

(c) **Managing turn-taking**

Further, body posture also helps to manage turn-taking within conversational exchanges. Shifting body orientation or posture can indicate that a signer has completed a turn and is prepared to yield the floor to the other speaker. On the other hand, maintaining a more assertive posture can indicate a wish to hold onto a conversational turn or to interrupt it.

2.9   Iconicity and arbitrary signs

2.9.1   Iconicity

Iconicity – the fact that signs bear a striking visual relationship to the things they denote – is easier to acquire and easier to process than arbitrary signs. This is because iconic signs directly map the form of the referent onto the sign. Iconicity arises naturally in the visual-motor modality of sign languages, where gestures and visual forms can be directly mapped to the corresponding objects and actions in the world (Figure 2.10).

(a) **Visual representation**

Iconic signs are marked by handshapes, movements, and locations that resemble the physical features or actions of the signs' referents. For example, in ASL, the sign for yes is signed by extending the fingers and holding the hand straight, then moving it up and down like a nodding head, while no uses a pinched gesture from the fingers. These signs are illustrated in Figure 2.10, which demonstrates the hand and facial movements for both.

Figure 2.10   Head movements representation for the signs 'Yes' and 'No' in ASL

(b)   **Advantages of iconicity**
Iconicity offers several advantages in sign language acquisition and use:

- **Ease of learning:** Iconic signs are often easier for beginners to grasp because their meanings are visually self-explanatory: the form is transparent and acts as a mnemonic.
- **Quick recognition:** even non-signers can often guess the meaning of iconic signs, so these signs can convey basic meaning and allow basic communication and interaction.
- **Expressiveness:** Iconic signs can be very expressive, providing vivid imagery that enriches storytelling and descriptive discourse.

(c)   **Limits of iconicity**
Iconicity is a characteristic of many signs, but not all signs are iconic, and the level of iconicity can vary – what is iconic for one person might not be iconic to another person. Finally, some iconic signs might become more abstract over time as they lose their more obvious visual relationship with the things they represent.

(d)   **Examples of iconicity**

- **Tree:** In many sign languages, the sign for 'tree' literally consists of raising the fingers of a hand straight up, to represent the branches of the tree, while the arm represents the trunk.
- **House:** Sign language for 'house' can include a roof-shaped sign, where the hands make the shape of a triangle for the typical shape of a house.
- **Eat:** This sign is made by bringing your hand up to your mouth in an action that is instantly recognizable as eating.

2.9.2   *Arbitrary signs*

Arbitrary signs are devoid of visual or gestural connection to their referents. Any meaning they might convey is entirely dependent on convention, and they must be taught through exposure and drill since their forms are not informative about their meanings.

(a)   **Nature of arbitrary signs**
But in arbitrary signs, the connection between the sign and meaning exists only because of social convention, not any form of visual resemblance between the sign and its meaning. For example, one sign in ASL shown in Figure 2.11 for 'why' is made by forming a certain handshape and holding it in front of your forehead, where the letter 'Y' would be. There is no visual resemblance between the sign and the underlying concept of 'why'; understanding the sign requires knowing what it means by convention.

(b)   **Learning arbitrary signs**
Arbitrary signs are harder to learn because learners cannot use pattern-matching to infer what they mean. Instead, they must memorize the signs and how they are used by repeatedly practicing their meanings. This is similar to

Figure 2.11   Understanding arbitrary signs with the ASL sign 'why'

learning vocabulary in spoken languages, in which words usually have no connection with what they mean.

(c) **Importance of arbitrary signs**

While iconic signs evoke their meanings and have the potential to be understood without a word order, arbitrary signs have to be learned and are the key to linguistic richness and flexibility as they can be used to express every kind of abstract concept, technical term, and idea that has no natural visual representation. Arbitrariness is what has made sign languages develop complex and nuanced vocabularies, which are necessary for advanced communication.

(d) **Examples of arbitrary signs**

- **Why:** The ASL sign for 'why' is made with a movement in front of the forehead that transforms into a Y, without any visual association to querying.
- **Because:** 'Because' in many signs, languages are represented with a handshape near the forehead followed by a particular movement, which is conventionalized, but not iconic.
- **Government:** The sign for government is made by rotating the fingers in a circle in front of the forehead (who knew?) but, of course, it doesn't look anything like government. It is the convention that tells you this sign means government and not, say, the French Revolution.

2.9.3   Balancing iconicity and arbitrary signs

Sign languages make judicious use of both iconic and arbitrary signs to create a balanced and efficacious means of communication. Icons are particularly useful because they offer direct visual links and are easy to learn; on the other hand, arbitrary signs are needed in order to accommodate a broad range of concepts.

(a) **Evolution of signs**

But, over time, some of these signs might have evolved, from iconic to arbitrary, or vice versa. This evolution might be the result of a sign evolving through a process of increasing standardization and abstraction or as a result of cultural and linguistic changes undergone by the deaf community. For example, a sign that used to be iconic might be simplified in its use, losing some of its visual resemblance to the referent.

(b) **Cultural and linguistic influences**
Development and use of iconicity are also culturally and linguistically influenced. Different sign languages can contain more or fewer iconic signs depending on cultural preferences and/or the historical development of the language. A sign that is considered iconic in one culture might not be interpreted as such in another. We can see that the world of sign languages is diverse.

(c) **Teaching and learning approaches**
Educators take advantage of the iconicity of a sign to help new learners acquire language more easily. Iconic signs are learned first and build a basic vocabulary that learners can memorize and recognize more easily. They then gradually incorporate arbitrary signs to expand their vocabulary and communicate.

2.10   Challenges and considerations

2.10.1   Cross-linguistic studies

Cross-linguistic studies are essential for appreciating the diversity and similarities of sign languages across the globe. Not only do they help us identify universal features and language-specific characteristics of sign languages, but they're valuable for both sign linguists and computer scientists working on AI translation systems.

(a) **Identifying universal features**
Universal features are elements that are found in more than one sign language. For instance, there might be similar handshapes, movement patterns, or syntactic structures found in many or all sign languages. Some examples in ASL include the use of a bent index finger and thumb to express a number or the use of a side-to-side action to express 'eat' or 'drink'. By identifying these universal features, researchers can come up with more generalized models for AI translation systems to recognize.

(b) **Language-specific characteristics**
These universal features form a backbone, but each sign language also has idiosyncratic features – such as unique signs, idioms, or grammar – that reflect the culture, society, and history of that language. For example, the sign for 'thank you' in ASL looks quite different from the equivalent in BSL. AI systems that can translate and interpret these subtleties are crucial for the future of sign language technology.

(c) **Informing AI development**
Cross-linguistic studies are particularly helpful for those who develop artificial intelligence (AI) automated translation systems. If the researchers know which aspects of signing are the same across sign languages and which are

unique to some of them, they can make sure that the AI algorithms that they design are more flexible and robust. The algorithms must be able to handle the variety of forms and patterns that are found across sign languages. Ultimately, such insights should contribute to developing more powerful AI models that can handle the diversity of actual sign language communication.

2.10.2   Documentation and preservation

Finally, documenting and preserving sign languages are an integral part of linguistic diversity and cultural heritage. Documentation involves the creation of descriptions of sign languages (e.g., corpora, dictionaries, pedagogical materials, etc.) to allow for the sharing of such languages. Preservation of these languages ensures that sign languages with fewer speakers or less institutional support do not fade into obscurity over time.

(a)   **Creating comprehensive corpora**
A linguistic corpus is a collection of texts or recorded speech (in the case of sign languages, recorded video) used for linguistic study. To develop truly encyclopedic resources, we must assemble and annotate enormous datasets of sign language data. These resources are indispensable to researchers, teachers, and AI developers alike. They provide an extremely valuable dataset of naturally occurring language use, which is necessary for training AI systems to operate on sign language and for undertaking linguistic research.

(b)   **Developing dictionaries**
This makes the dictionary an important reference tool for sign language learners and researchers who need to know what signs look like and how to produce them. The process of creating a dictionary starts with documenting signs, their meanings, and how they are expressed. It's complicated because a single sign can have different meanings depending on how it is performed. That's where detailed descriptions, pictures, and videos showing the movements that make up each sign come in. Digital dictionaries with video examples work particularly well for sign languages because the movements of signs are inherently dynamic.

(c)   **Educational resources**
Educational resources (e.g., textbooks, videos, and online courses) are a vital tool in safeguarding and promoting sign languages, helping new learners to acquire the language, and helping them to pass this knowledge on to future learners, as well as helping teachers and community leaders to educate others about sign languages and deaf culture.

(d)   **Community involvement**
We also need to involve deaf community members in documenting and archiving. They offer perspectives and genuine language use that documenters need to understand. Most importantly, they ensure that documents are culturally sensitive and reflective of the language being documented.

2.10.3   Ethical considerations

This also means that research and application in sign language linguistics – in particular, the use of sign languages for AI technologies – needs to be mindful of these ethical issues and doesn't violate the rights and interests of the deaf community. Since the risks and dangers of potential misuse or harm are especially high when it comes to AI technologies, ethical concerns in this area are of utmost importance.

(a) **Informed consent**

   One of the most basic ethical standards of research is to get informed consent from those who participate. Researchers need to make sure that participants fully understand what the research is about, what is involved, and its potential benefits and risks. This could mean, for example, telling participants in sign language research how the data will be used, who will have access to it, and how the data will be safeguarded. Participants should have opportunities to ask questions, and the decision to participate should be voluntary, with no coercion involved.

(b) **Data privacy**

   Steps need to be taken to protect the privacy of research participants, including those whose data contribute to sign language corpora and other research projects. Procedures for the collection, storage, and use of personal data need to implement robust data protection measures to avoid inappropriate access and misuse. Data should be anonymized where possible, and all identifying information should be kept separately from the research data and only accessible by people authorized to do so.

(c) **Impact of AI technologies**

   The design and rollout of AI systems for sign language translation and other purposes must be done in consultation with members of the deaf community, to expand access and opportunities, not replacing human interpreters or deaf professionals.

(d) **Community engagement and empowerment**

   Including the deaf community in the research and development process is another important step for ethical practice. This means consulting with the deaf community, incorporating their feedback, and ensuring that they have a stake in the research outcomes. One way to empower the deaf community is to give them the tools and resources to participate in the research and development process. This way, the deaf community can help shape AI technologies so that they foster respect for their needs and rights.

(e) **Addressing bias and fairness**

   AI systems can perpetuate existing biases in the training data, so researchers and practitioners must be aware of potential biases to minimize the risk of creating unfair or inaccurate translations. Increasing diversity and representative training data sets, regularly auditing AI systems, and creating teams with a diversity of perspectives and competencies are all possibilities.

Exercises

(I) **Multiple choice questions**
1. Which of the following is an example of an iconic sign?
    (A) The sign for 'why'
    (B) The sign for 'tree'
    (C) The sign for 'book'
    (D) The sign for 'name'

2. What is a chereme?
    (A) A type of facial expression used in sign language
    (B) A basic unit of meaning in sign languages
    (C) A grammatical structure in spoken languages
    (D) A method of teaching sign language

3. Which of the following sign languages is primarily used in the United Kingdom?
    (A) ASL
    (B) BSL
    (C) DGS
    (D) JSL

4. In sign language, what does the parameter 'orientation' refer to?
    (A) The location of the sign
    (B) The movement of the sign
    (C) The direction the palm and fingers face during the sign
    (D) The handshape used in the sign

5. Which of the following is a non-manual signal in sign languages?
    (A) Handshape
    (B) Movement
    (C) Location
    (D) Facial expression

(II) **Short questions**
1. What is a chereme in sign language linguistics?
2. Why are non-manual signals significant in sign languages?
3. Describe the difference between iconic and arbitrary signs in sign languages.
4. List the parameters of signs in sign languages.
5. Why is studying sign language phonology important for AI translation systems?

(III) **Think and answer**
1. Why is documenting and preserving sign languages important? How can this benefit the deaf community and linguistic research?

2. How do cross-linguistic studies help in understanding universal and unique features of sign languages? How do these studies contribute to AI translation systems?
3. What are the ethical considerations in sign language research and AI application? What measures should researchers and developers take to address these issues?

(IV) **Practical exercise**
1. Watch the following ASL video on ASL Lesson 01 (https://www.youtube.com/watch?v=k9cFqNYlV1A).
    (a) List the cheremes (handshapes, locations, movements, and orientations) used in each sign.
    (b) Classify the non-manual signals accompanying each sign.
2. Find examples of iconic signs and arbitrary signs on handspeak.
    (a) Create a table listing at least five iconic signs and five arbitrary signs, including their meanings.
    (b) Explain why each sign is considered iconic or arbitrary.
3. Watch the following ASL video on ASL University Lesson 01.
    (a) Identify the sentence structure (e.g., subject-verb-object, topicalization).
    (b) Describe the role of non-manual signals in the sentence structure.
4. Watch the video on sign formation (https://www.youtube.com/playlist?list=PL6akqFwEeSpiLwRFA3ZvuOWMwPXwI7NqA).
    (a) Identify examples of derivation (e.g., adding prefixes or suffixes) and inflection (e.g., modifying signs for tense, number, aspect).
    (b) Create a diagram showing the base sign and its derived and inflected forms.
5. Read about ethical considerations in sign language research on the Global Sign Languages Corpus Project website (https://www.sign-lang.uni-hamburg.de/dgs-korpus/index_en.html)
    (a) List the key ethical principles researchers must follow.
    (b) Discuss how these principles can be applied in a hypothetical research project involving sign language users.

References

[1] https://www.steppingstoneschool.com/platinum-learning-for-life/program-enrichments/american-sign-language/.
[2] ASL University: https://www.lifeprint.com/asl101/.
[3] https://www.signdummy.com/.
[4] https://www.signbsl.com/sign/christmas.

Chapter 3
Sign language datasets

3.1 Dataset description

In sign language AI translation, the quality and coverage of the dataset are the basis for any robust and effective model, which means that working on a sign language dataset is an essential part of developing an algorithm that can convert hand signs into spoken or written words. Sign language datasets need to be captured, annotated, and processed, derived from potentially three types of datasets: (images, video, and multimodal – a combination of video, audio, and text).

Datasets are the ones that determine the world of AI for sign language translation. Any given dataset will make sure that the AI model learns the specific articulation of units and combinations in sign language in terms of the shape and movement of the hands, movements of the head, facial expressions, and the gestalts of the context of usage. This chapter will explore the various types of data, the way they are collected, the different preprocessing algorithms, and the linguistic challenges associated with the curation of the data.

3.2 Types of datasets

3.2.1 Image-based datasets

Image-based datasets are static images of sign language gestures. Each image comprises a different sign, shot from different angles and lighting conditions, collected together to form a training set. These datasets can be used for the early stages of training and for tasks that focus on the recognition of individual signs or hand-shapes. Table 3.1 illustrates different image-based SL datasets available in various regions.

Advantages

- **Simplicity:** Image-based datasets are relatively cheap to acquire and annotate compared with more complex datasets, such as video.
- **Cost-efficient:** Smaller and easier to store and compute, they can assist in small projects or initial research phases.
- **Training:** Ideal for training a model to recognize single gestures or hand-shapes, the starting point for more complex systems.

Table 3.1   Image-based sign language datasets

Dataset	Country	Class	Total signs	Signers	Sign level	Availability
ASL	USA	29	2,230,74	10	Alphabet labels	Publicly available [1]
ISLAN	India	26	700	6	Alphabets, numbers, words	Publicly available [2]
JSL	Japan	20	13,200	11	Words	Contact authors [3]
SignsWorld Atlas	Arabic	26	Not available	10	Handshapes, words, sentences	Contact authors [4]
STK LS	France	Not specified	1-h recording	Not specified	Alphabet labels, grammatical phenomena	Contact authors [5]

Limitations

- **Lack of context:** A static image cannot show signers moving through space and time, nor can it convey the transitions occurring between signs.
- **Minimal realism:** They are not representative of real-world variability, such as variation in speed, context, and variation among users.

3.2.2   Video-based datasets

Unlike the static nature of word-level data, video-based datasets contain time-sequenced representations of sign language gestures, which are inherently dynamic due to the moving nature of hands and the continuous evolution of a sign. This prolonged duration is what gives us access to the rhythms of language and the variety of movements that can be used to convey meanings. It's this information that's lost if we focus exclusively on word-level data. Table 3.2 illustrates different video-based SL datasets available in various regions.

Advantages

- **Temporal dynamics:** The sequential motion of signs from one moment to the next in a video enables models to learn how gestures unfold and morph into each other to create coherent communicative actions.
- **Contextual:** They provide context to help understand the meaning of a sign relative to the preceding and following gestures.
- **Real-world data:** More representative of real-world usage, capturing differences in speed, style, and environmental conditions.

Limitations

- **Complexity:** Video data are more complex to acquire, annotate, and process than static images.

Table 3.2   Video-based sign language datasets

Dataset	Country	Class	Signers	Total signs	Sign level (annotations)	Availability
RWTH-PHOENIX-Weather 2014	Germany	1200	9	45,760	Sentences (glosses)	Publicly available [6]
ASLLVD	USA	3300+	6	9800	Words (end/start)	Publicly available [7]
LSA64	Argentina	64	10	3200	Gesture labels	Publicly available [8]
DGS corpus	Germany	40	15	3000	Words	Publicly available [9]
SIGNUM	Germany	450	25	33,210	Sentences	Contact authors [10]
CSL daily	China	2000	10	20,654	Sentences (glosses, spoken language translations)	Publicly available [11]
KETI Sign language	Korea	524	14	14,672	Words, sentences (glosses)	Contact authors [12]
LSFB-CONT	Belgium	6883	100	85,000+	Hand, start/end, translation	Publicly available [13]
PSL ToF 84	Poland	84	1	1680	Words, depth from ToF camera	Publicly available [14]
WLASL	EEUU	2000	119	21,083	Words	Publicly available [15]
ISL-CSLTR	India	100	7	18,863	Sentences (glosses)	Publicly available [16]
MS-ASL	USA	1000	222	25,513	Word and sentences (glosses)	Publicly available [17]
LSE corpus	Spain	Not specified	20	2400 signs, 2700 non-signs	Word and sentences (glosses, phonological, grammatical, articulatory information)	Publicly available [18]

- **Resource intensive:** Requires significant storage and computational resources for processing and model training.
- **Harder to annotate:** Continuous nature of the data, need for accurate temporal markers.

3.2.3   Multimodal datasets

Multimodal datasets combine data from different modalities (e.g., video, audio, text) as an attempt to capture the full picture of sign language communication. Multimodal datasets can be particularly helpful for creating models that combine different information modalities, such as hand gestures, facial expressions, and spoken language. Table 3.3 illustrates different multimodal SL datasets available in various regions.

Advantages

- **Multimodal context:** Multimodal datasets are richer contexts within which to learn, as they include visual, audio, and text components.
- **Enhanced accuracy:** Models can leverage multiple data sources to improve recognition accuracy and robustness.
- **Training:** Good for creating more complex systems that can do sign-language translation in a manner closer to how human interpreters do.

Limitations

- **Data collection complexity:** Collecting and synchronizing different types of data (video, audio, text) is complex and time-consuming.
- **More expensive:** Costlier to gather and process because of the requirement of extraordinary equipment and tools.

Table 3.3   Multimodal sign language datasets

Dataset	Country	Total signs	Video duration	Signers	Type	Sign level (annotations)	Availability
How2Sign	USA (ASL)	16,000	80 h	11	Video, RGB-D, 3D, text	Sentences (gloss, pose, depth, translation, audio)	Publicly available [19]
Dicta-sign	EU (BSL, GSL, LSF, Greek)	~1000 per language	~25 h	~60	Video, stereo	Sentence and Words (gloss, segmentation, gaze, clause boundaries, HamNoSys)	Publicly available [20]
RWTH-PHOENIX-Weather Multimodal	Germany	1080	Extensive coverage of 386 editions	9	Video, Speech, Text	Sentence (Gloss annotations, translation, audio)	Publicly available [21]
AUTSL	Turkey	38,336	Not specified	43	RGB, Depth, Skeleton	Word (gloss)	Publicly available [22]
LIBRAS-UFOP	Brazil	56 isolated, 37 continuous	Not specified	Not specified	RGB, depth, skeleton	Sentence and Words (gloss annotations, minimal pairs)	Publicly available [23]

- **Modelling difficulties:** Models that can combine and process multimodal data effectively are challenging to develop and can tax computation.

3.3   Data collection methods

3.3.1   Controlled environments

Recordings are made in controlled environments – in a studio as shown in Figure 3.1 – in order to get clean and consistent data. This allows us to have complete control over variables like lighting, background, and camera orientation. Controlled environments are ideal for this task because high-quality sign language data is needed to train accurate and reliable sign language recognizers.

Example: A laboratory environment in which signers are recorded in front of a plain wall with stable lighting to generate high-quality gesture data. In the RWTH-PHOENIX-Weather dataset, all recordings are performed in a controlled studio environment using the same setup to minimize the impact of external variables.

Advantages

- **Consistency:** Implements uniform lighting, background, and recording angles to produce an excellent-quality dataset.
- **Accuracy:** Ensures that the details of gestures are captured, which is critical for training robust models.
- **Repeatability:** Easier to recreate the recording environment to collect new data, ensuring consistency.

Figure 3.1   Data collection in controlled environments [24]

Disadvantages

- **Lack of naturalism:** Might not capture the variation and spontaneity of how sign language is used in the real world.
- **Limited context:** Often lacks the environmental context that can influence gesture meaning and usage.

3.3.2   Real-world environments

Real-world data collection tries to capture sign language usage by being out in the world as shown in Figure 3.2. In the real world, you can record data in a public space, in a home, or in a workplace. In the real world, we make signs, so it is likely going to be more varied and realistic. Of course, it also comes with more noise and variability.

Example: Filming sign language users in the wild, during ordinary interactions – such as conversing in a park or working in a shop, to obtain naturalistic and spontaneous gestures. Now, MS-ASL has recordings from natural environments, so people are doing sign language in a wide variety of backgrounds and recording conditions.

Advantages

- **Realism:** It allows for natural variation in sign language use, leading to data sets that better match actual communication scenarios.
- **Contextual richness:** Environmental context is relevant – a property that can be vital for sign meaning and use.

Disadvantages

- **Noise and variability:** Adds uncertainty and background noise that can make data processing and model training more difficult.
- **Control:** Difficult to control external variables, which can affect data quality and uniformity.

Figure 3.2   Data collection in controlled environments [25]. Image source [26].

3.3.3   Synthetic data generation

Synthetic data generation refers to the creation of artificial data from scratch, for example, using techniques such as computer graphics or through simulation as shown in Figure 3.3. Synthetic data can be used to augment incomplete data sets; for example, when there are gaps in the available real-world data. Synthetic data can also be useful for training models, especially when it is difficult or expensive to collect real-world data.

Example: Synthetically generated motions of sign language created with motion capture technology, with the goal of building up a reference corpus that can augment or supplant real-world data. A computer-generated avatar in the Synthesis of Signed Language project creates synthetic data for sign language. The summary of data collection methods is shown in Table 3.4.

Advantages

- **Cost-effective:** Reduces the need for extensive real-world data collection, saving time and resources.
- **Controlled variability:** Models can generate a wide range of variable data with controlled differences in gestures, angles, and backgrounds.

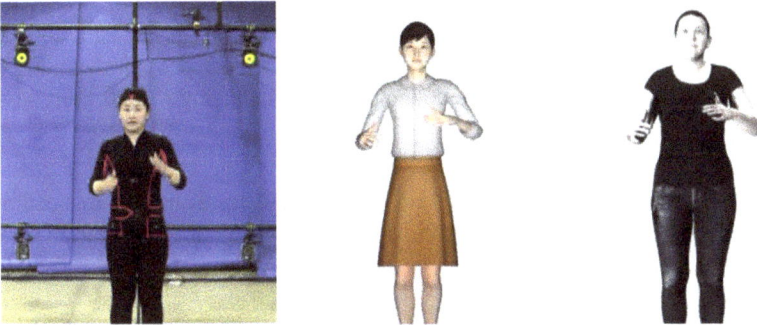

Figure 3.3   Synthetic sign data generation [27]

Table 3.4   Data collection methods

Method	Environment	Example dataset	Advantages	Disadvantages
Controlled environments	Studio	RWTH-PHOENIX-weather	Consistency, precision, reproducibility	Lack of naturalism, limited context
Real-world environments	Natural	MS-ASL	Realism, contextual richness	Noise and variability, control issues
Synthetic data generation	Virtual	Synthesis of signed language	Cost-effective, controlled variability, gaps filled	Lack of realism, community acceptance issues

- **Fill-in-the-blanks:** Aid in developing data for rare or infrequent signs that can be challenging to collect in real-world settings.

  Disadvantages

- **Unreality:** Possible that the movements are not natural signs.
- **Acceptance:** Synthetic data are not likely to be accepted by the community as easily as real data because of a sense of artificiality.

3.4   Data preprocessing

Data preprocessing is the process of transforming raw datasets into a form suitable for training machine learning models. It is usually one of the first steps in machine learning, consisting of a number of tasks such as noise reduction, cleaning (e.g., handling missing values), data reduction, and labeling. Performing preprocessing well can make all the difference in the quality and performance of the trained model, allowing it to learn and generalize to new data and the summary of the preprocessing strategies is shown in Table 3.5.

3.4.1   Data cleaning

Data cleaning involves cleaning up noisy data, correcting errors, and standardizing the data format – for example, ensuring that all dates are stored in the same format. This step is important because noisy data or other types of errors can degrade the quality of a dataset, and therefore degrade the performance of any models built on it.

Steps in data cleaning

- **Noise removal/cleaning:** Finding and removing irrelevant or misleading points of data, such as a blob of dust in a video recording or a digitization error in an annotation.

Table 3.5   Data preprocessing strategies

Step	Description	Example
Data cleaning	Removing noise, correcting errors, and standardizing data formats	Removing background noise from MS-ASL videos, correcting mislabeled signs, and standardizing video resolutions and frame rates
Data annotation	Labeling data with relevant information, such as gesture identification and timing	Labeling ASL signs in the How2Sign dataset with start/end times, specific signs, and contextual information like accompanying spoken sentences
Data augmentation	Using techniques like rotation, scaling, and flipping to increase the dataset size	Rotating, scaling, and flipping video frames in the RWTH-PHOENIX-Weather dataset to create diverse training examples and improve model robustness

- **Error correction:** Correcting any mistakes in the signal, like display signs labeled wrong, timestamps misread, or files corrupted.
- **Standardization:** Making all the data into one format, through consistency checks, for example, when all video data resolutions, frame rates, or color schemes are already normalized.
- **Data Imputation:** Missing data handling in which some method is applied to fill in missing observed values or remove completely filled-in observations.

Example: In the MS-ASL dataset, data cleaning might include culling videos that have too much background noise or poor annotations, so that the data remaining are truly representative of the signs in question.

3.4.2 Data annotation

The process of annotating data – such as identifying the gesture, the timing, and the context – is called data annotation. Data annotation is essential for supervised learning models because it tells them what information to look for and how to learn from it.

Steps in data annotation:

- **Annotation/labeling:** Attaching tags to each of the gestures in the dataset (e.g., the sign that is being made, the person who is making it, or any other contextual data).
- **Timing information:** Indicating when in time each gesture starts and ends, to allow the alignment of the gestures with their labels.
- **Contextual annotations:** Adding more context (e.g., the face, body, location of production) to give models more training data.

Example: In the How2Sign dataset, annotators might label each clip with the ASL sign being performed, when it starts and when it ends, and what (if anything) it is being used to convey (e.g., if it is accompanied by some words or sentences in spoken English) and the same is shown in Figure 3.4.

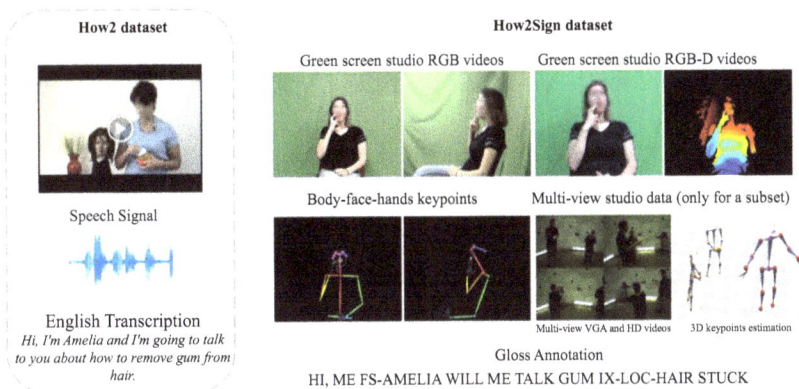

Figure 3.4   Example of sign data annotation from How2Sign. Image source [28].

Original	Horizontal Flip	Rotation	Color Space Transformation

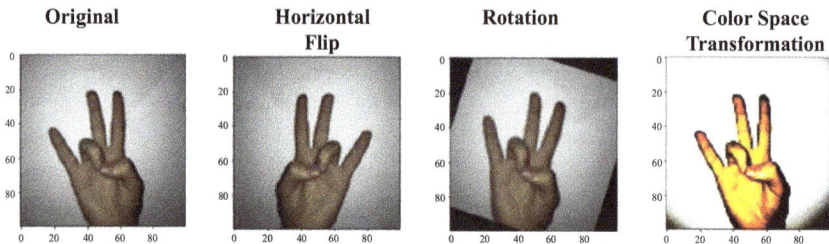

Figure 3.5   Data augmentation techniques in sign language [29]

3.4.3   Data augmentation

Data augmentation, such as rotating, scaling, or flipping the original image artificially, as shown in Figure 3.5 to increases the size of the dataset to make your model more robust – that is, more likely to generalize to new images that you've never seen before.

Common data augmentation techniques

- **Rotation:** Rotating images or video frames to different angles to simulate different perspectives.
- **Scaling:** Zooming in and out on images or video frames to simulate how far away the signer is from the camera.
- **Flipping:** Horizontal or vertical flipping of images or video frames to create mirrored images, increasing the diversity of the dataset.
- **Cropping:** Randomly cropping parts of images or videos to simulate different framing conditions.
- **Color jittering:** Altering the contrast, saturation, or brightness of images at random to simulate different lighting settings.

Example: Data augmentation for the RWTH-PHOENIX-Weather dataset might include rotating and flipping frames of video footage showing sign language gestures to create additional training examples, which make the model more robust to different camera angles and signer positions.

3.5   Challenges in dataset curation

There are important inclusions, exclusions, and generalizations to consider with any dataset curated for sign language recognition. These challenge us to create more complete, ethical, robust, and representative AI models and the summary of the challenges is shown in Table 3.6.

Table 3.6 Summary of challenges in dataset curation

Challenge	Description	Example dataset
Diversity and representation	Ensuring the dataset includes a wide range of users (age, ethnicity, regional dialects)	Dicta-Sign (multilingual and regional variations)
Ethical considerations	Adhering to ethical guidelines, ensuring privacy, and consent	How2Sign (informed consent and privacy protection)
Data quality and consistency	Maintaining high-quality and consistent data, especially in real-world data collection	RWTH-PHOENIX-Weather (controlled studio recordings)

3.5.1 Diversity and representation

Building an inclusive AI model that represents all sign language users, such as children, older adults, and people of diverse ethnicities and regional dialects, is crucial. Having a diverse dataset makes the model better at generalizing to multiple real-world scenarios and reduces the possible bias that could have an impact on the model's performance.

Key considerations

- **Age groups:** The training data should contain participants of different age groups, as this increases the likelihood that the model can detect a sign performed by either a younger or an older signer, who could use different styles.
- **Ethnicities:** The more ethnicities included in the dataset, the better. Greater ethnic diversity in the dataset should help to mitigate differences in ways that skin tone and facial features can affect the recognition of facial expressions and hand movements.
- **Regional dialects:** Sign language might differ quite considerably between regions even within the same country. Adding dialects helps the model to be more general and accurate.

Example: Data from the Dicta-Sign dataset features signers from across Europe, encompassing British sign language (BSL), German sign language (DGS), Greek sign language (GSL), and French sign language (F allegedly less represented in the dataset, but these differences can help develop more generalizable models.

3.5.2 Ethical considerations

Responsible data collection necessitates ethical considerations about privacy and consent in real-world settings, and protecting the rights and well-being of citizens who are part of the dataset and being modelled.

Key considerations

- **Informed consent:** Participants must be clearly told about the purpose of the data collection, how the data will be used, and their right to withdraw their consent at any time.

- **Privacy guard:** Personal information should be anonymized, and the data should be securely stored such that it cannot be accessed without permission.
- **Cultural sensitivity:** Respect for the cultural importance and variation of sign languages in different cultures. The researchers need to engage with the deaf community and represent it with respect and accuracy.

Example: The How2Sign dataset was gathered through informed consent, ensuring that all recordings were authorized by participants, with their awareness of privacy and rights.

3.5.3   Data quality and consistency

Data quality and consistency can be difficult to achieve for many reasons, such as working in the real world where there is more variability and noise than in lab experiments, and ensuring the quality of the data you collect. High-quality data are essential for training good models.

Key considerations

- **Noise reduction:** Techniques used to remove or minimize irrelevant background information (such as noise) during the actual collection of data.
- **Standardization:** Collecting data in the same way and with the same instruments every single time will reduce variability and thus increase the reliability of the dataset.
- **Validation and verification:** Frequent validation and verification to identify and correct the errors and inconsistencies in the data help maintain the validity and accuracy of the dataset.

Example: The controlled studio environment reduces variability and produces more similar individuals whose facial gender is clearly visible and with a high resolution. Data collected this way is of higher quality in terms of consistency than everyday data from the world.

Exercises

(I)   **Multiple choice questions**
1.   What are the three main methods of data collection for sign language datasets?
   (a) Controlled environments, real-world environments, and synthetic data generation
   (b) Text, audio, and video
   (c) Manual, automatic, and semiautomatic

2.   Why is data cleaning important in preprocessing sign language datasets?
   (a) It increases the number of samples
   (b) It removes noise, corrects errors, and ensures consistency
   (c) It adds more annotations

3. What is a key challenge in ensuring diversity and representation in sign language datasets?
   (a) Reducing noise in recordings
   (b) Including a wide range of sign language users (age, ethnicity, regional dialects)
   (c) Increasing the number of cameras used

(II) **Short answer questions**
   1. Write the advantages and disadvantages of data collection in controlled environments and real-world environments for sign language datasets. Provide an example of a dataset collected using each method.
   2. Describe the main goal of data annotation in sign language datasets.
   3. What is synthetic data generation and why is it used in sign language dataset curation?

(III) **Discussion questions**
   1. Describe the steps involved in data preprocessing for sign language datasets. How does each step contribute to the overall quality of the dataset?
   2. Analyze the impact of using synthetic data generation in sign language dataset curation. Discuss its advantages and potential limitations.
   3. Analyze the ethical considerations involved in the collection of sign language data. Why is informed consent and privacy protection critical?

(IV) **Practical exercise**
   Design a small-scale data collection plan for a sign language dataset.
   Objective: To create a diverse, high-quality, and ethically collected dataset for sign language recognition.
   Steps:
   1. Participant recruitment:
      • Recruit 20 participants from various age groups, ethnic backgrounds, and regions.
      • Ensure balanced representation to capture diverse signing styles and dialects.

   2. Ethical guidelines:
      • Obtain informed consent from all participants, explaining the study's purpose, data usage, and their right to withdraw.
      • Ensure data anonymity and secure storage to protect participant privacy.

   3. Data collection setup:
      • Use high-resolution cameras and consistent lighting in a controlled environment.
      • Implement a standard protocol for recording, including multiple angles and consistent frame rates.

- Record each participant signing a predefined set of words and sentences.

4. Data quality assurance:
    - Regularly review the recordings to remove noise and correct any errors.
    - Standardize the video formats and resolutions to maintain consistency.

5. Data annotation:
    - Label each video clip with the specific sign, start/end times, and contextual information.
    - Use gloss annotations to ensure accurate labeling and validation by sign language experts.

References

[1]   https://www.kaggle.com/datasets/debashishsau/aslamerican-sign-language-aplhabet-dataset/code.

[2]   Elakkiya, R., and Rajalakshmi, E. (2021). ISLAN, *Mendeley Data*, V1, doi:10.17632/rc349j45m5.1.

[3]   Ito, S.I., Ito, M., and Fukumi, M. (2019). Japanese sign language classification is based on gathered images and neural networks. *International Journal of Advances in Intelligent Informatics*, 5(*3*), 243–255.

[4]   Shohieb, S.M., Elminir, H.K., and Riad, A.M. (2015). Signsworld Atlas: benchmark Arabic sign language database. *Journal of King Saud University-Computer and Information Sciences*, 27(*1*), 68–76.

[5]   Reverdy, C., Gibet, S., and Le Naour, T. (2024). STK LSF: a motion capture dataset in LSF for SignToKids. In *Proceedings of the LREC-COLING 2024 11th Workshop on the Representation and Processing of Sign Languages: Evaluation of Sign Language Resources* (pp. 315–322).

[6]   https://www-i6.informatik.rwth-aachen.de/~koller/RWTH-PHOENIX/.

[7]   https://www.bu.edu/asllrp/av/dai-asllvd.html.

[8]   https://facundoq.github.io/datasets/lsa64/.

[9]   https://www.cvssp.org/data/KinectSign/webpages/downloads.html.

[10] https://clarin.phonetik.uni-muenchen.de/BASRepository/index.php?target=Public/Corpora/SIGNUM/SIGNUM.1.php.

[11] https://paperswithcode.com/dataset/csl-daily.

[12] Ko, S.K., Kim, C.J., Jung, H., and Cho, C. (2019). Neural sign language translation based on human keypoint estimation. *Applied Sciences*, 9(*13*), 2683.

[13] https://lsfb.info.unamur.be/.

[14] https://ds.gpii.net/content/psl-tof-84.

[15] https://github.com/dxli94/WLASL.

[16] https://data.mendeley.com/datasets/kcmpdxky7p/1.

[17] https://paperswithcode.com/dataset/ms-asl.

[18] http://lse-sign.bcbl.eu/web-busqueda/.

[19] https://how2sign.github.io/.

[20] https://www.sign-lang.uni-hamburg.de/dicta-sign/portal/.

[21] https://www-i6.informatik.rwth-aachen.de/~koller/RWTH-PHOENIX-2014-T/.

[22] https://cvml.ankara.edu.tr/datasets/.

[23] https://paperswithcode.com/dataset/libras-ufop.

[24] https://www.femalevoicenarrator.com/voiceover-blog/sign-language-video-production-recording-tips.

[25] Pisharady, P.K., Vadakkepat, P., and Loh, A.P. (2013). Attention-based detection and recognition of hand postures against complex backgrounds. *International Journal of Computer Vision*, 101, 403–419.

[26] Eid, A., and Schwenker, F. (2023). Visual static hand gesture recognition using convolutional neural network. *Algorithms*, 16, 361.

[27] Miura, T., and Sako, S. (2021). SynSLaG: synthetic sign language generator. *In Proceedings of the 23rd International ACM SIGACCESS Conference on Computers and Accessibility* (pp. 1–4).

[28] https://www.bsc.es/news/bsc-news/bsc-develops-database-the-automatic-sign-language-translation-thanks-ai.

[29] Kothadiya, D.R., Bhatt, C.M., Saba, T., Rehman, A., and Bahaj, S.A. (2023). SIGNFORMER: deepvision transformer for sign language recognition. *IEEE Access*, 11, 4730–4739.

Chapter 4

Text translation in sign language

4.1 Introduction

4.1.1 Importance of text translation in sign language

Sign language translation is a critical field of research between the hearing and deaf populations. It is most important when you want to translate text from written or spoken language into sign language. It is important, since it allows deaf people to learn in their language of choice, which decreases barriers they encounter in education, social interactions, healthcare and employment.

Translation from text-to-sign language has a distinct advantage over traditional translation systems because sign languages are structurally and linguistically different. Sign languages are a visual-gestural language, with grammatical, syntactic and semantic distinctions from spoken languages. Sign languages, for example, typically have no written language, and it is often hard to translate text into gestures. In several ways, the significance of text translation can be explained:

- **Education accessibility:** By offering learning content in sign language via translation from text, deaf learners gain access to the information they need. A lot of textbooks are printed and only published on paper, and translation into sign language ensures equal learning.
- **Social inclusion:** Sign-language translation of texts also enables social inclusion and enables the deaf to engage in day-to-day conversations, news, and entertainment with subtitling or real-time translation.
- **Professional and administrative services:** In professional settings, text translation technology allows deaf users to communicate effectively, both in daily job operations and when entering information at healthcare or government portals.
- **Cultural heritage:** Text translation into sign language preserves and spreads the richness of various sign languages across borders. With automated translators, languages could share content across different sign languages without compromising linguistic variety.

4.1.2 Applications and use cases

The sign language translation of texts can be used in different fields, but some major uses are:

- **Media and entertainment:** Captioning and transcribing films, TV series and online videos to sign-language help deaf people enjoy the same visual experiences as hearing viewers. Live sign language interpreters or automated systems on live streams can drive participation.
- **Textbook tools:** There are internet services that provide automatic texting from textbooks and educational materials to sign language for training purposes. For instance, e-learning websites with sign language translation can make studying more engaging for deaf students.
- **Healthcare:** Sign Language Translation of Patient Records, Physician's notes and Diagnostic Reports in Hospitals and Medical Appointments – Sign language interpretation of healthcare records and diagnostic documentation improves communication between the healthcare workers and deaf patients. It can also be applied to telemedicine networks.
- **Customer services:** In customer care, the translation of text into sign language can enhance the user experience of deaf customers. Systems could automatically convert texts or live chats into sign language, providing immediate assistance to end users.
- **Government and legal services:** Sign language translation software for official records, forms, and documents in the courts can help deaf people to use government services, fill out forms, and learn about their rights under the law. That helps break down communication obstacles in formal environments.
- **Public notices and alert systems:** Convenient translation of emergency announcements, public safety messages, and warnings into sign language can reach many deaf participants during a natural disaster, public health emergency, or emergency.

In these instances, however, text translation is not just a medium of communication but also a vital facilitator of inclusivity and self-determination for the deaf. The creation of reliable and accessible text-to-sign language translation tools can give people power through democratizing access to knowledge.

4.2   Data collection and preprocessing

When building a model for text-to-sign language translation, data collection and preprocessing are necessary to provide the model with quality, varied, and structured data. This section discusses how this is done using examples from **PHOENIX-2014T**, **RWTH-BOSTON-50** and other datasets such as American Sign Language Lexicon Video Dataset (**ASLLVD**), as well as specific techniques and algorithms used in each approach.

4.2.1   Text data sources

To create realistic models of translation, the information must come from varied and relevant corpora and reflect both syntactic and semantic complexity of the target language. Here are some specific ones:

- **PHOENIX-2014T (German sign language):** German text together with sign language gestures is presented in this dataset. It includes weather information, a reasonably orderly area in which scholars can work to fix the match between German sentences and their signs.
- **RWTH-BOSTON-50 (American sign language):** ASL video and corresponding English text in this dataset. Due to the smaller dataset size, data augmentation techniques for modeling efficiency should be applied.
- **ASLLVD:** It is a great dataset for isolated signs with rich linguistic annotations. It works very well for training models for the recognition of single signs or gestures and later applies to continuous sign-language processing and translation.

Other potential data sources:

- Broadcast media with sign-language captioning (news broadcasts).
- Course textbooks to create sign language translations in specific domains.

4.2.2   Data cleaning and preprocessing

Cleaning of data is very important to clean the text and sign language data to use in training. Below, we will discuss the cleaning, normalization, and data segmentation techniques across datasets.

(a) **Data organizing:**
- **PHOENIX-2014T:** To prepare this dataset, we need to eliminate noise and inconsistencies by applying OpenPose to skeletal frames to extract meaningful sign language gestures. Video artefacts like motion blur and low light are smoothed with Gaussian blurring or Median filtering applied to the video frames.
- **RWTH-BOSTON-50:** For text, methods such as Rule-based noise filtering can be applied to eliminate irrelevant metadata like timing markers or speaker annotations. Missing information of the gesture sequences is inferred using the Forward or Backward Fill Imputation method; no gaps exist in the gesture sequences for translation.

(b) **Tokenization and text normalization:**
PHOENIX-2014T and RWTH-BOSTON-50 both use BPE tokenization to split text into units of subwords. This technique tamely fixes neural machine translation (NMT) out-of-vocabulary issue by having the model break rare words into well-used subword units. Further, the text is normalized with TF-IDF (Term Frequency-Inverse Document Frequency) vectors so that frequent but irrelevant words such as "the" or "a" are weighted less than useful words such as "storm" or "temperature."

(c) **Dealing with non-verbal indicators in sign language:**
Non-verbal Indicators in sign language may include facial expressions, eye gaze and mouth expressions. They are essential for a correct grasp of what signs are about.

- OpenPose and MediaPipe are widely used for pose estimation in both PHOENIX-2014T and ASLLVD datasets. These tools extract keypoints from human body joints (hands, face) so models can identify non-manual aspects of signing.
- Time Convolutional Network (TCN) or Recurrent Neural Network (RNN) is useful for gesture segmentation, parsing continuous sign videos into discrete sign units using time series data from skeletal keypoints.

4.2.3   Data augmentation approaches

Data augmentation can be used to scale the dataset, which becomes more important for low-resource sign languages that do not provide a lot of data. This becomes crucial, especially for datasets such as RWTH-BOSTON-50 which are quite small. Here are some advanced methods:

(a) **Text data augmentation:**
    Figure 4.1 shows the illustrations of text data augmentation.
    - **Back-translation:** Back-translation in PHOENIX-2014T is applied to add variability to text data. The German words, for example, are encoded into English with transformer-based NMT systems, and back into German. This method is done with models such as MarianMT (an open-source NMT engine), and paraphrased sentences are semantically still based on the original.
    - **Contextual data augmentation:** Using models like BERT (Bidirectional Encoder Representations from Transformers), contextual variants of sentences are created. For instance, synonymizing some words but maintaining their meaning contributes to data diversity.

(b) **Sign language data enhancement:**
    Figure 4.2 shows the illustrations of sign language data augmentation.

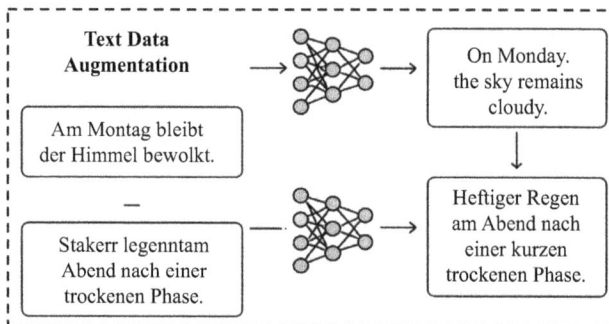

Figure 4.1   Text data augmentation PHOENIX-2014T

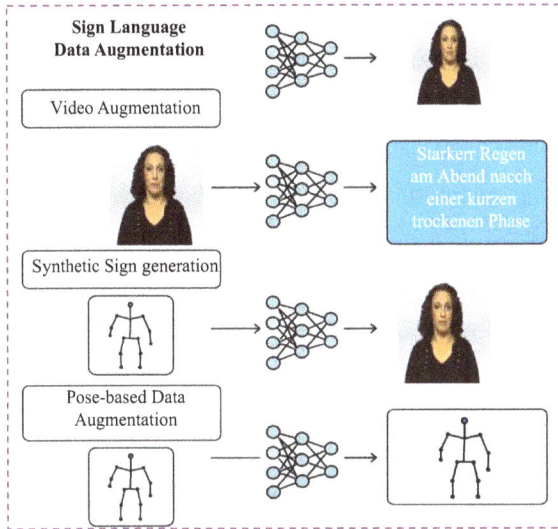

Figure 4.2   Sign data augmentation PHOENIX-2014T

- **Video augmentation:** Video augmentation methods include spatio-temporal cropping and random video rotations in the PHOENIX-2014T dataset. This technique is integrated with generative adversarial networks (GANs), especially Video GANs, to create novel patterns of sign language gestures that preserve the body's natural motion.
- **Synthetic signs:** RWTH-BOSTON-50 produces synthetic sign videos through Conditional GANs (cGANs). When training the GAN on skeletal information extracted from actual videos, new gestures can be made to approximate the actual use of sign language.
- **Pose augmentation**: Skeletal keypoints in datasets, such as ASLLVD, can be enhanced with Affine transformations, providing an unpredictability to gestures by adjusting, scaling or rotating the keypoint data. This method increases the model's resilience to slight alterations in hand position and body orientation.

4.2.4   Dataset annotation and alignment

Proper annotation and mapping of text-to-sign are needed to train models to associate written words and gestures correctly. Here are a few examples of annotation and mapping methods on datasets.

(a) **Text annotation:**
- In PHOENIX-2014T data, spaCy is used for part-of-speech tagging, entity recognition and dependency parsing. These markings make

sentence structure more visible to the model and facilitate faster synchronization between German words and accompanying sign gestures.
- RWTH-BOSTON-50 leverages NER with BERT-based NER models to recognize objects like names, addresses and dates. This is critical to translating contextually dependent signs better.

(b) **Sign language annotation:**
- PHOENIX-2014T and ASLLVD support FACS, which codes for non-manual actions such as eyebrow raises or lip gestures, which convey crucial grammatical information in signs. For PHOENIX-2014T, FACS annotations supplement manual gestures to capture the full meaning of the sentence.
- SignAligner application is used to mark gesture edges in RWTH-BOSTON-50, linking each sign to the corresponding text unit.

(c) **Alignment techniques:**
- **Dynamic time warping (DTW):** PHOENIX-2014T uses DTW to coordinate text sentences and their sign sequences. This algorithm calculates the best alignment route between the time series information (sign gestures) and the text when there is a temporal variation of signing rate.
- **Connectionist temporal classification (CTC):** In RWTH-BOSTON-50, CTC loss functions are used in the RNNs for variable length sequences in sign language translation. It is a technique that enables the model to coordinate text and sign gestures by computing alignment between the most likely text tokens and gesture frames, in the absence of temporal coherence.

4.3   Features extraction and modeling

Feature extraction is crucial for converting text-to-sign language because the model needs to be able to comprehend and model both the semantic characteristics of the text and the expressive gestures of sign language. In the following, we explore more sophisticated methods, along with the ones discussed earlier, to enhance the quality of the translation.

4.3.1   Advanced methods to unpick features from text

Apart from the traditional Bag of Words (BoW) or TF-IDF, features extracted from text are now taken into consideration by using deep learning to extract rich, context-aware features of language. Such approaches make text understandable for the model in relation to sign language etiquette.

(a) **Transformer-based models (BERT, GPT, RoBERTa):**
- BERT: In the PHOENIX-2014T data, BERT is used to generate context-sensitive embeddings. BERT determines the meaning of the word using

its surrounding words, which make it the best tool to translate ambiguous or polysemous words into the right sign language gesture. For instance, "bank" can be the bank or the bank of a river; BERT guesses the right word in the context. Figure 4.3 shows the embedding illustrations by the BERT model.

- Generative pre-trained transformer (GPT): GPT, GPT-3 is used to make coherent sentences. We can use such models to produce text paraphrases in augmentation and to produce contextual embeddings of whole phrases instead of single words, providing for improved translation.
- RoBERTa: An optimized version of BERT, RoBERTa can be tuned to higher-resolution data sets, such as RWTH-BOSTON-50. This framework also helps in the extraction of small-scale contextual information from texts – essential for sign languages that rely on fine-grained grammatical variation.

(b) **Sequence-to-sequence models (Seq2Seq):** For datasets such as PHOENIX-2014T, Attention-Based Seq2Seq Models are implemented to extract features from sequences of text data and match them with associated sequences of sign language. Seq2Seq algorithms read full sentences or paragraphs, learning the sequence patterns – this helps in the translation of longer words into continuous sign language movements.

(c) **Character-based models (Char-CNN and CharRNN):** Character-based models (Char-CNN/RNN) on the ASLLVD dataset extract features directly from characters, rather than words or subwords. This method is especially useful in scarce languages or dialects where word-level models are not always effective because they lack vocabulary. Character models render the text in

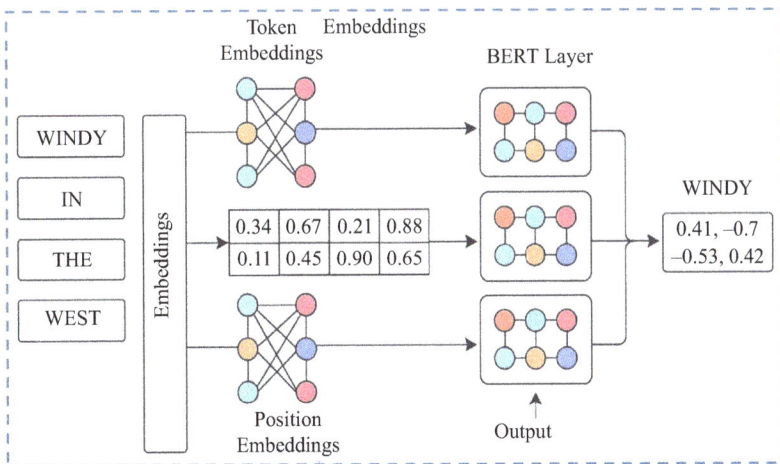

Figure 4.3   Token and positional embeddings illustration in BERT architecture

small units, making difficult or unfamiliar words easier to process in translation.

4.3.2   Specialized methods to decode sign language features

Since sign language is visually gestural, it is important to extract spatiotemporal features. The following advanced methods help the model learn elaborate gestures, shapes of hands, movements and facial expressions.

(a)   **3D convolutional neural networks (3D-CNNs):** 3D-CNNs provide a way of visualizing the spatio-temporal evolution of sign language. In the PHOENIX-2014T dataset, 3D-CNNs compute video scenes by overlapping both spatial (height, width) and temporal (time). This approach allows the model to learn how hands, faces and body positions move in the future while detecting similar signs but different actions (fast vs. slow, circular vs. linear).

- Temporal 3D convolutions: C3D (Convolutional 3D Networks) is an extension of 3D-CNN that is used for video recording. In the RWTH-BOSTON-50 dataset, for instance, C3D detects temporal dependencies between hand movements so that the model can distinguish underlying, temporal changes in gestures.

(b)   **Spatial-temporal graph (ST-GCN):** ST-GCN enables us to derive spatial and temporal correspondence in the skeletal data for sets such as ASLLVD. Sign language movement is associated with many joints, and ST-GCN generates a graph of joints (e.g., elbow, wrist, hand), where nodes are each a joint, and edges are the relations among joints. This network learns both how joints move in relation to each other (spatial) and how those movements change over time (temporal). ST-GCN works best with sign languages that are very seated/moving with body posture.

(c)   **RNNs Long short-term memory (LSTM):** LSTMs are commonly employed to read sequential data, making them well suited for video-based sign language datasets like RWTH-BOSTON-50. LSTMs can record continuous dependencies between gestures, which means that the sentence-long chain is being considered, instead of sign-along single signs.

- Bidirectional LSTMs (BiLSTMs): BiLSTMs are applied for continuous sign language recognition in PHOENIX-2014T to learn the context before and after each gesture. This is crucial to avoid confusing signals with the same appearance, which translate to something different from the underlying gestures.

(d)   **Optical flow/motion estimation:**

- Optical flow algorithms such as Horn-Schunck or Farneback Optical Flow determine the rotation of a pixel of a video frame between frames. The hand movement is tracked using optical flow on the RWTH-BOSTON-50 dataset and is essential for the classification of signs that share handshapes but do not make a difference (i.e., walking in a straight line vs. a curve).

- Dense optical flow: By measuring the motion of each pixel in a video, Dense Optical Flow will be able to extract motion features for sign language. This is especially handy for defining fast and slow signs in sign language.

(e) **Video processing using attention mechanisms:** In PHOENIX-2014T, attention is used to treat video frames to select those features that have the highest significance (e.g., hands, expressions) and filter out the rest (e.g., noise). Incorporating this technique into RNN models or transformer models enables the system to pay special attention to key gesture points so that the translation output is precise and contextual.

(f) **Handshape and movement feature extraction using convolutional pose machine (CPM):** For example, on datasets such as ASLLVD, CPM is applied to extract fine-grained handshape features. Such robots identify joint positions and hand poses at varying levels of refinement, increasing the handshape detection rate with time. It works particularly well for reading complicated signs with complicated movements in the hands.

4.3.3   *Word emblems and contextual expressions*

The success of a text-to-sign language translation scheme is closely tied to the ability of the machine to interpret the content of the text. Using word embeddings is important to capture the semantic and syntactic properties of the text in a form that can be used by the model to generate associated gestures.

(a) **Contextual embeds with embeddings from language models (ELMo):** ELMo produces rich contextualized word representations by considering the context of both the word and sentence. The ELMo embeddings in PHOENIX-2014T data show the forward and backward contexts, which are particularly useful when the ambiguous words could have multiple interpretations depending on the sentence.

(b) **Self-attention-based embeddings:** Self-attention processes, such as those in transformer and BERT, compute the relations between each word of a sentence so that the model can target the most relevant segments of the text for translation. On RWTH-BOSTON-50 data, attentional embeddings are used to match words with the associated gestures to help translate text that retains the subtle details of its content.

(c) **Multimodal embeddings:** Multimodal embeddings integrate both the text and sign modalities. In PHOENIX-2014T, for example, the model learns joint embeddings of text and gesture patterns, thus it can capture cross-modal relationships. Such embeddings enable the model to match the spoken or written words with their visual representation in sign language to better align the spoken or written words with their visual representation in sign language.

4.4   Machine translation techniques

Machine translation (MT) is the foundation of text-to-sign transformation. They use two main paradigms: statistical machine translation (SMT) and NMT. They both employ different methodologies for learning and translating, with NMT being the leading practice because it has better control over sophisticated linguistic forms.

4.4.1   Statistical machine translation

SMT is one of the first attempts at text-to-sign language translation. SMT systems model the probability of translating one sentence from language a to b. Well, here is how SMT works, and it is used to translate sign language:

(a)   **Parallel text alignment:** SMT needs a large amount of parallel data (i.e., sentence pairs in one language, for example, English text and the other language, such as sign language gloss or gestures). For instance, in PHOENIX-2014T datasets, pairs of German sentences and matching sign language gestures are aligned using parallel corpora.

(b)   **Phrase-based SMT:** Phrase-based statistical machine translation (PB-SMT) models split sentences into phrases instead of just words, providing better translation. This system identifies phrases in the source text that co-occur statistically with corresponding phrases of sign language (usually several gestures) and aligns them. These phrases receive probability values from the model, which estimates the most probable succession of gestures that will represent a given sentence.

(c)   **Drawbacks of SMT in SLT:**
- **Contextual handling:** SMT cannot handle long-range dependencies and context in the text, making it problematic for sign language as many signs rely heavily on context to fully convey meaning (especially polysemy).
- **Non-spoken aspects:** Sign languages are very visual, and SMT does not have the ability to represent non-manual features like facial expressions or body gestures.
- **Word Reordering:** If the word order of a source language is very different from the word order in the target language, then which SMT systems would not work. This presents a particular issue for languages such as ASL, which has an entirely different syntactic structure than the English language.

Despite these limitations, SMT formed a fundamental part of early sign language translation algorithms but has largely been replaced by tools like NMT.

4.4.2   Neural machine translation

NMT revolutionized machine translation by utilizing deep learning to automatically infer sentence-to-sentence mapping between different languages. Neural networks and NMT models excel in sign language translation because they capture the nuances of language and gesture.

(a) **Encoder-decoder structure:** NMT models largely adopt an encoder-decoder structure. In this architecture:
  - The encoder reads the input text and converts it to a single-byte vector (code) that contains the text's meaning.
  - The decoder takes this representation and creates the appropriate target sequence (in this example, a sequence of sign language gestures).

    For example, in the PHOENIX-2014T dataset, NMT models learn German sentences via an encoder network (sometimes RNN or LSTMs). The decoder outputs a set of sign gestures, either as keypoint sequences (for video creation) or glosses (text representations of signs).

(b) **NMT for continuous sign language:** NMT models are particularly useful in continuous sign language, where the input is a moving, continuous stream of signs. NMT is implemented in RWTH-BOSTON-50 on an RNN encoder-decoder framework with attention mechanisms to allow the model to pick out the most meaningful chunks of the input text and produce the sign accordingly.

(c) **Attention:** Attention enables NMT models to pay attention to certain words or phrases when they are translating. For instance, if a German sentence has a word with a good sign gesture attached to it, attentional processing means that the decoder places greater emphasis on that word when it is drawing the sign. This is particularly useful in sign language translation, where some words in one language might be translated into a larger number of gestures in the other.

(d) **Transformer-based NMT:** Transformers have been the dominant NMT model for a bit, thanks to its parallelization and the ability to catch dependencies from a very long distance. PHOENIX-2014T uses transformer models to translate whole sentences or paragraphs, with multiple attention layers enabling the model to translate long lines of text to sophisticated sign language gestures.
  - **Self-attention mechanisms:** Transformers do not use RNNs to learn a sequence in steps; they leverage self-attention to learn all the words in the sentence. This is particularly effective in sign language since the model can pick up on the associations between distant words in the sentence and produce better gestures.

4.4.3   NMT methods for sign language translation

Several sophisticated NMT techniques have been developed specifically for text-to-sign translation:

(a) **Seq2Seq models:** Seq2Seq LSTMs and attention models are commonly applied to data sets such as RWTH-BOSTON-50. These models work well when you want to translate a text into glosses (simplified sign symbols) or simply into sign gestures. The model encodes the input text and translates it into a continuous sign language sequence, with attention algorithms making sure that the correct parts of the input text are emphasized throughout the translation process.

(b) **Sign2Pose and Pose2Sign:** In the PHOENIX-2014T dataset, Pose2Sign models create sign language gestures from the text. These models associate the text with skeletal pose representations of gestures in sign language. For example, OpenPose learns keypoint coordinates from videos, and NMT is trained to get keypoints from words. This facilitates real-time translation of words into sign language videos.

(c) **Hybrid models (SMT + NMT):** A combination of SMT and NMT is sometimes applied in a hybrid fashion. An SMT model can, for instance, pre-translate text into glosses and then enhance them using NMT models to get fluent, natural-looking sign language chains. This has been implemented in PHOENIX-2014T, where initial SMT outputs are filtered through NMT for better gesture alignment.

4.4.4   Handling inconsistencies in sign language translation

NMT models must deal with a few challenges that are unique to sign language translation:

(a) **Non-manual signs:** Non-manual signs, including facial expressions, eye gazes, and head tilts, contribute significantly to meaning in sign languages. Multimodal attention-based transformer models work on both text and video signals, registering the flow between manual signs and non-manual signs. Such models employ attention layers encompassing both the textual aspects of the text and the visual aspects of sign language videos.

(b) **Multimodal neural networks:** Multimodal NMT models merge textual and visual inputs to produce sign language translations. These models both employ the input words and features that are gleaned from videos of sign language (handshapes, facial expressions). For PHOENIX-2014T, NMTs using both CNNs and LSTMs incorporate text embeddings and pose embeddings extracted from sign language videos. This allows the model to take full advantage of the meaning offered by text and visual representations.

4.4.5   NMT advanced attention mechanisms for sign language

By focusing on specific segments of the input sequence, NMT systems have been able to redefine how they process translations. In sign language translation, where the connection between words and gestures is more difficult to resolve, attentional functions are particularly useful.

Some of the advanced attentional methods used in sign language translation are outlined below:

(a) **Self-attention (in transformers):** Self-attention forces the model to map every word of the input sequence on every other word, to capture long-range dependencies. In sign translation, it's particularly useful for sentences in which the meaning of a gesture is derived from context within more than one part of the sentence.

For instance, with the PHOENIX-2014T dataset, a transformer-based model that pays attention to itself may pay attention to the relationship between subject and verb so that gestures are meaningful and contextually correct. The model could need to consider word-order differences between German and the target sign language.

(b) **Multimodal attention:** In multimodal NMT systems, the model's attention is directed toward text and image signals. When it comes to sign language translation, this means that the model can simultaneously extract the linguistic structure of the input text and visual structural features (i.e., gestures, facial expressions) from sign language videos.

Multimodal attention layers in datasets such as RWTH-BOSTON-50 use features derived from text and pose sequences. This enables the model to dynamically alternate between the spoken sentence and the keypoint information in the sign language video, thereby having both modes play a role in the final translation result.

(c) **Hierarchical attention:** We can leverage hierarchy to apply attention at multiple levels of information (phrase, sentence, paragraph). This can be useful in situations where a single gesture could have been associated with a phrase or clause, instead of a word.

For the PHOENIX-2014T data set, top-down attention allows the model to focus on larger linguistic units like phrases or clauses so that the sign language translation retains both fine and coarse level meaning. This approach can be used to make gestures flow across longer passages of text.

4.4.6 *Multimodal NMT sign language translation*

Multimodal neural machine translation (multimodal NMT) combines multiple input signals (e.g., text, image or video) to enhance translation performance. In sign language translation, multimodal NMT systems employ both the text and the visual information from sign language gestures to produce more precise translations.

(a) **Combining text and video features.**
- **Text-to-sign translation (Sign2Pose):** In multimodal NMT models, text first goes through an encoder (for BERT or LSTMs), and the video passes through a visual encoder (for 3D-CNNs or Graph Convolutional Networks (GCNs)). Both modalities are then stitched together with attentional processing to generate a sequence of sign language gestures from the input text.

For instance, in the PHOENIX-2014T dataset, text is processed with transformer while the video of sign language is processed with 3D-CNN to recognize hand gestures and body movements. The two encodings are combined in a multimodal attention layer that produces the sign gesture output.

- **Pose and gesture-based sign translation:** A multimodal pose-based NMT can extract skeletal pose sequences from the input text. The poses can be transcribed into sign language videos. This is achieved in PHOENIX-2014T by using a GCN to simulate the bones and joints and to produce poses that mimic the natural movements of human sign language.

(b) **Multimodal alignment:** The major difficulty with multimodal NMT is the reshuffling of the different input modalities. For sign language translation, the text must be compatible with both manual and non-manual signs. In doing so, models use cross-modal alignment, which means the text has meaning not just in hand motions, but also in facial expressions, eye movements and other non-manual signals. In the RWTH-BOSTON-50 dataset, for instance, a multi-modal NMT model can utilize alignment networks to map specific phrases in the input sentence with phrases in the video. This ensures that the facial expression used to describe a question or feeling corresponds to the appropriate part of the text.

4.4.7 Handling non-manual signals in NMT

Sign language consists of both manual (hand signals) and non-manual cues (facial expressions, body movements). These non-manual signals are a challenge in NMT sign language translators.

Incorporating non-manual features:

- **FACS**: Non-manual facial movements can be simulated using the facial action coding system (FACS), which converts expressions into action units (e.g., eyebrow raising, mouth movements). These action units can be trained on NMT models to match them with linguistic features in the input, thus creating facial expressions for the sign that corresponds to it. The PHOENIX-2014T dataset, for instance, incorporates FACS annotations along with manual gesture annotations to produce hand movements and facial expressions, thus yielding a more complete translation.

- **Multimodal attention for non-manual signals:** Multimodal attention is employed to interpret both the text input and the visual aspects of non-manual signals. It enables the model to pay attention to portions of the text that prompt specific facial expressions or movements. As in the RWTH-BOSTON-50 dataset, non-manual gestures such as head nods and eye movements are coded in addition to manual gestures, and attentional filters enable the model to choose when and how to use non-manual signals in the resulting sign sequence.

4.4.8 Pretraining and transfer learning for low-resource sign languages

The biggest hurdle for sign language translation is the lack of large annotated datasets. To counter this, scientists have developed pretraining and transfer learning algorithms to take known resources from high-resource languages and translate them to low-resource sign languages.

(a) **Pretraining on related tasks:** NMT models can be pre-trained on large sets of data for related problems (e.g., machine translation between spoken languages), and then trained on smaller sign language sets. For instance, a model could be trained on the Europarl (speech language) and then tuned on the PHOENIX-2014T (German sign language) dataset.

(b) **Multilingual transfer learning:** Multilingual NMT models like mBART or mT5 can be pretrained across multiple language sets and optimized for sign language datasets. The latter method enables the model to generalize across text and sign language, even when sign language information is sparse. In the RWTH-BOSTON-50 dataset, for instance, a multilingual NMT model trained on English, Spanish and French text can be trained to decode English text into ASL by taking advantage of the language-specific structure common to all three languages.

(c) **Few-shot and zero-shot learning:**
- **Few-shot learning:** Few-shot learning is used in low-resource environments to generalize the model using only a small amount of labelled sign language inputs. Pretrained on a resource-intensive language and fine-tuned using just a few samples of the target sign language, this model can be used to produce reliable translation systems with low amounts of data.o GPT-3 and T5 models, for instance, have been deployed in few-shot training experiments, in which a model trained on large text corpora can be tuned with only a few sign language translations to give good results.
- **Zero-shot learning:** Sometimes models can perform zero-shot learning by translating into sign language without having been trained on the sign language data. These models draw on collective representations that have been learned from pretraining on other languages and tasks.

4.5 Attention mechanisms and transformer models

The transformers implemented through self-attention mechanisms have become a fundamental element in NMT, including those for sign language translation. This enables models to capture long-range dependencies and attend to the most salient parts of an input while producing translations. This section will cover how attention works text-to-sign language translation, as well as an in-depth look into how transformer models have an architecture and its applications.

4.5.1   *Attention mechanism in text translation*

The main purpose of an attention mechanism is to allow the model to pay attention to or focus on specific parts of the input while predicting the output. It is important in text-to-sign language translation as some words need more focus during the generation of the sign language gesture for accurate and relevant translation. Here's how attention works for translation:

- **Attention for focusing on selective input words:** In the traditional Seq2Seq model setting without attention, the entire input sentence is encoded into a fixed-length vector, leading to performance degradation, especially for long sentences. The attention mechanism addresses this issue by enabling the model to "attend" to various portions of the input sequence during every decoding step. For example, if one were training a model to translate the sentence "The weather is beautiful today" into sign language, the model may choose to really focus on the words "weather" and "beautiful" when converting the meaning into gestures because these are the words that provide the most "meaning" to this translation.
- **Soft and hard attention mechanisms:** Two popular types of attention mechanisms are:
  - o **Soft attention:** This enables the model to put different weights on all input words, homing in on the most relevant ones. For example, soft attention used for translation toward sign language will allow the model to focus more on important gestures (for instance, on facial expressions that usually come with some signs).
  - o **Hard attention:** On the other hand, hard attention requires that the model pay attention to the exact portion of the input at each time step. It is useful in interpreting isolated signs, in which the words and gestures correspond in a clearer way.

4.5.2   *Transformer architecture and its application*

By now, everybody is familiar with the transformer architecture introduced in Vaswani *et al.* (2017), which marked a breakthrough for machine translation, leveraging self-attention to read the input sequences in parallel. Recently, transformers have become the conformal choice for text-to-sign language translation due to their ability to model long-range dependencies and complicated sentence structures. In this section, we describe the main elements of the transformer architecture and its applications in sign language translation.

(a) Components of the transformer architecture
The transformer model is composed of two key components, namely the encoder and decoder, both of which contain several layers of self-attention and feed-forward networks (FFNs).

- **Self-attention mechanism:** The self-attention mechanism is the heart of the transformer. This enables the model to assess how significant each word in the input sequence is in relation to every other word. This allows the model to learn relationships between distant words. Self-attention is crucial in sign language translation because the meaning of a gesture may depend on multiple words in a sentence. In the PHOENIX-2014T dataset, let's say we need to translate a sentence like "It will rain tomorrow," the self-attention mechanism would allow the model to understand the relationship between "rain" and "tomorrow" to ensure that the corresponding gesture for "rain" gets generated with the correct temporal marker.

- **Positional encoding:** Unlike RNNs which sequentially process input, transformers can process the whole input sequence in parallel. Positional encodings are added to the input embeddings to provide the model with information about the relative positions of words. These encode where each word is in the sentence. Positional encoding is used in sign language translation to make sure the gestures are created in the exact order. For instance, for the sentence "John is playing football," "John" comes first, and positional encoding ensures the "John" gesture comes before "football."

- **Multi-head attention:** Transformers utilize multi-head attention to enable the model to attend to various sections of the input sequence at once. Each "head" learns to recognize different characteristics of the sentence. For example, in translating sign language, the model must be able to attend to many signs or facial expressions simultaneously. For example, in the RWTH-BOSTON-50 dataset, given a sequence of words to translate, multi-head attention can be applied to generate the gestures for both the parts that need manual signs (e.g., hand movements) and non-manual signals (e.g., face expressions) together. This ensures that while generating sentences, the model will consider both gestures.

- **Feed-forward networks (FFNs):** A fully connected FFN for each layer that processes the output of the self-attention mechanism. It makes training the model to understand more complex correlations between the input text and the target signs easier.

- **Layer normalization and residual connections:** Transformers include layer normalization and residual connections between layers to stabilize training and help the model learn. By employing mechanisms such as multi-head attention and residual connections, upset problems like vanishing gradients are prevented, enabling the model to learn representations of deeper aspects of the input sequence.

(b) Encoder-decoder model for sign language translation

Transformers' encoder-decoder architecture is well suited to sign language translation, as it requires the model to generate a sequence of gestures in correspondence with input text. Here's how the two parts work:

- **Encoder:** The input text sequence is processed and transformed into a sequence of representations by the encoder. These features encode the semantic information of the input sentence. For instance, in the PHOENIX-2014T dataset, the encoder processes a German sentence and gives the output as a sequence of context vectors that contain the meaning of a word relative to the others.

- **Decoder:** These context vectors are then used by the decoder to produce the sequence of target sign language. At each step of the decoder, an element of the output sequence is generated (e.g., gesture or keypoint) based on the context from the encoder and the outputs generated so far. The decoder outputs the sequence of body gestures (hand movements, facial expressions, and other non-verbal signals) corresponding to the complete sign language translation.

4.5.3   Applications of transformers in sign language translation

- **Text-to-sign language translation system:** In datasets such as PHOENIX-2014T, transformer-based models are employed to translate spoken or written language into sign language gestures. These new models have resulted in significant improvements with respect to translation accuracy over standard NMT models. Transformers can produce coherent and natural sign language videos that maintain a contextual representation via multi-head and self-attention.
- **Text-to-sign video generation:** For example, transformers are also applied in video generation systems, such as the sign language video generation system, in which the text input is translated to sign language videos. The generated sequences of skeletal poses or key points are rendered to sign language videos through pose estimation models like OpenPose by the systems that adopt the encoder-decoder architecture of transformer. In RWTH-BOSTON-50, we use this approach from text to create a high-quality sign language video.
- **Real-time translation systems:** Transformer-based approaches are also used in real-time scenarios to translate text into sign language in real-time during live events or video calls. Such models take an input text and process it in a continuous manner generating the relevant gestures and displaying them as an animated Avatar or video.

4.6   Summary

In this chapter, the important components related to the text-to-sign language translation process, methodologies, techniques, and real-world applications that enhance accessibility for the deaf community have been explored. It emphasized the critical need of translating text into sign language for access to education, media and healthcare, among other areas. This helps deaf people read the information, take part in social gatherings and be more independent. Translation approach works on large datasets, such as PHOENIX-2014T and RWTH-BOSTON-50, and hand gestures pose estimation, optical flow, and data augmentation to deal with specific challenges with sign language translation that consider facial expressions and other non-manual signals. Feature extraction is important in both text and sign language, and various techniques were employed to learn powerful features from the input data including Word2Vec, BERT, and GCNs. Thus, the contextual representations and attention mechanisms are useful for obtaining relationships between the text and gestures. It includes reviews of SMT and NMT, as well as comparing them in terms of sign language translation. In contrast, NMT models, and especially transformer-based architectures, have demonstrated a higher efficiency level when dealing with these complexities. It was about Seq2Seq models, Pose2Sign techniques and hybrid SMT–NMT models for improving outputs of translation. These mechanisms, particularly self-attention and multi-head attention, allow the model to consider the relevant parts of the input sequence, which makes transformers a very effective option for sign language translation, as they can capture long-range dependencies and context.

Chapter 5

Speech-to-sign language translation

5.1 Introduction

Assistive technology has come a long way in enhancing the lifestyles of people with hearing disabilities. Although text-to-sign language translation has emerged successfully, the task of translating speech to sign language provides a much more natural and consistent medium of communication. For most hearing individuals, speech is the most common and intuitive form of communicating, making just translating speech into sign language a powerful form of inclusive communication.

Speech-to-sign language translation systems try to converge the gap between spoken-word communication and visual gestural languages. These systems are critical to enabling real-time communication anywhere – classrooms to public venues, emergency alerts and healthcare environments, virtual meetings, and beyond. But translating from speech to sign language is not a clear-cut challenge. It comes with challenges that are not present in text-based systems. Spoken language is more than just changes in pitch, tone, speed, emotion, and accent. In addition, spoken language contains extraneous words, hesitations, and non-standard structures that do not have a direct corresponding mapping onto grammatical or semantic constructs in sign languages.

Typically, this involves two steps where automatic speech recognition (ASR) is employed to convert the audio signal into text, which is later translated into sign language representations. Recent research in this area is focusing on training models to translate directly from speech to sign, bypassing the traditional text intermediate, and using deep learning models that can learn mappings from audio to gesture.

This chapter details the basic features of speech processing, outlines the widely used ASR models, and explains how speech recognition works with sign language translation models. The goal is to establish a technical foundation for converting speech input into expressive and accurate sign language output.

5.2 Speech processing fundamentals

At its core, speech processing is the critical first step in understanding and interpreting human speech, making it an essential component of systems designed for applications such as speech-to-sign language translation. Speech, in contrast to text, is an indefinite and time-varying analogue signal that contains much more complex information than just the semantic meaning of the words spoken, including tone, emotion, accent, speaker characteristics, etc.

To interpret speech features, it should be pre-processed and converted into numerical representations, which are then input to statistical or deep learning models. In this section, we will investigate the stages of speech processing: The nature of speech signals, preprocessing techniques, feature extraction, and creation of the data ready for training the model.

5.2.1   Speech signals

A speech signal is termed a non-stationary signal, i.e., the characteristics of the speech signal change over time scale. It is created by the human vocal tract, which functions as a resonator system. The articulatory motion of the mouth, lips, tongue, and nasal cavity shapes the vibrations of the vocal cords. This results in complex waveforms across frequencies, amplitudes, and durations. A typical waveform of a spoken sentence is shown in Figure 5.1. You can see the amplitude change as the speaker goes from saying one word/phoneme to another. The important features of the speech signal are:

- **PITCH**: How high or low a voice sounds, determined by the speed of vibra-tions of the vocal folds.
- **Formant**: Resonant frequencies in the vocal tract that give their identity to vowels.
- **Prosody**: Patterns of rhythm, stress, and intonation, which can convey emotion or intent.

The diversity of these properties among speakers, languages, and contexts makes speech processing a difficult but rich task.

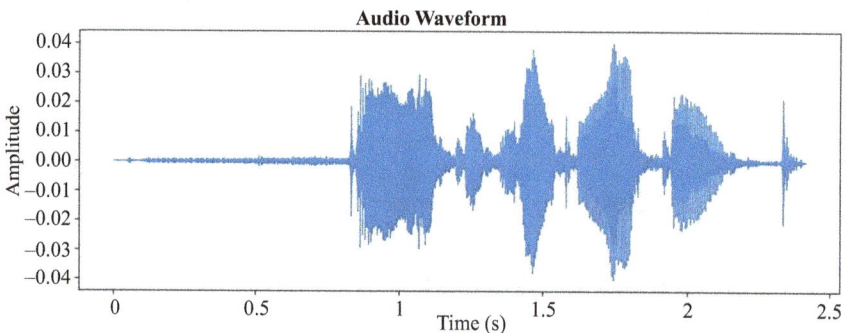

Figure 5.1   A typical waveform of a spoken sentence "I want to drink Water"

5.2.2 Speech signal preprocessing

When raw audio data are captured by a microphone or another input device, it typically comes with some sorts of distortion, such as background noise, silence, and signal amplitude variation. These conditions severely impact the performance of the downstream speech recognition and translation models. As a result, preprocessing is a necessary procedure to make sure the input audio is free of noise, normalized, and segmented to allow easy feature extraction and research.

(a) **Noise removal**

Recent innovations in speech enhancement techniques have transitioned beyond conventional techniques, encompassing deep learning-based speech denoising methods. For example, models like Deep Complex Convolution Recurrent Network (DCCRN) and Speech Enhancement GAN (SEGAN) are state of the art in terms of removing background noise and retaining speech intelligibility.

DCCRN, proposed by Hu *et al.* [1], functions directly within the complex domain, enabling effective modeling of the phase information related to speech signals. In the meantime, real-world telephony and voice-assistant systems have benefitted from architectures such as DeepFilterNet2 [2] and winning models from the DNS Challenge. Such techniques are critical in applications like speech-to-sign language translation, where background noise can cause a cascade of errors in recognition and translation.

(b) **Voice activity detection (VAD)**

Very recent advancements in VAD have focused on adopting end-to-end neural models that achieve high robustness across the language and noise types as well as the intra-speaker differences. Examples of this are the Silero VAD [3] and WebRTC VAD++ (with neural post-filtering), which are well-liked for their high accuracy and low latency. Meanwhile, systems based on wav2vec 2.0 [4,5] have been shown to learn speech segment representations in a self-supervised manner. These models therefore work well in multilingual or spontaneous speech scenarios, which are common in real-time assistive applications.

(c) **Normalization**

Normalization processes ensure that the waveform is preserved across recordings, yielding similar amplitude and loudness for the resulting signal. While classic approaches such as RMS or peak normalization are still used, deep learning models will often embed automatic gain control (AGC) as an online pre-processing module or learn invariance to amplitude during training. Normalization in data preprocessing involves in:

- Per-sample statistics for amplitude scaling
- Loudness units full scale (LUFS) loudness normalization for broadcast-compliant applications
- Compression of a very wide dynamic range for very uneven speaking volumes.

Finally, normalization is sometimes combined with data augmentation (e.g., SpecAugment [6]), leading to increased robustness during model training.

(d) **Framing and windowing**

Speech is non-stationary; however, so it is analyzed in short-time frames over which it can be considered quasi-stationary. This core framing principle still holds for deep learning models such as convolutional or transformer-based architectures, though they typically substitute manual windowing with learned convolutional kernels. However, the Hamming window can still be used in traditional feature extraction pipelines such as Mel-frequency cepstral coefficient (MFCC) or spectrogram calculation. For deep ASR, any framed and windowed audio is typically processed through fast Fourier transform (FFT) layers or used directly as input pointwise in CNN (and in transformers too, e.g., in Whisper by OpenAI, 2022).

5.2.3   Feature extraction

After the raw speech signal is processed with respect to noise reduction, segmentation, and normalization, it must be converted into a numerical representation that computers can read. It is called feature extraction. It aims to transform the information-rich, high-dimensional time series nature of the waveform signal into a low-dimensional representation that captures as much of the relevant embedding space structure of the original waveform during the duration of the signal as possible, whilst filtering out irrelevant or unnecessary information.

Feature extraction plays a crucial role in speech-to-sign language translation in the context of this detection. These features act as the initial input of ASR systems, whose outputs are inputted into downstream generative sign translation models. Features of low quality can potentially lead to errors in the transcription, which then carry through to incorrect or confusing signs being output.

We will now analyze the most common feature extraction methods in both classic and recently proposed ASR pipelines, and methods that were used within the generator component only.

(a) **Mel-frequency cepstral coefficients**

MFCCs are one of the most well-known and commonly used acoustic features in speech processing. They are specifically designed to mimic the nonlinear perceptual scale of human hearing, known as the mel scale, which gives much more weight to lower frequencies – where most of the phonetic information in speech is concentrated. Figure 5.2 illustrates Mel-frequency cepstral damping of a short segment of a speech sound. The steps that constitute calculating MFCCs, in the proper order, are as follows:

(i)   **Framing and windowing**

Therefore, the continuous speech signal gets split into frames with some overlap between consecutive frames (typically of the order of 20–40 ms) based on the assumption that speech is stationarity within each frame. Each frame is then multiplied by a window function (e.g., Hamming window) to reduce spectral leakage.

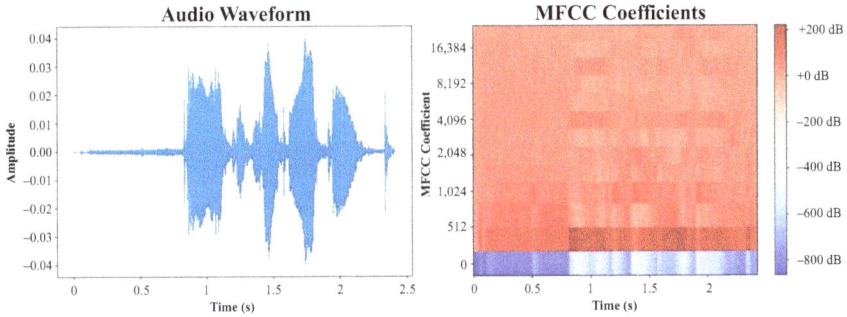

Figure 5.2 *Spoken sentence considered "I want to drink Water". Audio waveform (left) and Mel-frequency cepstral damping of a speech sound (right).*

(ii) **Fast Fourier transform**

Next, we use the FFT to transform each windowed frame we used in the time domain to the frequency domain.

(iii) **Mel filter bank application**

The output of the FFT is fed through a bank of triangular filters arranged at mel-spaced intervals. This mimics the ear, which is less sensitive to changes in loudness at higher frequencies, in a logarithmic manner.

(iv) **Logarithmic compression**

The energies in each Mel filter are then compressed logarithmically. This emulates the dynamic range of human hearing and improves the feature robustness to the amplitude variability.

(v) **Discrete cosine transform (DCT)**

In the final step, the log-Mel energies are decorrelated using DCT. This gives us a series of coefficients (commonly the first 12 or 13) that represent the form of the spectral envelope, which we call MFCCs.

The GMM-HMM architectures have widely adopted MFCCs as the de facto standard in many classical ASR systems. Even though modern deep learning systems can do without MFCCs, instead using their raw or log-Mel form, MFCCs remain prevalent because they are compact, interpretable, and convenient for resource-limited applications.

(b) **Spectrogram and log-Mel spectrograms**

The plot is visualizing the frequency content over time, which is called a spectrogram. This is built by generating the short-time Fourier transform (STFT) of successive overlapping frames of the signal, yielding a 2D matrix where the *x*-axis represents time, frequency on the *y*-axis, and the color or brightness corresponds to the amplitude (power) at each time-frequency bin. Spectrograms can be a good input to CNNs since they resemble grayscale images and maintain spatial (i.e., temporal and spectral) patterns inherent in speech. A log-Mel spectrogram expands this concept by implementing a Mel-scaled filter bank and amplitude scaling in logarithmic scale, to obtain a 2D projection that highlights perceptually significant frequencies while sacrificing the dynamic range. Figure 5.3 represents the spectrogram on the left and the log-Mel spectrogram on the right of the same audio input.

(c) **Chroma features**

Chroma features, or pitch class profiles, summarize the energy of the twelve semitone pitch classes (C, C#, D, ... B) of the musical octave. So, each chroma vector represents the distribution of energy in these 12 pitch classes over all octaves. Although they are mainly used for music information retrieval and tonal analysis, chroma features can prove useful for specific speech applications that hinge on prosody, intonation, or tonal distinctions – namely, tonal languages (e.g., Mandarin, Thai), analysis of expressive speech (e.g., storytelling, affective tone), and translation from singing to sign or synthesis of musical gesture. However, they are less popular in the ASR tasks as it lacks sensitivity in fine-grained phonetic detail. Figure 5.4 shows the chroma features of the speech signal.

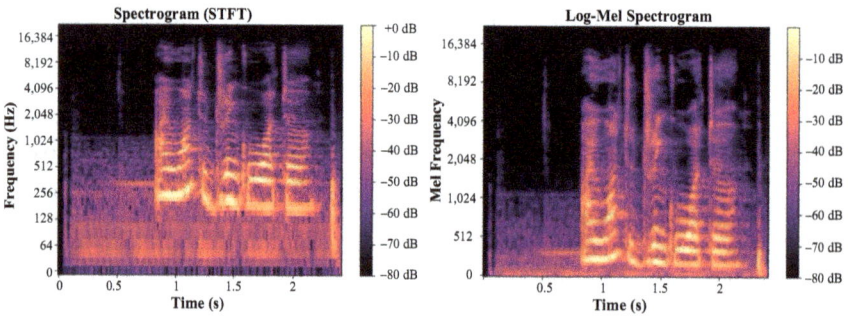

Figure 5.3   Spoken sentence considered "I want to drink Water". Spectrogram (left) and log-Mel spectrogram (right).

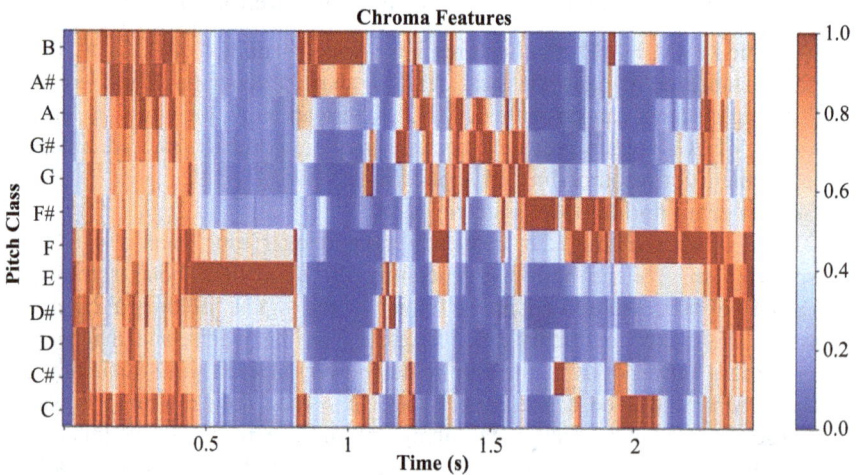

Figure 5.4   Chroma features of the spoken sentence "I want to drink Water"

5.3 ASR in sign language translation

For sign language translation, ASR is often used as the first step in generative AI to convert spoken word into an accessible form for individuals with hearing impairments. ASR systems first transcribe the audio signal into text and then use a second generative model to convert it into sign language sequences. The Speech → Text → Sign Language pipeline remains the architectural choice for most systems simply due to the robustness of ASR technologies and the variety of large-scale speech datasets.

5.3.1 Components of ASR systems

An ASR system in its most architectural sense, especially in the context of generative AI pipelines for sign language translation, consists of various optimized submodules that collaborate to transcribe audio information into precise text representations. While recent end-to-end architectures tend to include all previously mentioned components into a single neural model, an understanding of their individual roles is key – both for how one interprets the system and for how one adapts them within a speech-to-sign translation context.

A typical ASR pipeline consists of the following three main components: (a) acoustic model; (b) language Model; and (c) decoder.

(a) **Acoustic model**
The acoustic model takes incoming audio features like MFCCs, spectrograms, etc., and maps them to probabilities of phonetic or linguistic units. These early systems used Gaussian mixture models (GMMs) and nowadays these systems use deep learning models such as CNNs, Long short-term memory networks (LSTMs), or transformers. These models are trained to find correlations between time-frequency features and sub-word units (phonemes, graphemes, or characters).

Given an input acoustic feature sequence X, the acoustic model (AM) estimates the posterior probability of a linguistic unit y_n (a phoneme or character). In probabilistic terms:

$$P(y_n|X) = AM(X) \qquad (5.1)$$

The most common example of this is an acoustic model, where the model learns to compute a distribution over the possible speech units given a sequence of audio frames. In end-to-end systems (e.g., connectionist temporal classification (CTC), or encoder–decoder models), this is implemented via neural networks $f_\theta(X)$ where θ denotes learned parameters.

In a self-supervised manner, a model like Wav2Vec 2.0 uses an encoder to learn contextual representations z_t from masked raw waveform input X:

$$z_t = f_\theta(X) \qquad (5.2)$$

which are then being mapped during fine-tuning to phoneme/character labels [4].

(b) **Language model**

A language model defines the probability of a word sequence in terms of given grammar and semantics. This helps to guarantee that the end transcription coheres with how things would look naturally in syntax and context. Instead, traditional models employed statistical n-grams, but they have now largely been supplanted by neural language models, like LSTMs and transformers (Bidirectional encoder representations from transformers (BERT), Generative pre-trained transformer (GPT) variants), that learn to compose words in proper order, capturing long-range dependencies and context.

The language model gives a probability to a sequence of words $Y = (y_1, y_2, \ldots.y_N)$. In the case of an autoregressive model, this is decomposed as:

$$P(Y) = \prod_{n=1}^{N} P(y_n | y_1, \ldots \ldots y_{n-1}) \tag{5.3}$$

In transformer-based models (e.g., GPT, Whisper), this is achieved through masked self-attention, where the prediction of each token is conditioned on past context [7].

(c) **Decoder model**

The decoder model combines the acoustic and language model predictions to produce the final transcription. It does a search over possible output-word sequences and picks the one with the best joint probability, i.e., the one with the best phonetic fit and best linguistic coherence. In classical systems, decoding is usually performed using beam search, which maintains a preset number of best candidate sequences at each time step. The decoder computes:

$$\widehat{Y} = \underset{Y}{\operatorname{argmax}} P(Y|, X) = \underset{Y}{\operatorname{argmax}} \prod_{n} P(y_n | y_{<n}, X) \tag{5.4}$$

where X is the input audio, Y is the expected output sequence, and y_n is the token at time t. The decoder at an end-to-end ASR model is like: a CTC layer, which produces sequences of labels without requiring explicit alignment, an attention-based sequence decoder in encoder–decoder architectures, and a CTC-attention hybrid decoder with joint decoding benefits. Both real-time performance and semantic accuracy are paramount for live sign language generation systems; hence, the efficiency and correctness of the decoder play a critical role in it.

5.3.2 Neural ASR architectures

Deep learning has revolutionized ASR from hand-engineered pipelines to data-driven systems. Current ASR systems have the capability of learning such representations from raw audio data, allowing for adaptation to speaker variability, noise, and language diversity. These neural ASR models are critical components in speech-to-sign translation systems as they need to accurately transcribe the linguistic symbols of the speech input that are to be transformed into sign gestures.

Here are the three influential neural ASR approaches: hybrid convolutional neural network–recurrent neural network (CNN–RNN) architectures, CTC, and the transformer networks – together reinforcing the successes of generative sign translation pipelines.

(a) **CNN–RNN hybrid models**

Convolutional recurrent neural networks (CRNNs) are one of the first deep learning models used for ASR. These architectures join convolutional layers, which are good at capturing local acoustic patterns in features such as MFCCs or spectrograms, and recurrent layers that model temporal dependencies over the speech signal. This architecture underlays early end-to-end ASR systems like DeepSpeech. CNN–RNN hybrids are simple and relatively lightweight, but tend to suffer from long-range dependencies, and train less efficiently due to their sequential nature. Yet, they do have utility in real-time applications or cases where compute is constrained – for example, mobile or embedded sign language systems. Figure 5.5 shows the architecture of the CNN–RNN hybrid models.

(b) **Connectionist temporal classification**

CTC enabled speech recognition by making models be trained without the need for manual alignment of audio frames with textual transcriptions. Rather, a CTC-based model learn to predict the right output tokens able all the auto-alignments stations. This reduced some of the burdens of having to train an ASR system on a large dataset and allowed it to handle variable-length input and output sequences far more easily. CTC models are frequently incorporated within a modular pipeline of sign language translation systems, in which it is essential to generate accurate word-level transcription for the generation of gestures in the following steps. They are also preferred for their simplicity and interpretability. Figure 5.6 shows the architecture of the CTC neural network model.

(c) **Transformer-based models**

The largest gains in ASR have been from transformer architectures. By using self-attention mechanisms, transformers can capture local and global dependencies of the speech data and allow for processing across time steps in parallel, leading to faster and more accurate training. Figure 5.7 illustrates the

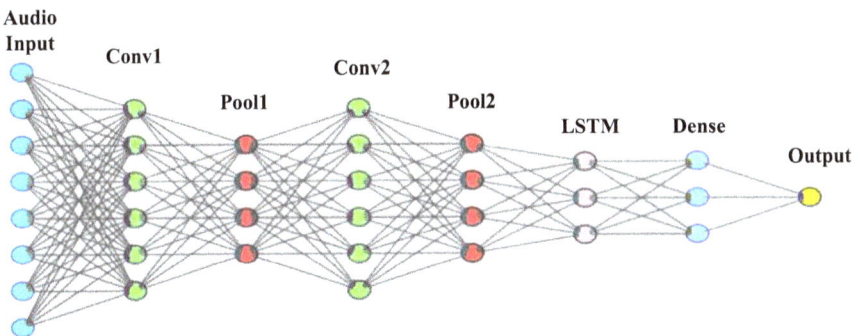

Figure 5.5   Basic architecture of the CNN–RNN hybrid model

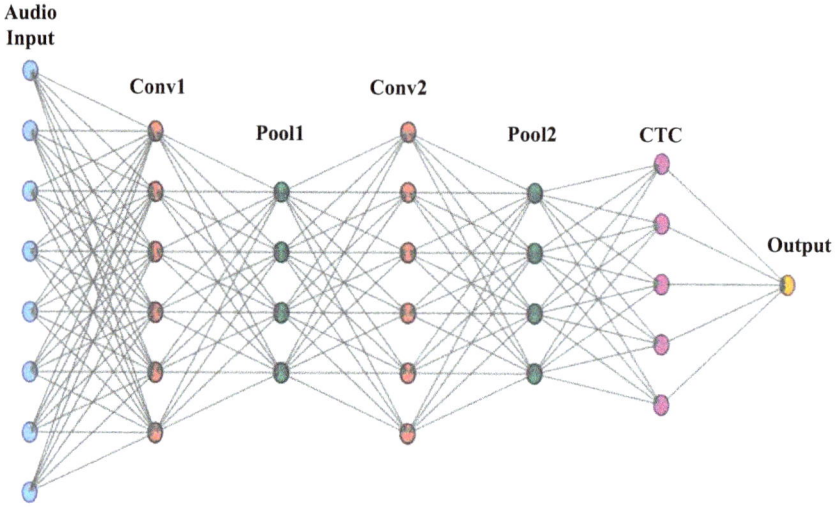

Figure 5.6   Basic architecture of the CTC neural network model

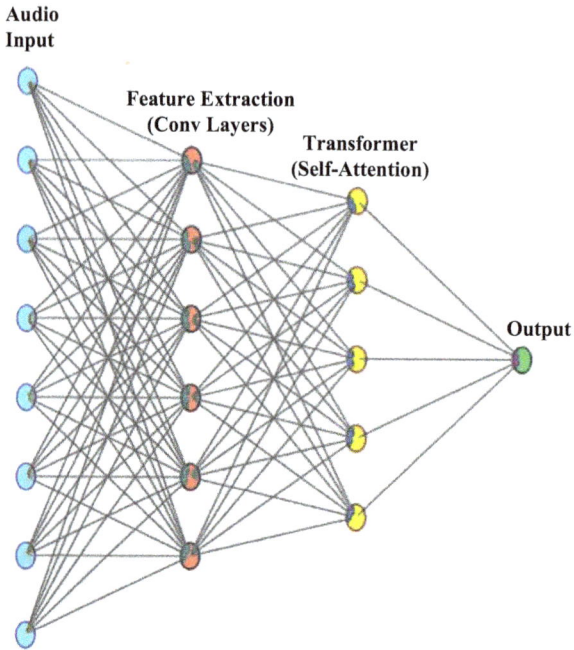

Figure 5.7   Basic architecture of the transformer-based model

transformer model architecture. Two notable transformer-based models that have emerged in recent literature are Wav2Vec 2.0 and Whisper:

- Wav2Vec 2.0 is a self-supervised model trained by Meta AI on unlabeled audio data. It does this by learning general-purpose representations of speech, which can then be fine-tuned for a transcription task. It is well suited for multilingual or low-resource speech-to-sign as it can work without the availability of large amounts of labeled data.

- OpenAI's Whisper is trained on hundreds of thousands of hours of audio in multiple languages and multitasks. It does direct transcription, translation, and even timestamped outputs in a single model. The strength of Whisper across languages, accents, and noise conditions makes it especially well-suited as the backbone for generative sign language systems deployed in the wild.

Transformer models have become standard in state-of-the-art ASR systems and they are commonly found in research and commercial products. They boast a high level of flexibility and accuracy and are typically integrated as front-end modules in SLT chains.

5.3.3   ASR evaluation metrics

The accuracy of ASR systems needs to be evaluated to know how accurately spoken language is being converted into text. Word error rate (WER) and character error rate (CER) are two key metrics that are used for this purpose. These metrics offer a precise way to evaluate an ASR system's effectiveness, aiding developers in improving its accuracy.

(a) **Word error rate**

The most common way of evaluating ASR systems is to calculate WER. It calculates the percentage of errors compared to the original content on a word basis. The WER is computed based on the minimum number of single-word edits (insertions, deletions, or substitutions) needed to convert the transcription into the reference text, which can be derived from the Levenshtein distance. The formula for WER is:

$$WER = \frac{S + D + I}{N} \tag{5.5}$$

where S is substitutions, D is deletions, I is insertions, and N is the reference text word count. A WER of 0 per cent means that the transcription has no errors, and a higher WER means worse performance (more errors).

(b) **Character error rate**

CER is a measure in which the accuracy is calculated on a character basis instead of on the whole word. It is also based on the Levenshtein distance but from the character level, where the Levenshtein distance is the minimum number of edits (characters substituted, deleted, or inserted) that is required to convert the ASR output to the reference text. CER is computed using a formula similar to WER, except that the unit of measurement used is now the characters:

$$CER = \frac{S + D + I}{N} \tag{5.6}$$

where S, D, and I mean substitutions, deletions, and insertions of characters, respectively, and N is the number of characters in the reference text. Zero CER represents a perfect character level match. CER is especially valuable for languages with complex orthographies or in tasks where character-level precision in recognition is vital (e.g., legal or medical transcription).

Both WER and CER are important metrics used to evaluate the performance of an ASR system, as they help to identify the weaknesses in the system so that improvements can be made. Through the exploration of these various metrics, developers can revise and improve their systems over time, leading to higher levels of accuracy in speech-to-text functionality. The continuous cycle of assessment and enhancement is crucial for the evolution of speech recognition systems.

5.4   Speech-to-sign language translation

Speech-to-sign language translation is an emerging approach in human–computer interaction and accessibility research. It is a new paradigm rather than following the conventional pipeline of getting audio and converting it to text, which is further translated to sign, and it rather directly maps spoken audio to sign language gestures. Such systems are promising in terms of reducing translation latency and preventing error propagation, two challenges associated with such sequential pipelines [8].

Conventional ASR-to-sign pipelines exhibit an error propagation phenomenon, where the mistakes made in the speech-to-text step propagate into the sign language translation step, leading to semantically incorrect output. In contrast, the direct systems (speech-to-sign) are made to encode the acoustic signal and translate it instantly into a visual, gesture-based modality. But overcoming these hurdles brings considerable architectural and linguistic challenges with it.

5.4.1   Emerging models for direct translation

State-of-the-art models here leverage multi-modal neural architectures that can learn from both audio features and visual cues in a joint learning framework. These architectures are normally trained in an end-to-end manner, bypassing for the most part the use of intermediate text labels, thus allowing the model to learn more direct relationships between segments of speech and signs. Camgoz *et al.* [8] proposed an end-to-end transformer-based speech-to-sign translation model that inputs spectrogram features of speech and generates sign glosses and pose sequences simultaneously.

5.4.2 Multi-modal neural architectures

This is grounded in multi-modal models. They are used to take and align inputs from multiple modalities for expressive sign language generation: most commonly audio (e.g., MFCCs, log-mel spectrograms) and visual cues (pose keypoints, hand trajectories). The models typically leverage convolutional neural networks (CNNs) or pretrained audio encoders (e.g., Wav2Vec 2.0, Whisper) plus graph-based or transformer decoders to produce pose sequences that correspond to sign gestures. The benefit of multi-modal learning is that it enables the model to exploit co-occurring signals (e.g., the pitch, duration, and rhythmic structure of speech) alongside learned mappings to spatial gestural patterns in sign language, which is important specifically for producing expressive and context-sensitive signs.

5.4.3 Attention mechanism: encoder–decoder

For direct speech-to-sign translation, the encoder–decoder with attention is one of the most common frameworks adopted. The encoder takes the raw or preprocessed audio as input and produces a latent representation in this setup. Then at each output step, the attention mechanism allows the decoder to focus on only relevant parts of the input signal to output a sequence of sign gestures (i.e., a sequence of glosses or 2D/3D skeletal pose sequences in most cases) [9]. This is where the attention mechanism shares its magic, enabling the model to capture such complex alignments between the acoustic entities with the visual-spatial modality that often does not have a one-to-one word mapping with spoken language.

5.4.4 Audio + visual embeddings

Building on top of the above performance improvement, more recent approaches used joint embeddings of audio and video information, enabling the system to learn unifying representations across modalities. For instance, in the study done by Afouras *et al.* [10], speech inputs were converted to spectrogram features and the corresponding gesture outputs were encoded in 3D pose embeddings. Intersecting all modalities in a shared embedding space can help the system to model the semantic and temporal relationships better. Embedding spaces also lend some degree of invariance to speaker and signer identities, which helps in performing better across different users – an important consideration for real-world deployments.

5.4.5 Issues in direct translation

Still, temporal synchronization becomes a significant pain point even with the architectural improvements. In addition to grammar and structure, speech and sign language also differ in their rhythms and duration. Most spoken utterances differ by an order of magnitude in speed and prosody, and aligning these with gestures – which may represent higher-order concepts spanning multiple words – requires advanced temporal modeling. Work on using dynamic time warping, monotonic attention, and sequence alignment loss functions has recently been explored to improve synchronization of the two modalities. Attention-based systems, which are proposed by Saunders *et al.* [11], propose a solution, but they limit output ordinality; on the other hand, transformers adapt well to have different lengths in inputs and outputs while also keeping translational ordinal consistencies.

5.5 Datasets for sign language translation

To train systems that translate speech directly to sign languages, one must consider the relevance and diversity of the datasets available. But despite significant progress in ASR in the last decade, the combined processing modalities of spoken language and sign language have been challenging primarily because of the lack of paired spectra between the two modalities.

5.5.1 Foundational resources: ASR datasets

ASR datasets are foundational to many of the machine learning models used for speech. This is especially useful for speech-to-sign translation, where speech models can be pretrained as strong encoders that can learn useful phonetic and semantic features from raw audio. Then, these representations are used for conditioning generative models that generate sign language sequences.

One of the most commonly used corpora is LibriSpeech, which contains ~1000 h of English read speech extracted from public domain audiobooks. The clean and segmented structure of the datasets combined with accurate transcriptions makes it appropriate for training models in both supervised and self-supervised learning frameworks [12].

A very useful dataset is Mozilla's Common Voice [13], which is a crowd-sourced, multilingual dataset of speech recordings and speech transcription. It encourages the emergence of inclusive models that can address the linguistic diversity of the world's sign languages, with contributions available in more than 100 languages.

In using TED-LIUM [14], the audio comes from TED talks, which injects more value in spontaneous speech. These training data stem from an aligned corpus whose transcript and speaker metadata allow for models to attain better generalization to conversational as well as expressive speech, which form key components of realistic signing generation.

5.5.2 Speech translation using pretrained encoders

Commonly used transformer architectures are pretrained using large ASR datasets in a self-supervised manner (e.g., Wav2Vec 2.0 [4], HuBERT [15], Whisper [7], and SpeechLM [16]). These models learn a mapping from speech to high-dimensional representations that reflect phonetic and prosodic information.

These encoders serve as audio front ends in speech-to-sign pipelines, passed to decoder modules for gloss sequences, 2D pose trajectories, and sign videos. The support for auxiliary surpasses a strong dependence on text transcribing; language encoders therefore operate without any direct representation of intermediate text, making pretrained language encoders ideal for running translation designs.

5.5.3   Aligning speech and sign

The main bottleneck in building datasets is that the speech and the sign are spoken at different times. The rules of grammar and rhythm of spoken languages and those of sign languages are radically different from each other. Spoken phrases usually correspond to single gestures (e.g., "I don't know" → one shrugging sign), and speech prosody seldom linearly corresponds to the gestural flow of signs. This asynchronicity becomes problematic at model training, particularly in the case of encoder–decoder architectures, which depend on sequence-level alignment. Methods such as monotonic attention, dynamic time warping, and forced alignment are often used to reduce this, but they come with their own drawbacks. In addition, sign language annotations are typically at the gloss level and thus, the expressiveness of signed communication may not always be accurately represented. This expert annotation of glosses with audio is a labor-intensive process that makes very large datasets challenging to collect.

5.5.4   Data scarcity and paired corpora

But perhaps the most urgent need is for datasets with synchronized speech and sign video. Although a great number of corpora are dedicated specifically to speech or sign language, not many contain both with parallel annotation. Such scarcity becomes particularly problematic for the training of end-to-end models that map audio waveforms directly to gestures. The scarcity of such paired datasets constrains not only the training of generative models but also the assessment of their capabilities in realistic and multimodal settings. The research community is increasingly united in the opinion that new benchmark corpora are urgently required, which incorporate high-quality audio, speaker diversity, gloss annotations, and 2D or 3D pose data of signers.

5.5.5   Synthetic pairing and data augmentation techniques

To fill this gap, data augmentation techniques have been evaluated by researchers. These include synthesizing speech using text-to-speech (TTS) systems aligned to existing gloss corpora, the use of pose estimation models to convert sign video into skeletal frames for greater flexibility in modeling, and hoping to apply transfer learning from ASR and text-to-sign translation to bootstrap initial models. These strategies are helpful but ultimately are temporary fixes. The prospective long-term answer remains a collection of genuine, diverse, and context-rich speech-sign paired datasets across languages and areas.

5.6   Summary

In this chapter, the key advances, challenges, and architectural approaches in the speech-to-sign language translation field, a crucial subset of accessibility-oriented generative AI have been discussed. The chapter first provided an overview of ASR techniques, detailing classical methods for ASR and new neural architectures that have emerged (CNN–RNN hybrids, CTC-based models, transformer-based architectures such as Wav2Vec 2.0 and Whisper). These form the basis of how we map spoken language into intermediate representations (like text or even features).

Next, the chapter investigated the emerging interest in translating spoken word directly into sign without the use of an intermediate text representation, alluding to a potential way to reduce latency and the accumulation of error propagation. It stressed the usage of multi-modal neural architectures, encoder–decoder models with attention, and joint audio-visual embeddings that allow a direct mapping from speech waveforms to its sign gestures. In addition, key challenges like temporal alignment, grammatical divergence between languages, and the asynchronous nature of spoken and signed modalities were also discussed, showcasing the need for robust end-to-end systems.

The chapter finally highlighted the vital importance of speech datasets in training these models. It evaluated foundational ASR corpora such as LibriSpeech, Common Voice, and TED-LIUM, and addressed their integration with pretrained self-supervised encoders for downstream sign generation. A significant limitation cited was the relative lack of paired speech-sign corpora, leading to the call for new multimodal datasets specifically designed for speech-to-sign translation. See Chapter 3 for an extensive discussion on datasets and annotation approaches in the specific case of sign language.

Exercises

(I) **Multiple choice questions**
   1. Which of the following models is commonly used in self-supervised speech representation learning?
       (a) BERT
       (b) GPT-2
       (c) Wav2Vec 2.0
       (d) ResNet

   2. CTC-based models assume that:
       (a) Input and output sequences are always the same length
       (b) The decoder needs alignment with the text
       (c) The output is aligned using a monotonic mapping
       (d) Audio and video embeddings are fused

   3. True or false: word error rate (WER) is calculated using insertions, deletions, and substitutions at the phoneme level.
   4. Which of the following is a major challenge in direct speech-to-sign translation?
       (a) Low vocabulary in sign language
       (b) Lack of sign gloss standards

(c) Temporal alignment between audio and gestures
(d) Excessive pretraining data availability

5. Which dataset is primarily used for English ASR tasks?
   (a) RWTH-PHOENIX-Weather
   (b) TED-LIUM
   (c) CSL
   (d) Phoenix-2014T

(II) **Short answer questions**
   1. Define word error rate (WER) and explain how it is computed.
   2. What is the role of attention in encoder–decoder architectures for speech-to-sign translation?
   3. Why is temporal synchronization critical in speech-to-sign translation systems?
   4. List two limitations of using a sequential speech → text → sign translation pipeline.
   5. Name any two pretrained ASR models commonly used in direct speech-to-sign systems.

(III) **Discussion questions**
   1. Evaluate the impact of error propagation in multi-stage pipelines (Speech → Text → Sign). Would a direct approach be more reliable?
   2. Discuss the linguistic differences between spoken and signed languages. How do these affect the training of generative models?
   3. In the context of accessibility, what are the ethical considerations when developing speech-to-sign systems for global deployment?
   4. How can self-supervised learning improve data efficiency in speech-to-sign applications, especially in low-resource languages?
   5. Given the lack of paired speech-sign datasets, how would you design a project to bootstrap a usable corpus for a new language?

(IV) **Practical/Hands-on exercises**
   1. **Audio feature extraction task**
      Use a Python library (e.g., librosa) to extract Mel spectrogram and MFCC features from a sample .wav audio file of the phrase "I want to drink water". Visualize and compare both.
   2. **WER and CER calculation**
      Write a function in Python to compute WER and CER between two strings:
      Reference: "I want to drink water"
      Hypothesis: "I want drink water."
   3. **Model architecture sketching**
      Design a neural network architecture using blocks (CNN + BiLSTM + Dense) for a simple speech-to-sign pipeline. Label input/output shapes at each stage.

4. **Dataset review**
    Pick one ASR dataset (LibriSpeech / Common Voice / TED-LIUM) and review:
    - Type of speech
    - Language coverage
    - Annotation format
    - Suitability for speech-to-sign tasks

References

[1]   Hu, Y., Liu, Y., Lv, S., *et al.* (2020). "DCCRN: Deep complex convolution recurrent network for phase-aware speech enhancement". arXiv preprint arXiv:2008.00264.

[2]   Schröter, H., Maier, A., Escalante-B, A. N., and Rosenkranz, T. (2022, September). "Deepfilternet2: Towards real-time speech enhancement on embedded devices for full-band audio". In *2022 International Workshop on Acoustic Signal Enhancement (IWAENC), IEEE* (pp. 1–5).

[3]   Silero AI. (2022). *Silero Voice Activity Detector (VAD)*. GitHub Repository, https://github.com/snakers4/silero-vad.

[4]   Baevski, A., Zhou, Y., Mohamed, A., and Auli, M. (2020). "wav2vec 2.0: A framework for self-supervised learning of speech representations". *Advances in Neural Information Processing Systems* 33, 12449–12460.

[5]   Bovbjerg, H. S., Jensen, J., Østergaard, J., and Tan, Z. H. (2024). Self-supervised pretraining for robust personalized voice activity detection in adverse conditions. In *ICASSP 2024-2024 IEEE International Conference on Acoustics, Speech and Signal Processing (ICASSP), IEEE* (pp. 10126–10130).

[6]   Park, D. S., Chan, W., Zhang, Y., *et al.* (2019). "Specaugment: A simple data augmentation method for automatic speech recognition". *arXiv preprint arXiv:1904.08779*.

[7]   Radford, A., Kim, J. W., Xu, T., *et al.* (2022). Robust Speech Recognition via Large-Scale Weak Supervision. OpenAI. https://openai.com/research/whisper.

[8]   Camgoz, N. C., Koller, O., Hadfield, S., and Bowden, R. (2020). "Sign language transformers: Joint end-to-end sign language recognition and translation". In *Proceedings of the IEEE/CVF Conference on Computer Vision and Pattern Recognition* (pp. 10023–10033).

[9]   Liang, Z., Li, H., and Chai, J. (2023). "Sign language translation: A survey of approaches and techniques". *Electronics* 12(12), 2678.

[10] Afouras, T., Chung, J. S., Senior, A., Vinyals, O., and Zisserman, A. (2018). "Deep audio-visual speech recognition". *IEEE Transactions on Pattern Analysis and Machine Intelligence* 44(12), 8717–8727.

[11] Saunders, B., Camgoz, N. C., and Bowden, R. (2020). Progressive transformers for end-to-end sign language production. In *Computer Vision–ECCV*

2020: 16th European Conference, Glasgow, UK, August 23–28, 2020, Proceedings, Part XI 16, Springer International Publishing (pp. 687–705).

[12]   Panayotov, V., Chen, G., Povey, D., and Khudanpur, S. (2015, April). Librispeech: An ASR corpus based on public domain audio books. In *2015 IEEE International Conference on Acoustics, Speech and Signal Processing (ICASSP), IEEE* (pp. 5206–5210).

[13]   Ardila, R., Branson, M., Davis, K., *et al.* (2019). "Common voice: A massively-multilingual speech corpus". *arXiv preprint arXiv:1912.06670.*

[14]   Hernandez, F., Nguyen, V., Ghannay, S., Tomashenko, N., and Esteve, Y. (2018). TED-LIUM 3: Twice as much data and corpus repartition for experiments on speaker adaptation. In *Speech and Computer: 20th International Conference, SPECOM 2018, Leipzig, Germany, September 18–22, 2018, Proceedings 20, Springer International Publishing* (pp. 198–208).

[15]   Hsu, W.-N., Bolte, B., Tsai, Y.-H. H., *et al.* (2021). "HuBERT: Self-supervised speech representation learning by masked prediction of hidden units". *IEEE/ACM Transactions on Audio, Speech, and Language Processing* 29, 3451–3460.

[16]   Zhang, Z., Chen, S., Zhou, L., *et al.* (2024). SpeechLM: Enhanced speech pre-training with unpaired textual data. *IEEE/ACM Transactions on Audio, Speech, and Language Processing.* 20(32), 2177–2187.

Chapter 6

Generative AI models for sign language translation

6.1 Introduction

Sign language translation system development has usually taken the form of either discriminative or sequence modeling approaches. While both have performed admirably in recognition and translation tasks, they are generally not able to model realistic and human-like translation videos. This gap is particularly important when the goal changes from mere interpretation of text to the generation of visuals, in which both manual (hand movements) and non-manual characteristics (facial expressions, body posture) are critical.

6.1.1 Generative AI for sign language

Generative AI (GenAI) models are meant to create new, synthetic data that follows the distribution of real data. In the case of sign language, generative models can create continuous, consistent expressive video sequences automatically from text or speech input. This is useful for creating accessible technologies for social good, including:

- Digital access, such as websites or devices for digital content delivery, that can translate content into sign language video.
- Educational platforms, where course content can be automatically generated for hearing-impaired students.
- Interactive communicative technology, like virtual avatars that translate spoken input into real-time, dynamic sign language.

Generative models such as generative adversarial networks (GANs), variational autoencoders (VAEs), diffusion models, and transformers have shown the ability to generate realistic, high-fidelity video sequences at scale that are temporally consistent. These generative models go beyond classical models with a series of static images or a rule-based synthesis model since generative models such as GANs, VAEs, diffusion models, and transformers include globally coherent and semantically aligned representations over time that represent actions that are syntactically valid to sign but also exhibit natural-looking and expressive semantics.

Recent works [1,2] illustrate that methods can generate video sign poses or frames of video directly from speech or text input, using multi-modal embeddings, and attention-based encoder/decoder architectures, addressing the simultaneous complexity of language structure, motion dynamics, and expressing sign language far better than previous rule-based or frame-based classifiers.

6.1.2   Limitations of discriminative or sequence-only models

Discriminative models concern class-label or sequence-mapping from a worker's input and are best suited for purely recognition tasks. In a generative context, there are several challenges with discriminative models:

- **No content generation:** Discriminative models cannot create new video frames or a sequence of gestures continuously.
- **Frame-by-frame prediction:** Temporal inconsistencies emerge where each frame is often treated independently.
- **Lack of expressiveness:** Subtle variations in signing styles, expressions, or transitions of the hand are not well expressed.

For example, sign language transformers [3] are good at translating sign sequences into glosses or vice versa, but are strict about their predetermined intermediate representations and have no capability for generating photorealistic sign language videos.

GenAI models can alleviate these issues since they learn the distribution of data, so they can create new samples from their latent space conditioned on the input modality (e.g., text, speech). This shift is very significant, as it changes the paradigm from deterministic decoding to multi-modal, probabilistic generation, and can lead to new opportunities in sign language accessibility and interaction with computers. Figure 6.1 illustrates a conceptual comparison of classic discriminative pipelines versus GenAI models in the task of sign language translation. With respect to classic models, we focused on predictions represented as static

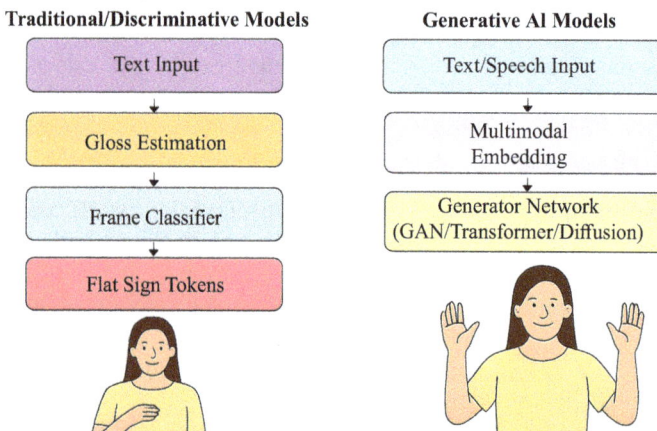

Figure 6.1   A conceptual comparison between traditional discriminative pipelines and generative AI-based models for sign language translation

tokens as the outcome of a frame-wise classification and connected discrete communicated messages together, but GenAI models learn how to produce realistic and continuous sign videos from textual or speech input.

6.2 Core GenAI techniques

GenAI models have transformed the ability of machines to produce human-like outputs in text, image, and video. In the case of sign language translation, GenAI can create synthetic, but realistic, sequences of gestures by mapping spatial and temporal parameters to semantic inputs. The main generative models that are useful in this context are GANs, VAEs, diffusion models, and transformer-based generative models. Figure 6.2 illustrates the overview of core sign language generative architectures. Each model has its strengths – GANs for realism, VAEs for latent representations, diffusion for fidelity, and transformers for multi-modal alignment.

6.2.1 Generative adversarial networks

First introduced by Goodfellow *et al.* (2014), the concept of GANs [4] consists of two elements: a generator and a discriminator that play a minimax game. The generator draws from a latent space to generate sample data, and the discriminator learns to discriminate between real samples and fake ones. Collectively, the generator and discriminator utilize adversarial training; this enables the generator to produce output that is indistinguishable from real samples. For sign language

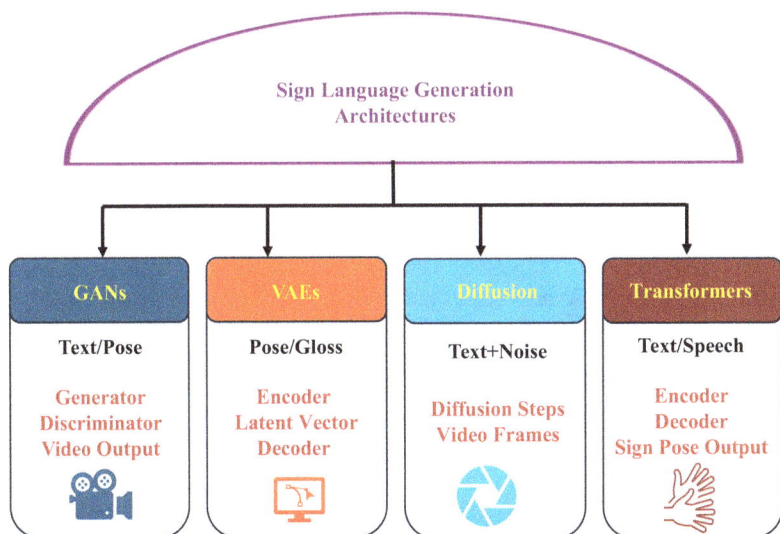

Figure 6.2   Overview of core generative architectures used in sign language generation

translation, GANs are used to translate gloss or pose sequences into sign videos. Temporal GANs and Video GANs can produce a sign video that uses motion continuity. For example, a dynamic GAN [5] was used to generate natural quantity sign language videos from skeletal pose sequences built from gloss inputs, enabling the natural transition of hand motion.

6.2.2   *Variational autoencoders*

VAEs are generative models that encode inputs to a latent representation and reconstruct from learned probability distributions. VAEs are useful for exploring compact representations that can be continuously represented and decoded to visual sequences. In applications for sign language, VAEs have been used as pose interpolators or gesture smoothing, especially during intermediate gloss-to-pose translation approaches. However, VAEs alone may produce blurry or low-resolution frames, and are frequently used in hybrid architectures with GANs (VAE−GANs, etc.).

6.2.3   *Diffusion models*

Diffusion models produce structured data by incrementally converting random noise to structure through steps of iterative denoising. Diffusion models have gained popularity for producing high-fidelity versions of images and video and can rival GANs in visual quality. In sign language translation, Diffusion models produce temporally consistent and smooth sign language frames, which can be particularly useful in long gesture sequences. Text-to-video diffusion models like VideoFusion, or Pix2Video, can be repurposed for sign synthesis with text input, while maintaining the fluency of both linguistics and visuals [6].

6.2.4   *Generative models based on transformers*

Transformers have been repurposed for implementing video generation tasks, as well as for text generation (e.g., GPT, T5). Employing self-attention, transformers can model long-range dependencies in sequences. In the context of sign language generation, transformer encoders process the text or speech input, and decoder modules output pose sequences or gesture embeddings. The output will often use visual token prediction heads to output frames. For example, a dual-attention transformer developed [2] functions as a direct speech-to-sign translator, allowing for input across the audio and visual modalities for optimal gesture predictions.

6.3   Text-to-sign video generation

Text-to-sign video generation is one of the most influential applications for generative models for sign language processing. Rather than applying recognition or gloss translation techniques, this task is the full, continuous generation of sign language videos from spoken/written language. The task is unique because of both the visual-spatial grammar that sign languages encompass and the need to create temporally and human-like coherent signing.

Not only does this task demand a linguistic comprehension of the original text, but it also requires accurate movements, correct pose articulation, and synchronized nonmanual cues (e.g., facial expressions, head movements). While the conventional approach falls short in capturing these multimodal aspects of signing, generative methods have emerged as useful for synthesizing realistic sequences of sign language directly from text.

6.3.1 End-to-end generation pipeline

A conventional text-to-sign video generation system shown in Figure 6.3 includes three main components:

(a) **Text encoding:** Natural language sentences are represented as intermediate representations, which can be:
- Gloss sequences (a canonical form of signs),
- or semantic embeddings using a transformer-based encoder such as BERT or T5.

This stage establishes the source text within context before the generation process begins.

(b) **Pose sequence generation:** The intermediate representation is translated into a sequence of kinematic keypoints that represent the signer's body, hands, and facial landmarks. The related concepts include:
- regression-based models, where the goal is to directly map the embeddings into poses,
- or sequence generation models using RNNs, transformers, or GANs.

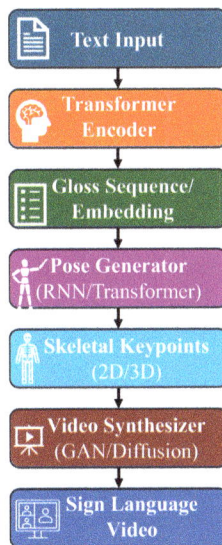

Figure 6.3   Text-to-sign video generation pipeline

The primary objective at this step is to establish the handshapes, movements, and transitions in a way that preserves the semantic meaning of the sentence.

(c) **Video synthesis:** The generated pose sequences are passed onto a video synthesizer, usually a GAN, VAE-GAN, or diffusion model will generate the video frames. The synthesizer renders (in real-time) the signer avatar that performs the generated hand motions, facial expressions, and overall body postures such that the signer articulates naturally.

6.3.2   Notable architectures

(a) **SignGAN:** SignGAN [7] is a GAN-based model that synthesizes videos of sign language from skeletal poses. The generator takes in pose keypoints and produces visual frames, and a discriminator assesses for temporal realism. The components of the SignGAN include:
- Pose2Frame generator
- Spatio-temporal discriminator

Advantage: Generates a video that is very high fidelity, which is a good case for avatar-based systems.

Use case: Commonly used in gloss-to-sign systems with pose intermediates.

(b) **Sentence2SignGesture:** Sentence2SignGesture architecture [5] is built on previous work by the author [8], which is a hybrid text-to-sign system that uses text embeddings, as well as gloss representations to produce experts of video from GANs. The different stages of this architecture include:
- Sentence encoder for context embedding
- Intermediate gloss prediction
- Keypoint trajectory generation
- Dynamic GAN for frame generation

Advantage: Support temporal alignment between sign transitions and semantic boundaries [5].

(c) **Dynamic GAN:** The dynamic GAN [8] architecture focuses on transitions between frames of fluid motion, by making up the temporal process of continuous gesture dynamics between gestures.
- Input: Glosses or semantic embeddings.
- Output: Video phrased from the frame-level of gesture.

Advantage: Improves coarticulation and avoids the robotic movements seen in traditional pipelines.

6.3.3   Pose estimation and skeleton generation

A crucial step in generation is mapping intermediate outputs to pose sequences. This enables:

- Abstracting signer identity.
- Focusing on handshape, location, and movement.
- Data augmentation and normalization.

Popular tools and techniques include:

- **OpenPose** [9]: Extracts 2D body, hand, and face keypoints.
- **MediaPipe** [10]: Real-time hand and body tracking optimized for deployment.
- **HRNet** [11]: High-resolution human pose estimation, useful for detailed gesture synthesis.

These tools generate standardized keypoint formats (e.g., COCO or MPII) for further use in rendering engines or generative pipelines.

6.3.4   Challenges in text-to-sign generation

Despite the advances, several challenges exist:

- **Linguistic ambiguity**: Text often lacks spatial cues and grammar required in sign language. Mapping "I went there" to a spatially grounded sign sentence needs context does not present in plain text.
- **Non-manual cues**: Lip movements, eye gaze, eyebrow movement, and head tilts are essential grammatical markers in sign language but are difficult to synthesize convincingly.
- **Dataset limitations**: Most datasets like RWTH-PHOENIX-2014T or SignStream are either gloss-aligned or lack expressive diversity. Large-scale parallel datasets with gloss, pose, and video are rare.
- **Signer variability**: Signers differ in style, articulation speed, and region-specific expressions. Models must generalize across signer-specific patterns.

6.4   Pose/skeleton to video generation

Sign language generation systems generally rely on representing signs with sequences of 2D or 3D skeletal poses. Pose-based representations allow for compact representation of the spatial relationships between the hands, body, and face, allowing the researcher to have a signer-invariant representation of signing motion. However, pose sequences lack the visual detail needed for real-world ability applications. To produce usable content, the skeletal structure needs to be transformed into a realistic sign language video.

While the generation of pose sequences captures the motion and structure of signs, it lacks the visual fidelity needed for user-facing applications. Generative models, especially GANs, VAE−GANs, diffusion-based architectures, and avatar-based neural rendering, are employed to render continuous video sequences from these skeletal inputs, and it is shown in Figure 6.4.

Skeletal representations serve as a language-agnostic intermediate format, reducing signer-specific biases and simplifying motion learning. These representations include:

- Hand keypoints (e.g., 21 per hand in MediaPipe)
- Body keypoints (e.g., 17–33 for full body)
- Facial landmarks (e.g., mouth shape, eyebrow, and eye position)

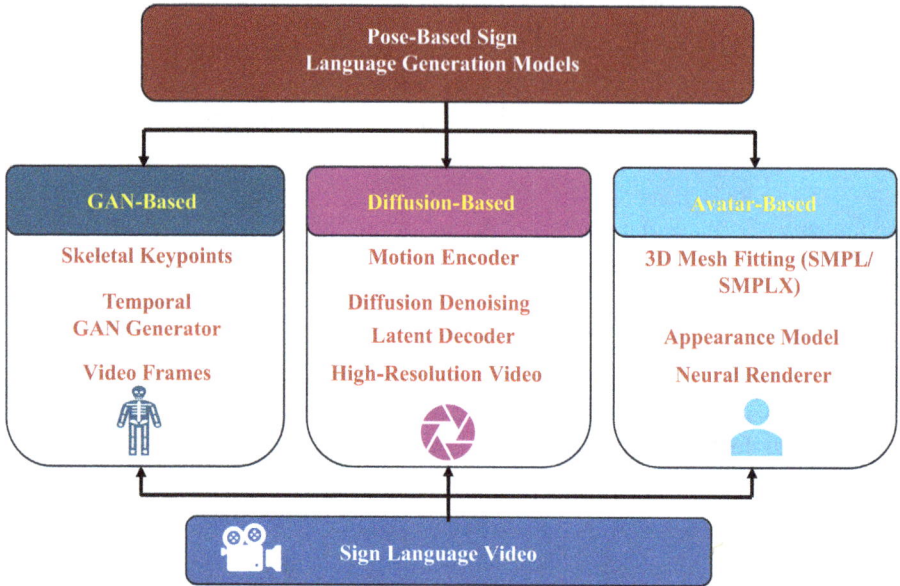

Figure 6.4   Different pose-to-video generation paradigms

However, for deployment in educational tools, digital interpreters, or accessibility apps, it is necessary to convert these skeletons into realistic video frames showing complete, expressive human signers.

6.4.1   GAN-based skeleton-to-video translation

GANs are widely used for translating skeletal keypoints into realistic video frames. A typical GAN architecture consists of a generator G, which maps pose sequences to video frames, and a discriminator D, which distinguishes between real and generated sequences. The training objective is adversarial, where G learns to fool D, and D learns to become more accurate at classification.

(a) **Everybody sign now (SignGAN)**
SignGAN [7] is one of the earliest full pipelines translating spoken input into photo-realistic sign language videos. It employs a pose-conditioned generator to synthesize individual video frames and a spatio-temporal discriminator to enforce motion consistency across time.

- Pose input: 2D keypoints (hands, body, face)
- Output: RGB video frames rendered with facial expressions and hand articulation
- Strengths: High frame quality and signer realism
- Limitations: Dependence on well-annotated pose-video pairs

This model was evaluated on the BSL Corpus and showed state-of-the-art results using Frechet video distance (FVD) and human preference studies.

(b) **Sentence2SignGesture**

A multi-stage architecture [6] where text is translated to gloss, then to pose, and finally to video using a temporal GAN. The temporal generator in this pipeline maintains frame-to-frame consistency, coarticulation of signs, and natural hand transitions.

- Input: Sentence → Gloss → Pose Sequence.
- Output: Continuous sign language video.
- Innovations: Use of gloss segmentation to improve semantic fidelity and temporal smoothing modules to reduce abrupt transitions.
- Performance: Improved fluency in sign transitions compared to direct frame prediction approaches.

(c) **MoCoGAN (Baseline)**

MoCoGAN [12] decomposes video generation into two latent spaces: (a) content and (b) motion. While not originally designed for sign language, it has been used as a baseline in multiple sign generation tasks due to its modularity.

- Input: Motion code from pose.
- Output: Video frames synthesized via recurrent latent sampling.
- Use case: Comparing temporal generation ability against more specialized models.

6.4.2   *Diffusion-based frame generation*

Diffusion models are a more recent addition to generative modeling, offering greater stability and visual fidelity than traditional GANs. These models gradually refine noise into structured outputs over multiple timesteps using a learned denoising function.

(a) **Pose-guided motion module (PGMM)**

PGMM [13], a dedicated pose-guided video generation system that utilizes two key components:

- Coarse motion module (CMM): Encodes temporal motion features from skeletal sequences.
- Pose fusion module (PFM): Integrates pose and motion features for fine-grained synthesis.

A novel metric called temporal consistency difference (TCD) is proposed to assess the smoothness of transitions. PGMM outperforms prior GAN models on metrics such as PSNR and LPIPS.

Advantages:

- Fine control over frame-level gesture transitions.
- Significant gains in temporal coherence and clarity.
- Training: Uses adversarial + reconstruction + temporal loss function.

(b) **SignGen**

SignGen [14] is a latent diffusion model conditioned on textual input. Instead of using glosses or posing as intermediate representations, SignGen learns to generate videos directly from sentence embeddings. The component of the SignGen architecture includes:

- Text encoder (e.g., T5).
- Latent diffusion decoder for video frames.
- Key Strength: Generates both manual and non-manual cues simultaneously.
- Datasets: Benchmarked on RWTH-PHOENIX-2014T and BSL-1K.
- Performance: Achieves superior FVD and BLEU scores compared to GAN pipelines.

6.4.3   Avatar-based neural rendering

Avatar-based methods aim to animate **3D models of signers** using skeletal motion data. These methods focus on personalization, realism, and controllability.

(a) **SignGAN with facial extensions**
In an extended setup of SignGAN [7], additional modules were incorporated to enhance facial expressiveness. These networks focus on mouth shape, eyebrow movement, and head tilts — essential features for grammaticality in sign languages.
- Pose input: Body + facial keypoints.
- Rendering: Dynamic facial synthesis using GAN-based refinement.
- Application: Useful in avatar-based sign language agents.

(b) **Disentangled appearance-pose models**
Some GAN pipelines, such as the extended pose-guided models, include the separation of appearance vectors (e.g., skin tone, clothing) from pose vectors. This disentanglement allows:
- Reusing one signer's identity across different gesture sequences
- Training identity-preserving models with fewer samples

These setups, while still 2D, represent the early stages of avatar-level sign synthesis. These methods separate pose dynamics from visual appearance, enabling consistent signer identity across generated videos, even when the gestures change:
- **Pose-based sign language appearance transfer** [15]: A model that transfers a signer's appearance onto pose skeletons processed from another signer. It preserves gesture content while obscuring identity, balancing privacy and utility.
- **Neural sign reenactor** [16]: A photorealistic retargeting pipeline that transfers both manual and non-manual signing elements (body motion, facial expressions, eye gaze) to a target signer. It achieves high-quality, identity-preserving sign language synthesis.

(c) **Future directions with SMPL-based models**
Current research is exploring 3D avatar synthesis using the SMPL family (SMPL or SMPL-X), which models the human body and hands as parametric meshes: SignAvatars [17] released with a dataset of 70K sign sequences annotated with SMPL-X mesh data. This benchmark sets the foundation for future 3D avatar-based sign language generation.

Though no complete SMPL-based video synthesis pipeline for sign language has been released yet, this dataset supports active research in:

- Mapping 2D pose sequences to 3D mesh animation
- Generating identity-containing avatars
- Animating fingers and facial expressions using parametric mesh deformation

This is a promising frontier for VR/AR sign language tutors and real-time avatar deployment − a growing direction that will likely yield practical systems soon.

6.5   Multimodal generative learning

Traditional sign generation models largely rely on single modality inputs like text or pose sequences. However, human communication is inherently multimodal − often combining speech, visual cues, and linguistic context. To emulate this richness, generative models have started integrating multiple modalities to improve fluency, expressiveness, and contextual accuracy of sign language outputs.

6.5.1   Foundational multimodal architectures

- Contrastive language–image pretraining (CLIP) learns a shared embedding space for text and images using contrastive loss. It enables flexible cross-modal alignment. In the context of sign generation, CLIP variants (e.g., SignCLIP) project glosses and video representations into a common embedding space for retrieval and weakly supervised translation tasks [18].
- Flamingo combines a frozen vision encoder (similar to CLIP) with a language model through gated cross-attention layers. It allows few-shot multimodal learning and supports sequential video-text interactions [19].
- BLIP-2 follows a modular design: frozen image encoder, large language model, and a lightweight Q-Former for bridging the two. This decoupling supports efficient multimodal fine-tuning for downstream tasks such as image-conditioned text generation or video retrieval [20].

6.5.2   Adaptation to sign language

- SignCLIP utilizes CLIP-style contrastive learning to encode both sign videos and text into a unified space. Trained on 500k+ sign video clips from 44 sign languages, it enables multilingual retrieval and text-to-sign matching. While not directly generative, it forms a key component in retrieval-augmented generation [18].
- Emerging diffusion models conditioned on multimodal signals (e.g., audio + text + pose) are under development. These models explore latent diffusion pipelines where phonetic features, glosses, and gesture priors guide realistic

sign video synthesis. Early efforts are reported in experimental setups but are yet to be standardized.

6.5.3   Integration strategies

• Encoder fusion: Each modality (text, audio, pose) is passed through individual encoders, followed by gated or attention-based fusion layers.
• Contrastive embedding alignment: CLIP-like architectures learn embedding alignment via contrastive loss for flexible modality interaction.
• Conditional generation: Generative backbones (GANs or Diffusion) are conditioned on fused multimodal embeddings to produce coherent sign gestures or videos.

6.6   Multimodal generative learning

This chapter focused on generative approaches for sign language translation, with specific attention to video generation from text, gloss, and pose sequences. The limitations of traditional discriminative models are discussed and motivate the need for generative techniques that produce continuous, expressive signing.

Core techniques covered

• **GAN-based models:** SignGAN, Sentence2SignGesture, and related architectures generate sign videos from skeletal inputs using adversarial training. These models learn temporal coherence and visual realism from pose-conditioned inputs.
• **Diffusion-based models:** Recent methods like PGMM and SignGen use latent diffusion for smoother video synthesis. These models are more stable than GANs, especially in long-sequence generation.
• **Avatar and neural rendering:** Methods explore disentangled appearance-pose pipelines and mesh-based animation using SMPL. While full sign avatar generation is under development, supporting datasets like SignAvatars are emerging.
• **Multimodal generative learning:** CLIP, Flamingo, and BLIP-2 frameworks demonstrate how text, audio, and visual cues can be integrated. SignCLIP adapts this for sign video alignment and generation.

Exercises

(I)   **Multiple choice questions**
    1.   Which component in a GAN architecture generates the output video from input pose sequences?
        (a) Discriminator
        (b) Encoder
        (c) Generator
        (d) Decoder

2. Which model explicitly separates content and motion for video generation?
    (a) SignCLIP
    (b) MoCoGAN
    (c) BLIP-2
    (d) SignGAN

3. What is the primary advantage of using diffusion models over GANs in sign language generation?
    (a) Lower training time
    (b) Higher compression
    (c) Improved stability and temporal smoothness
    (d) Better pose extraction

4. In BLIP-2, the Q-former is used to:
    (a) Perform temporal interpolation
    (b) Enhance facial rendering
    (c) Bridge visual and language embeddings
    (d) Normalize gloss sequences

5. Which dataset supports research in 3D avatar-based sign language generation?
    (a) RWTH-PHOENIX-2014T
    (b) BSL-1K
    (c) SignAvatars
    (d) ASL100

(II) **Short answer questions**
    1. What are the main differences between GAN-based and diffusion-based sign video generation methods?
    2. How does SignCLIP use contrastive learning in the context of sign language?
    3. Define the role of the coarse motion module in PGMM.
    4. Explain the significance of temporal smoothness in sign language video generation.
    5. What are appearance-pose disentangled models and why are they relevant for avatar-based synthesis?

(III) **Discussion questions**
    1. Discuss the challenges in synthesizing non-manual features (like facial expressions) in generative sign video systems. What are the existing solutions?
    2. Compare and contrast SignGAN and SignGen in terms of input modalities, architecture, and output quality.
    3. Evaluate the potential of SMPL-based models for real-time sign avatar generation. What are the current limitations?
    4. How does multimodal fusion improve the contextual accuracy of sign generation? Give examples from Flamingo or BLIP-2.

5.   Outline an ideal pipeline for generating sign videos from spoken input using generative AI techniques. Justify your design choices.

(IV)   **Practical/Hands-on exercises**

1.   Build a basic GAN pipeline for pose-to-sign video generation using synthetic 2D keypoint data (e.g., from MediaPipe or OpenPose). Train a simple generator and discriminator on a small pose-video dataset. Visualize a few generated frames. Evaluate temporal consistency manually or using frame difference metrics (tools recommended: PyTorch, TensorFlow, or Google Colab).

References

[1]   Zhao, J., Qi, W., Zhou, W., Duan, N., Zhou, M., and Li, H. (2021). Conditional sentence generation and cross-modal reranking for sign language translation. *IEEE Transactions on Multimedia, 24*, 2662–2672.

[2]   Yin, A., Zhao, Z., Liu, J., Jin, W., Zhang, M., Zeng, X., and He, X. (2021, October). Simulslt: end-to-end simultaneous sign language translation. *In Proceedings of the 29th ACM International Conference on Multimedia* (pp. 4118–4127). ACM: New York, USA.

[3]   Camgoz, N. C., Koller, O., Hadfield, S., and Bowden, R. (2020). Sign language transformers: Joint end-to-end sign language recognition and translation. *In Proceedings of the IEEE/CVF Conference on Computer Vision and Pattern Recognition* (pp. 10023–10033) IEEE.

[4]   Goodfellow, I. J., Pouget-Abadie, J., Mirza, M., *et al.* (2014). Generative adversarial nets. *Advances in Neural Information Processing Systems, 27*, 1–9.

[5]   Natarajan, B., Elakkiya, R., and Prasad, M. L. (2023). Sentence2-SignGesture: a hybrid neural machine translation network for sign language video generation. *Journal of Ambient Intelligence and Humanized Computing, 14*(8), 9807–9821.

[6]   Ho, J., Jain, A., and Abbeel, P. (2020). Denoising diffusion probabilistic models. *Advances in Neural Information Processing Systems, 33*, 6840–6851.

[7]   Saunders, B., Camgoz, N. C., and Bowden, R. (2020). Everybody sign now: Translating spoken language to photo realistic sign language video. *arXiv preprint arXiv:2011.09846*. https://arxiv.org/abs/2011.09846

[8]   Natarajan, B., and Elakkiya, R. (2022). Dynamic GAN for high-quality sign language video generation from skeletal poses using generative adversarial networks. *Soft Computing, 26*(23), 13153–13175.

[9]   Cao, Z., Hidalgo, G., Simon, T., Wei, S. E., and Sheikh, Y. (2019). Openpose: realtime multi-person 2d pose estimation using part affinity fields. *IEEE Transactions on Pattern Analysis and Machine Intelligence, 43*(1), 172–186.

[10] Lugaresi, C., Tang, J., Nash, H., *et al.* (2019). Mediapipe: A framework for building perception pipelines. *arXiv preprint arXiv:1906.08172*. https://arxiv.org/abs/1906.08172

[11] Sun, K., Xiao, B., Liu, D., and Wang, J. (2019). Deep high-resolution representation learning for human pose estimation. *In Proceedings of the IEEE/CVF Conference on Computer Vision and Pattern Recognition* (pp. 5693–5703). IEEE.

[12] Tulyakov, S., Liu, M. Y., Yang, X., and Kautz, J. (2018). Mocogan: Decomposing motion and content for video generation. *In Proceedings of the IEEE Conference on Computer Vision and Pattern Recognition* (pp. 1526–1535). IEEE.

[13] Shi, T., Hu, L., Shang, F., Feng, J., Liu, P., and Feng, W. (2024). Pose-guided fine-grained sign language video generation. *In European Conference on Computer Vision* (pp. 392–409). Cham: Springer Nature Switzerland.

[14] Qi, F., Duan, Y., Zhang, H., and Xu, C. (2024). SignGen: End-to-end sign language video generation with latent diffusion. *In European Conference on Computer Vision* (pp. 252–270). Cham: Springer Nature Switzerland.

[15] Moryossef, A., Sant, G., and Jiang, Z. (2024). Pose-based sign language appearance transfer. *arXiv preprint arXiv:2410.13675*. https://arxiv.org/abs/2410.13675

[16] Tze, C. O., Filntisis, P. P., Dimou, A. L., Roussos, A., and Maragos, P. (2022). Neural sign reenactor: Deep photorealistic sign language retargeting. *arXiv preprint arXiv:2209.01470*. https://arxiv.org/abs/2209.01470

[17] Yu, Z., Huang, S., Cheng, Y., and Birdal, T. (2024). Signavatars: a large-scale 3D sign language holistic motion dataset and benchmark. *In European Conference on Computer Vision* (pp. 1–19). Cham: Springer Nature Switzerland.

[18] Jiang, Z., Sant, G., Moryossef, A., Müller, M., Sennrich, R., and Ebling, S. (2024). Signclip: Connecting text and sign language by contrastive learning. *arXiv preprint arXiv:2407.01264*. https://arxiv.org/abs/2407.01264

[19] Alayrac, J. B., Donahue, J., Luc, P., *et al.* (2022). Flamingo: a visual language model for few-shot learning. *Advances in Neural Information Processing Systems*, *35*, 23716–23736.

[20] Li, J., Li, D., Savarese, S., and Hoi, S. (2023). Blip-2: Bootstrapping language-image pre-training with frozen image encoders and large language models. *In Proceedings of the 40th International Conference on Machine Learning, 202*, (pp. 19730–19742). PMLR. https://proceedings.mlr.press/v202/li23q.html

Chapter 7

Vision-based sign recognition and pose estimation

7.1 Introduction

Sign language recognition has shifted from pixel-level analysis to structured pose-based representation. By focusing on keypoints rather than raw RGB frames, pose-based systems reduce redundancy, improve generalization across signers, and enable real-time performance with lower computational cost. Sign languages involve coordinated hand shapes, facial expressions, head movements, and upper-body articulation. Capturing these features requires precise modeling of spatial and temporal information. Pose estimation frameworks address this by extracting 2D or 3D coordinates of joints from video, which are then used as input for gesture recognition models.

Tools like OpenPose [1] and MediaPipe [2] support real-time detection of body, hand, and face keypoints. OpenPose is suited for multi-person scenarios with high granularity, while MediaPipe provides efficient inference for mobile and embedded systems. Although 2D pose estimation is widely adopted, 3D estimation offers better context for signs involving depth-specific motion or spatial contrasts.

Skeleton-based models have gained prominence due to their ability to encode both structure and motion. Methods such as ST-GCN [3] and PoseConv3D [4] use graph or volumetric representations to model the evolution of joint positions over time. When combined with temporal networks like long short-term memory (LSTM), gated recurrent unit (GRU), or convolutional neural network–recurrent neural network (CNN–RNN) hybrids, these models achieve state-of-the-art performance in recognizing fine-grained gestures, including those found in continuous sign language.

This chapter focuses on pose estimation and vision-based gesture modeling for sign recognition. It covers 2D and 3D pose estimation techniques, keypoint tracking tools, skeleton-based feature learning, and temporal modeling approaches. Benchmark datasets and evaluation metrics relevant to pose-based recognition are also discussed.

7.2 2D and 3D pose estimation

Pose estimation involves detecting human anatomical keypoints (joints) from visual input. For sign language, this includes the detection of hand landmarks, body posture, and facial features that together convey semantic and grammatical information. The estimated keypoints are structured as skeletons, which serve as compact and informative inputs to gesture recognition models.

7.2.1   2D Pose estimation

2D pose estimation predicts joint coordinates in the image plane (x, y). It is computationally efficient and suitable for real-time applications. Widely used tools include:

- OpenPose is one of the first open-source systems to provide real-time multi-person 2D pose estimation. It employs part affinity fields to associate detected keypoints into full-body skeletons, including hands and face.
- MediaPipe provides high-speed, mobile-friendly pipelines for real-time body, hand, and face landmark detection. MediaPipe Hands outputs 21 keypoints per hand, while MediaPipe Pose provides 33 full-body landmarks.

2D models are particularly effective for recognizing isolated signs that occur in frontal views. However, they lack depth information, making it difficult to differentiate gestures that depend on spatial location, occlusion, or distance from the signer.

7.2.2   3D Pose estimation

3D pose estimation extends 2D detection by predicting depth (z-axis) for each joint, resulting in (x, y, z) coordinates. This provides richer spatial information, making it suitable for complex sign language gestures.

- VNect [5] performs real-time monocular 3D human pose estimation. It regresses 3D joint positions from a single RGB frame and fits a temporally stable skeletal model.
- VideoPose3D [6] is a temporal convolutional model that lifts 2D keypoints to 3D pose using 1D dilated convolutions across time. It is widely used in benchmark evaluations such as Human3.6M.
- In sign language recognition tasks, 3D pose helps disambiguate gestures involving forward/backward movement, crossing hand trajectories, and layered spatial references (e.g., classifier constructions in American sign language (ASL) or Deutsche Gebärdensprache (DGS) (German Sign Language)).

3D methods, however, are more resource-intensive and sensitive to camera viewpoint, occlusion, and depth ambiguity, especially when trained without multi-view or depth sensors. Pose estimation serves as the backbone for skeleton-based sign recognition. While 2D is sufficient for many real-time applications, integrating 3D enhances performance in recognizing continuous signs with spatial references. Figure 7.1 illustrates the representation of 2D and 3D models and Table 7.1 shows the comparison of these models.

7.3   Keypoint tracking and detection tools

Keypoint tracking involves extracting and maintaining consistent joint landmarks across video frames. For sign language recognition, this includes full-body pose, hands, and facial expressions. Recent advancements (2024–2025) have improved speed, accuracy, and cross-device compatibility, particularly relevant for real-time SLT systems and the comparison is shown in Table 7.2. Figure 7.2 illustrates

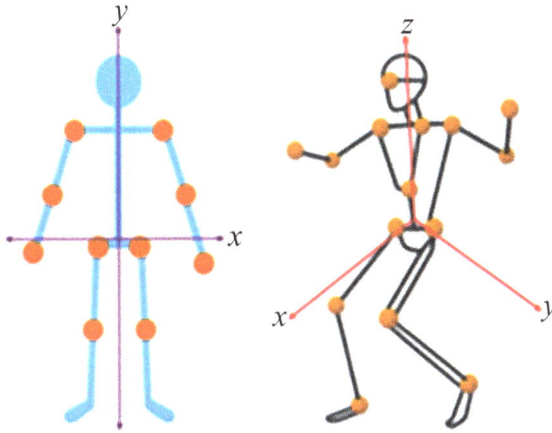

Figure 7.1   Illustration of 2D and 3D models

Table 7.1   Comparison of 2D and 3D models

Feature	2D pose estimation	3D pose estimation
Output	(x, y)	(x, y, z)
Tools	OpenPose, MediaPipe	VNect, VideoPose3D
Hardware	CPU/GPU, runs on mobile	Requires GPU, may need camera calibration
Accuracy	Effective for frontal signs	Better for spatially layered or occluded gestures
Limitation	No depth; occlusion-sensitive	Depth ambiguity; calibration complexity
Use in SLT	Isolated signs, handshape recognition	Spatial grammar, distance-based classification

Table 7.2   Comparison of keypoint tracking and detection tools

Model	Type	Strengths	Limitation
MediaPipe Holistic	2D + z	Unified tracking, edge deployment, 543 landmarks	Coarse depth, no full 3D lifting
OpenPose	2D	Robust, multi-person, high-quality face + hand	Heavy model, non-mobile friendly
DETRPose	2D	Transformer-based, real-time, high-precision	Requires transformer runtime
Greit-HRNet	2D	High-resolution, efficient, suitable for mobile	2D-only, no temporal modeling
LGM-Pose	2D	Fast, mobile-optimized, global-local fusion	Slight drop in accuracy on occlusion
HDiffTG	3D	Occlusion recovery, temporal + spatial modeling	Training complexity

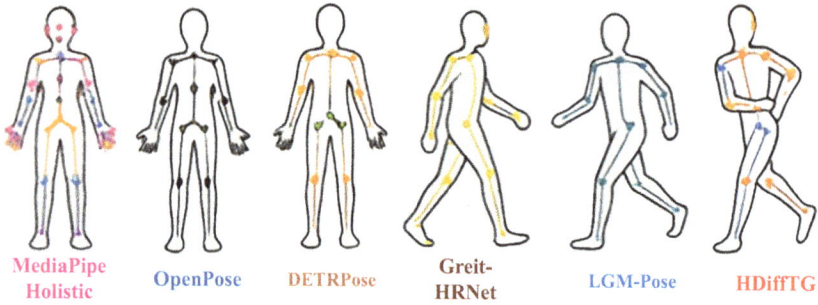

Figure 7.2   Visual comparison of recent keypoint tracking and detection models used in sign language recognition

differences in keypoint density, spatial articulation, and pose coverage across six models: MediaPipe Holistic (full-body, hands, and face tracking), OpenPose (2D multi-person with hand/body keypoints), DETRPose (transformer-based 2D estimation), Greit-HRNet and LGM-Pose (lightweight high-resolution and mobile-friendly models), and HDiffTG (3D pose estimation with temporal and occlusion handling).

7.3.1   MediaPipe holistic landmarker

The MediaPipe Holistic [7] solution integrates multiple models – Pose, Face Mesh, and Hand Landmarks – into a unified, lightweight inference pipeline capable of tracking 543 keypoints. In 2024, Google released a refined version using BlazePose GHUM for better anatomical accuracy and temporal filtering.

- Detects: 33 body landmarks, 21 per hand, and 468 facial landmarks
- Improved z-coordinate approximation with landmark depth ordering
- Runs in real-time on CPU/GPU and web/mobile environments

Although still limited in precise 3D estimation, it is suitable for embedded SLT applications and serves well in edge-deployable systems.

7.3.2   OpenPose

OpenPose remains a reference-standard tool for 2D multi-person body, face, and hand keypoint detection. While its core architecture has remained unchanged since 2018, it continues to be used widely for pre-processing and labeling SLT datasets.

- Uses part affinity fields to associate joints
- Robust to multi-person occlusion and camera variation
- Not suitable for lightweight or real-time mobile deployment

7.3.3   DETRPose

DETRPose [8] applies transformer-based architectures with set prediction objectives to estimate human poses end-to-end. By eliminating the need for heatmap decoding and anchor boxes, it offers high spatial precision and resilience to cluttered backgrounds.

- Global context via self-attention enables robust multi-person detection
- Architecture is based on DEtection TRansformer (DETR) + Pose heads
- Benchmarked on common objects in context (COCO) and PoseTrack with improved generalization

7.3.4 *Greit-HRNet*

Greit-HRNet [9] is a high-resolution network designed for lightweight pose estimation. It integrates Grouped Channel Spatial Attention (GCSA) to enhance spatial modeling while maintaining computational efficiency.

- Lightweight variant of HRNet with grouped feature encoding
- Achieves high AP on COCO and Max Planck Institute for Informatics (MPII) (Human Pose Dataset) datasets
- Suitable for SLT on constrained devices (Jetson Nano, smartphones)

7.3.5 *LGM-Pose*

LGM-Pose [10] introduces a Local-Global MobileViM-based architecture for efficient multi-scale keypoint estimation. It uses spatial shuffle and token reduction blocks, making it ideal for real-time mobile inference.

- Combines global attention with convolutional efficiency
- Maintains >70 FPS on ARM devices with minimal loss in AP
- Designed for resource-limited SLT deployments

7.3.6 *HDiffTG (2025)*

HDiffTG [11] is a hybrid framework combining diffusion models, temporal transformers, and graph convolutional networks (GCNs) for 3D pose estimation. It excels in occlusion recovery and cross-view generalization – key challenges in continuous SLT.

- Employs a denoising diffusion process to refine noisy 3D sequences
- Incorporates GCN layers for joint dependency modeling
- Outperforms prior models on Human3.6M and 3DPW datasets

7.4 Skeleton-based gesture recognition

Skeleton-based gesture recognition involves learning patterns from sequences of joint coordinates obtained from pose estimation tools. The goal is to recognize gestures by modeling spatial relationships between joints and temporal dynamics across frames. This method is particularly effective in sign language recognition due to its invariance to lighting, clothing, and background – focusing only on the structural and motion aspects of gestures.

7.4.1 *Feature representation*

Skeleton sequences can be encoded in various forms:

- **Joint coordinates** (x,y,z) over time
- **Relative joint angles** and **bone vectors** to capture articulation
- **Velocity** and **acceleration** features to represent dynamic aspects
- **Graph structures** where adjacency matrices define joint connectivity

Preprocessing often includes normalization (e.g., root-relative joints), resampling to fixed sequence lengths, and interpolation to handle occlusions.

7.4.2 Graph convolutional networks

(a) **CTR-GC** [12]: Channel-wise Topology Refinement Graph Convolution learns adaptive joint connectivity at each channel level, instead of relying on a fixed skeletal graph. It enables the model to capture fine-grained motion variations across joints in continuous sequences – essential for sign gestures involving subtle finger transitions.
- Each GCN layer learns a residual adjacency matrix over channels
- Supports frame-wise and global refinement
- Strong performance on NTU RGB+D 120 and UAV-Human

(b) **MS-G3D** [13]: Multi-Scale Graph 3D network improves temporal resolution by introducing multiple temporal convolution branches. It dynamically adjusts receptive fields for gestures with different motion durations (e.g., quick signs vs long holds).
- Multi-scale temporal kernels (e.g., 3, 5, 7 frames)
- Spatial graph remains fixed (body kinematic tree)

7.4.3 Transformer-based architectures

(a) **PoseFormer** [14]: One of the earliest pose-only transformer architectures, PoseFormer models temporal dependencies across full skeleton sequences using self-attention. It treats pose frames as tokens and uses a standard transformer encoder.
- Effective for gloss boundary modeling in continuous SLT
- Supports end-to-end training from keypoints to gloss labels
- Better than ST-GCN when long-term dependencies matter

(b) **ST-TR** [15]: ST-TR splits spatial and temporal attention into separate streams. This improves efficiency by reducing redundant attention calculations and supports long-frame modeling.
- Modular block design
- Works well on small-scale sign datasets (e.g., RWTH-BOSTON-50)

(c) **SignLLM** [16]: A multi-lingual SLP model using large language model architectures with reinforcement learning objectives. It supports MLSF and Prompt2LangGloss modes and achieves state-of-the-art SLP across eight sign languages.
- Combines prompt-conditioned gloss generation and pose synthesis
- Integrates multilingual gloss dictionaries with an LLM backbone
- Achieves best-in-class fluency and signer diversity in multilingual setups

7.5   Temporal modeling

Temporal modeling forms the backbone of sign language recognition, especially in continuous settings where signs are not isolated but occur in sequence. Understanding the motion across time – its rhythm, trajectory, and transition – is essential for correctly interpreting gestures. Unlike static image classification, sign language tasks require models that can capture the progression of joint movements, the duration and overlap of gestures, and the dependencies between signs.

7.5.1   Temporal models in SLT

Sign language is inherently dynamic. A sign's meaning often emerges not from a single frame, but from the evolution of hand and body positions over time. For example, the trajectory of a hand movement, the pause between signs, or the coarticulation between successive gestures carries important semantic information. Moreover, many signs share similar handshapes and differ only in motion pattern or duration. Therefore, models that ignore or inadequately represent temporal context fail to differentiate such signs. Temporal modeling also enables automatic segmentation in continuous sign language translation, identifying where one sign ends and another begins – an essential component in sequence-to-sequence translation pipelines.

7.5.2   Classical temporal encoders

Earlier models for sign language gesture recognition leveraged recurrent neural architectures such as RNNs, LSTMs, and GRUs. These models processed input pose or feature sequences in a time-step-by-time-step manner, learning dependencies via gated memory cells. For small-scale datasets or isolated sign recognition tasks, LSTMs performed reasonably well. CNN–RNN hybrid models were also proposed, where CNNs encoded spatial features per frame and RNNs modeled the temporal evolution. However, recurrent networks suffer from limited parallelism, vanishing gradient issues over long sequences, and often fail to retain long-range contextual dependencies – a drawback in modeling long continuous sign streams.

7.5.3   Temporal convolutional networks

To address the limitations of recurrent models, temporal convolutional networks (TCNs) were proposed. These models apply 1D convolutions along the temporal axis, enabling parallel computation and the capture of local and mid-range dependencies. MS-TCN++ introduced multi-stage refinement and dilated temporal convolutions to model both fine-grained and coarse temporal patterns. It was widely adopted in action segmentation and sign boundary detection tasks. Similarly, VideoPose3D employed temporal convolutions over 2D keypoint sequences to lift them into 3D pose space and was adapted in some SLT pipelines for gesture classification. TCN-based models offer lower latency and better gradient flow, making them more suitable for real-time systems.

7.5.4   Transformer-based temporal models

Recent advances have favored transformer architectures for temporal modeling due to their ability to model global dependencies without recurrence. PoseFormer, a transformer-based model for 3D pose estimation, treats each pose frame as a token and applies self-attention over time. This enables the model to capture both short-term variations and long-range semantic continuity, making it effective for isolated and continuous sign recognition tasks. ST-TR further extended this approach by decoupling spatial and temporal attention heads, improving efficiency and inter-pretability. Transformer-based SLT models offer scalability to long sequences, and their non-sequential computation makes them amenable to parallel hardware acceleration. A specialized model called Sign2Text Transformer was introduced to directly map sequences of poses to gloss-level outputs. It incorporates cross-modal attention to align sign trajectories with gloss semantics and achieves strong results on benchmarks like PHOENIX-2014T.

7.5.5   Diffusion-driven temporal modeling

Denoising diffusion models have recently been applied to temporal modeling in gesture synthesis. SignDiff is a representative model that generates smooth and expressive skeletal motion conditioned on gloss input using a denoising diffusion process. Unlike deterministic autoregressive models, diffusion-based approaches produce diverse and naturalistic outputs while still maintaining temporal coher-ence. In the context of SLT, such models are particularly useful for sign synthesis or for recovering motion segments in noisy or occluded pose sequences. Their integration into recognition tasks remains an emerging area of research, but they show promise in scenarios requiring high-fidelity motion representation.

Figure 7.3 presents four major categories of temporal modeling used in SLT pipelines: Recurrent Networks (e.g., LSTM, GRU), TCNs (e.g., MS-TCN++), Transformer-based models (e.g., PoseFormer, ST-TR), and Diffusion Models (e.g., SignDiff). Each block highlights the information flow and modeling depth over time. Recurrent models process frames sequentially, often struggling with long-range dependencies. TCNs apply parallel convolutions to capture local and

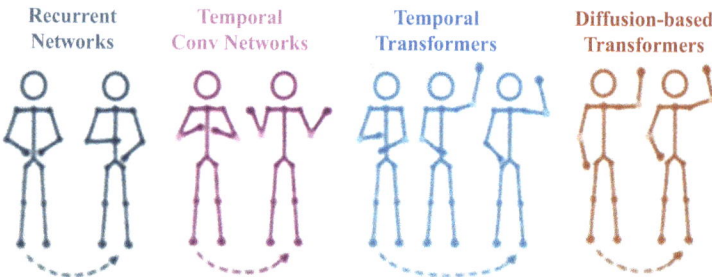

Figure 7.3   Comparative illustration of temporal modeling techniques in sign recognition and pose estimation

mid-range patterns efficiently. Transformers employ self-attention across the entire sequence, enabling global context modeling. Diffusion-based models iteratively refine temporal sequences to produce smooth and expressive motion trajectories, especially useful in sign synthesis and occlusion recovery tasks.

7.6   Summary

This chapter explored the evolution and advancements in vision-based sign recognition with a focus on pose estimation and skeletal modeling. Beginning with the fundamentals of 2D and 3D pose estimation, the chapter introduced tools such as MediaPipe and OpenPose that enable robust keypoint detection. These systems have paved the way for skeleton-based gesture recognition, where spatial configurations of joints form the primary modality for classification and translation tasks.

A detailed discussion followed on temporal modeling architectures – essential for capturing the sequential nature of sign language. The limitations of classical recurrent models were highlighted, leading to more recent methods such as TCNs (e.g., MS-TCN++), transformer-based encoders (e.g., PoseFormer, ST-TR, Sign2Text), and generative diffusion-based approaches (e.g., SignDiff). These models not only improve recognition accuracy but also support the synthesis of naturalistic signing motion with temporal coherence and expressiveness.

The chapter emphasized the shift from frame-wise static recognition to temporally aware architectures capable of modeling inter-sign dependencies, segmentation boundaries, and dynamic flow. This progression is essential for advancing continuous SLT systems that are both efficient and deployable on real-world datasets. Through selected figures and current literature, the chapter provided a comprehensive perspective on how temporal and spatial cues are jointly modeled in modern SLT pipelines.

Exercises

(I)   **Multiple choice questions**
1.   Which tool provides real-time 2D keypoint tracking for browser-based applications?
    (a) OpenPose
    (b) MediaPipe
    (c) HRNet
    (d) VIBE

2.   Which model applies self-attention across temporal keypoints in sign recognition?
    (a) GRU
    (b) TCN
    (c) PoseFormer
    (d) SignCLIP

3. Which of the following models uses a denoising process to model temporal sequences?
    (a) MS-TCN++
    (b) SignDiff
    (c) BiLSTM
    (d) PoseNet

4. What is the key limitation of LSTM-based models in SLT tasks?
    (a) Low accuracy
    (b) High variance
    (c) Poor long-range dependency modeling
    (d) Lack of supervision

5. Which dataset provides gloss-aligned 2D keypoints for continuous SLT?
    (a) RWTH-Boston-50
    (b) PHOENIX-2014T
    (c) SignAvatars
    (d) ASL100

(II)   **Short answer questions**
1. Explain the difference between 2D and 3D pose estimation in SLT.
2. What role does skeleton-based modeling play in gesture recognition?
3. Describe the benefits of using TCNs over RNNs in temporal modeling.
4. How does PoseFormer improve over traditional temporal models?
5. What are the challenges of using diffusion models for temporal pose generation?

(III)   **Discussion questions**
1. Discuss the evolution of temporal modeling techniques for sign gesture recognition. What are the trade-offs involved?
2. Compare transformer-based models with TCNs for long sequence modeling in SLT.
3. How do keypoint occlusions affect sign recognition? What are some recent solutions?
4. Evaluate the advantages of using diffusion models for gesture synthesis in sign language.
5. Propose an ideal architecture for combining skeleton-based recognition with temporal attention for real-time SLT.

(IV)   **Practical/Hands-on exercises**
1. Using MediaPipe, extract 2D keypoints from a set of sign language videos. Visualize the keypoints over time and evaluate the stability of tracking.
2. Implement a simple PoseFormer-like transformer using PyTorch to classify 2D keypoint sequences into glosses.
3. Compare TCN and LSTM architectures on a subset of the PHOENIX-2014T dataset for isolated sign recognition. Report accuracy and inference time.

4. Build a sign synthesis pipeline using SignDiff or a dummy denoising framework with noisy keypoints as input. Measure output smoothness.
5. Create an animation of a skeleton performing five signs using keypoints predicted from a temporal model. Use matplotlib or Blender for visualization.

References

[1] Cao, Z., Hidalgo, G., Simon, T., Wei, S. E., and Sheikh, Y. (2019). Openpose: realtime multi-person 2d pose estimation using part affinity fields. *IEEE Transactions on Pattern Analysis and Machine Intelligence*, *43*(1), 172–186.

[2] Lugaresi, C., Tang, J., Nash, H., *et al.* (2019). Mediapipe: a framework for building perception pipelines. *arXiv preprint arXiv:1906.08172.* https://arxiv.org/abs/1906.08172

[3] Yan, S., Xiong, Y., and Lin, D. (2018). Spatial temporal graph convolutional networks for skeleton-based action recognition. In *Proceedings of the AAAI Conference on Artificial Intelligence* (Vol. 32, No. 1).

[4] Duan, H., Zhao, Y., Chen, K., Lin, D., and Dai, B. (2022). Revisiting skeleton-based action recognition. In *Proceedings of the IEEE/CVF Conference on Computer Vision and Pattern Recognition* (pp. 2969–2978).

[5] Mehta, D., Sridhar, S., Sotnychenko, O., *et al.* (2017). VNect: real-time 3D human pose estimation with a single RGB camera. *ACM Transactions on Graphics (TOG)*, *36*(4), 1–14.

[6] Pavllo, D., Feichtenhofer, C., Grangier, D., and Auli, M. (2019). 3D human pose estimation in video with temporal convolutions and semi-supervised training. In *Proceedings of the IEEE/CVF Conference on Computer Vision and Pattern Recognition* (pp. 7753–7762).

[7] https://research.google/blog/mediapipe-holistic-simultaneous-face-hand-and-pose-prediction-on-device/

[8] Janampa, S., and Pattichis, M. (2025). DETRPose: real-time end-to-end transformer model for multi-person pose estimation. *arXiv preprint arXiv:2506.13027.* https://arxiv.org/abs/2506.13027

[9] Han, J., and Wang, Y. (2024). Greit-HRNet: grouped lightweight high-resolution network for human pose estimation. In *Proceedings of the Asian Conference on Computer Vision* (pp. 3771–3787).

[10] Guo, B., Guo, F., Luo, G., Luo, X., and Zhang, F. (2025). LGM-pose: a lightweight global modeling network for real-time human pose estimation. *arXiv preprint arXiv:2506.04561.* https://arxiv.org/abs/2506.04561

[11] Fu, Y., Huang, C., Li, J., Kong, H., Tian, Y., Li, H., and Zhang, Z. (2025). HDiffTG: a lightweight hybrid diffusion-transformer-GCN architecture for 3D human pose estimation. *arXiv preprint arXiv:2505.04276.* https://arxiv.org/abs/2505.04276

[12] Chen, Y., Zhang, Z., Yuan, C., Li, B., Deng, Y., and Hu, W. (2021). Channel-wise topology refinement graph convolution for skeleton-based

action recognition. In *Proceedings of the IEEE/CVF International Conference on Computer Vision* (pp. 13359–13368).

[13] Liu, Z., Zhang, H., Chen, Z., Wang, Z., and Ouyang, W. (2020). Disentangling and unifying graph convolutions for skeleton-based action recognition. In *Proceedings of the IEEE/CVF Conference on Computer Vision and Pattern Recognition* (pp. 143–152).

[14] Zheng, C., Zhu, S., Mendieta, M., Yang, T., Chen, C., and Ding, Z. (2021). 3D human pose estimation with spatial and temporal transformers. In *Proceedings of the IEEE/CVF International Conference on Computer Vision* (pp. 11656–11665).

[15] Plizzari, C., Cannici, M., and Matteucci, M. (2021). Skeleton-based action recognition via spatial and temporal transformer networks. *Computer Vision and Image Understanding, 208*, 103219.

[16] Fang, S., Wang, L., Zheng, C., Tian, Y., and Chen, C. (2024). SignLLM: sign languages production large language models. *arXiv preprint arXiv:2405.10718*. https://arxiv.org/abs/2405.10718

Chapter 8
Sign language generation and video synthesis

8.1 Introduction

Video synthesis and sign language generation are the last steps in the sign language translation (SLT) pipeline, converting abstract linguistic or skeletal representations into visually, temporally consistent, and expressive videos. The objective is to not only produce sign gestures that represent the correct semantics, but videos that closely approximate the fluidity, realism, and subtlety of human signing.

Unlike static gesture recognition or gloss-based translation, sign video synthesis requires the modeling of both detailed articulations (e.g., finger movement, facial expression) and global spatiotemporal coherence (e.g., body-spatial transitions, rhythm connected to a specific signer). In the early stages of work in sign video synthesis, the aim was simplistic and either elegantly or crudely mapped a signing gloss to a video notion of that gloss – often as frames, which resulted in either jittery or robotic outcomes if temporal modeling was absent. More recent work has been about generative adversarial networks (GANs), variational auto-encoders (VAEs), or diffusion models to generate higher fidelity video outputs from intermediate pose sequences or gloss inputs to ensure qualitative visual treatment at the same time as conveying entire sign language meaning.

A multi-stage pipeline is shown in Figure 8.1: gloss or text → 2D/3D pose sequence → RGB video. Notable models include:

- **SignGAN**, a transformer-based GAN conditioned on skeletal poses, produces photo-realistic sign videos with controllable signer appearance using a pose-conditioned synthesis network [1].
- **G2P-DDM**, a discrete denoising diffusion model, generates high-quality pose sequences from gloss annotations, achieving state-of-the-art results in gloss-to-pose modeling [2].
- **Gloss-driven conditional diffusion** models directly synthesize pose sequences through diffusion processes, improving temporal consistency in pose outputs [3].

Further, avatar-based synthesis using 3D human mesh models (e.g., Skinned multi-person linear model (SMPL)-X) allows for customizable and signer-independent video synthesis. These methods enable multilingual rendering and controlled avatar behaviour in sign video production [4].

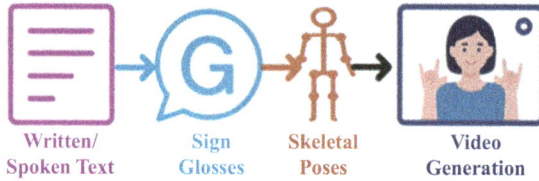

Figure 8.1   Pipeline of text-to-sign generation

This chapter delves into the fundamental aspects and methods of synthesis for sign language video, describes gloss-to-video and pose-guided generation methods, architectural choices (GANs, VAEs, diffusion), and the modeling of fine articulatory details such as the head/face area and hand shapes. By bringing together the last generation of low-level gesture modeling with high-level generative video synthesis, we can potentially make great strides toward improving accessibility for Deaf and hard of hearing future technologies.

8.2   Gloss-to-sign video generation

The gloss-to-sign video generation is a critical mediating layer in contemporary sign language synthesis pipelines. Gloss sequences are essentially normalized sign tokens that conceptually abstract the details of sign language grammar and articulation and represent a structure that streamlines modeling. The steps involved here can be summarized as follows: the glosses are first transformed into a series of pose frames, and then the pose frames are used to generate video output via photo-realistic or avatar-based synthesis. This section outlines the three primary stages of this process and it is shown in Figure 8.2: gloss embedding and temporal alignment, pose generation from sign gloss, and video synthesis from poses.

8.2.1   Temporal alignment and gloss embedding

To correctly embed gloss sequences, we need to capture both the linguistic meaning and the temporal rhythm, which is inherently multimodal. Hierarchical transformer-based encoders like TSPNet are able to simultaneously utilize gloss sequences at both global (entire sequence) and local (one sign) levels to ensure sign transitions are kept consistent semantically [5,6]. Prosody-aware encoders augment gloss embeddings by encoding timing-related cues (like pauses, repetitions, emphasis) to enable gloss sequences to have more natural motion pacing. In addition, contrastive learning approaches have been used to assist in aligning gloss embeddings with the corresponding pose sequences, so they are able to create richer, context-aware representations that enable more effective downstream synthesis.

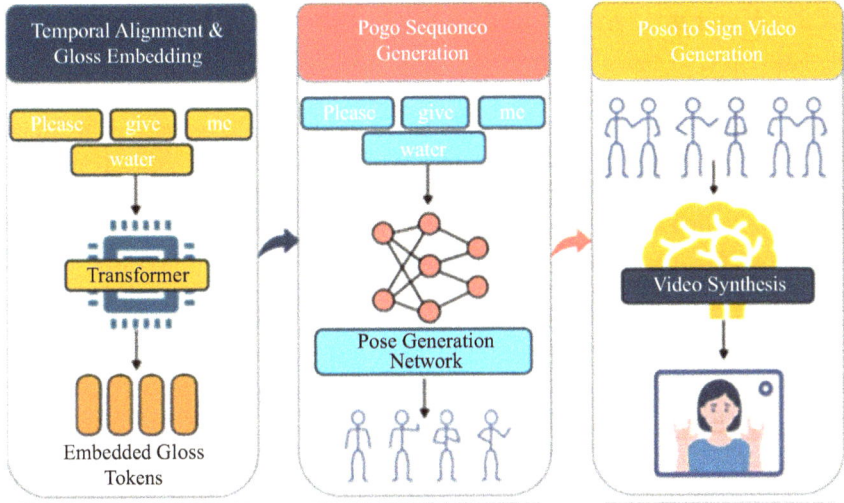

Figure 8.2   Gloss to video generation pipeline

8.2.2   Pose sequence generation from gloss

After being adequately encoded, gloss sequences are applied to recover skeletal pose sequences. One promising avenue relies on diffusion-based approaches, exemplified by gloss-to-pose (G2P) dynamic decoding module (DDM), which is a discrete denoising diffusion model that generates pose trajectories with discrete denoising steps. G2P-diffusion also utilizes the Pose-VQVAE framework, which quantizes pose data into discrete tokens and allows the transformer-based denoising backbone network to show good temporal coherence [2]. Another variant of diffusion models, called sign intermediate discriminator decoder (IDD), has a better-quality version of the pose generation paradigm by disentangling bone-length and joint-direction features to produce anatomically valid poses [7]. The advanced fidelity of these models provides improvements elusive with traditional methods like GANs or Recurrent neural networks (RNNs), with greater fluidity in the transitions, improved diversity, and reduced jitter.

In addition to the diffusion-based methods, the flow-based frameworks and temporal consistency models so far have not taken advantage of the flexibility of incorporating flow models constrained by optical flow, as gloss2pose flow [6] improved the consistency across gloss types. We hope that multi-stage constraint models across frames and gloss boundaries will further improve consistency and account for other gloss styles typical in sign. One of the transformer structures analyzed is Skeletonformer [8], which regresses skeletal clothes coordinates representing the joints directly by using masked temporal attention and is flexible and robust to different signing styles.

8.2.3   From pose to video synthesis

The last step is to create visual outputs from pose sequences. Classical techniques for creating visual outputs from pose to video include techniques like vid2vid, which synthesizes realistic RGB frames based on skeletal keypoints and reference images and is penalized and measured by flow and identity loss to maintain coherency in movement [5]. SignGAN improved realism by using spatially decoupled motion and appearance pathways (to preserve motion for pose correctness and appearance for signer-specific features like face, hand shape, and clothing) on the frontal-oriented signer [1].

Additional methods have fused separate streams of facial expressions and mouthing animations to generate even more realistic videos. Neural rendering avatars utilize 3D mesh avatars based on SMPL [4], which are animated using inverse kinematics and textured through learned neural mappings with 3D visualizations. The active field of research on neural rendering includes new models like TalkinNeRF [9], which use implicit volumetric representations for producing gesture outputs with high fidelity, including realistic lighting and shading (this model is complete with a full body NeRF and allows for hand deformation through individual meshes). Avatar-based systems like SignAvatars are derived from the blender-based SMPL mesh animations that support blendshapes, allowing for signer-independent multilingual outputs and allowing for large-scale outputs for 3D sign language production [10].

Most systems now include spatio-temporal adversarial losses, keypoint-based regularization, and appearance consistency constraints to ensure video frames will have smooth transitions and not create any visual artifacts. These features are essential for removing flickering and maintaining structure across frames.

8.3   Temporal modeling and pose-guided control in sign video generation

To generate a sign language video that is fluent and contextually appropriate, it is necessary to model the transitions of the static poses temporally. This entails predicting the movement dynamics of the hands, face, and body in coordination with one another. Cutting-edge temporal modeling approaches as shown in Figure 8.3 leverage transformer architectures, diffusion models, graph-based learning, and text-to-pose pipelines to improve the realism and control of the video generation.

8.3.1   Transformer-based temporal reasoning

Transformers have changed sequential data modeling by providing a way to capture long-range dependencies without requiring recurrent operations. In sign language synthesis, the use of such models can provide for accurate alignment between sequences of glosses and gesture trajectories.

- PoseFormer [11] employed spatial and temporal self-attention for 3D pose estimation that can be used to produce temporally coherent gestures.

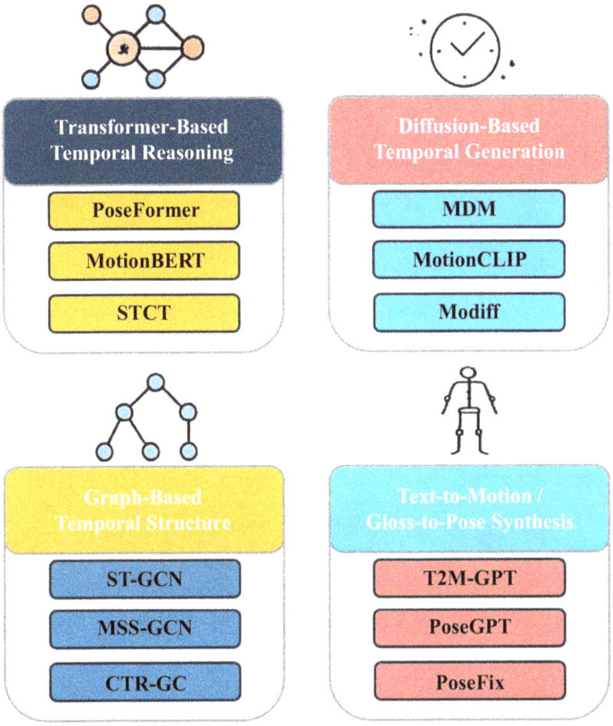

Figure 8.3   Temporal modeling and pose-guided control techniques in sign generation

- MotionBERT [12] unified 2D and 3D motion prediction into a framework using BERT-like transformers that produce rich spatiotemporal embeddings fit for pose-conditioned synthesis.
- Spatio-temporal channel transformer (STCT) [13] improved temporal motion modeling via two separate channels – spatial and temporal (and where temporal channels were separate and non-overlapped) – which increased the accuracy of long-horizon motion predictions.

These models can perform well at encapsulating the evolution of joint positions over time, which is important for sign language synthesis to achieve signs that occur in continuity without abrupt transitions.

8.3.2   Diffusion-based temporal generation

Diffusion models allow the generation of human motion sequences in the context of temporal sequences because they start with noise and convert that into motions incrementally. Because of their stochastic nature, they provide a good way to represent variability and styles of gestures.

- Motion diffusion model (MDM) [14] is a prominent way of using diffusion to generate realistic motions given a textual prompt, which is translatable into gloss-conditioned motion.
- MotionCLIP [15] guided motion synthesis given CLIP text embeddings, which provided some semantic control over the stylistic and content elements of gesture synthesis.
- Modiff [16] conditioned the action semantics of a sequence to add diversity and structure to motion generation, which still allows for some differentiation if context for signs in phrases.

Thus, diffusion-based techniques yield promise for quality and flexibility in modeling the motions developed in signs.

8.3.3   Graph-based temporal modeling

Modeling skeletal joints as graphs and movement over time as temporal sequences provides a greater structural basis to reason about signer kinematics.

- ST-GCN [17] was still one of the first to apply graph convolutional processing to human skeletons over time.
- Multi-scale skeleton graph convolution network (MSS-GCN) [18] was the first of its kind to extract multiple spatial scales (the display of gestural motion, for example, optimally uses the observed spaces) and also multiple temporal scales, and this improved expressive representations of hand and face motion.
- Channel-wise topology refinement graph convolution (CTR-GC) [19] has an additional preference for eliminating joint overlap and dynamically changes the graph structure to best reflect co-articulated gestures (expression of one limb impacts the other), which permits it for the modeling of signers as unique and personal representations of gesture users.

These models draw more upon the constructs of continuity, coordination, and articulation of the gestures by indulging the structural relationships among some interacting body parts.

8.3.4   Text-to-motion/gloss-to-pose synthesis

Connecting natural language or gloss input to pose trajectories is one of the most important tasks in sign language synthesis. Many of these models are based on transformer or language-conditioned generation.

- T2M-GPT [20] intervened in a discrete token framework to produce motion embeddings from text using a GPT-like model. This can easily be adapted for gloss sequences.
- PoseGPT [21] uses quantized pose codes and operates on an auto-regressive basis to generate long motion sequences from textual prompts.
- PoseFix [22] provides a novel twist by coupling natural language with correcting 3D poses. This could be particularly useful in the context of refinement of gloss-to-pose outputs with specific prompt styles or emotional cues.

These generative processes provide a form of controllability with sign generation, whereby a gloss or language entry becomes the driving factor of the pose sequence.

8.4 Gesture refinement and pose-to-video translation

After obtaining skeletal pose sequences from gloss-level inputs, the one last step still to be performed is transforming the abstract body keypoints into expressive, photorealistic signer videos. In this stage, which involves gesture refinement and pose-to-video conversion, we are connecting linguistic correctness and visual realism explicitly through gesture formulation, temporal coherence, visual clarity (given the variability of each subject), and emotional expression (through reflection of social interaction). This section explores four major components in this process: denoising/smoothing, GAN-based image translation, diffusion and flow-based video generation, and fine detail refinement for face and hands.

8.4.1 Denoising and temporal smoothing

There are motion sequences with sign language, and minimal differences in predicted pose frames can produce perceptually noisy motion or a stammer when synthesizing video. To address this issue, several denoising and temporal smoothing methods are in existence:

- Kalman filters [23] assume linear dynamics with a process and observation model and are often used in real-time systems to take a generative, or smooth, estimate of pose over time by filtering a sequence of observed, noisy frames. Kalman filters are particularly well suited for recursively estimating the spatial locations of the joints (e.g., right shoulder, right elbow, etc.) in a noisy pose prediction.
- Gaussian smoothing [24] is another common method that can smooth out a high-frequency jitter or noise in the output by applying a temporal kernel over a sliding window. Gaussian smoothing was particularly useful in the postprocessing of the skeletal outputs from keypoint extractors such as OpenPose and MediaPipe.
- Temporal convolution networks (TCNs) [25] offer one way to apply a learned smoothing method. TCN architectures, such as DynaBOA use causal convolutions to layer joint-pose estimates to predict smoothed future poses while capturing short-term dependencies, which eliminate certain abrupt trajectories of hand or shoulder motion.

All these techniques are important pre-processing for high-fidelity video synthesis, as we do not want erratic or noisy joint predictions to be passed downstream.

8.4.2 GAN-based pose-to-image translation

GANs are currently leading the way in generating photorealistic images based solely on the structure as information (e.g., the human skeleton); on the side of sign language generation, they provide the ability to translate pose sequence data into detailed visualizations of the signer:

- PoseGAN [26] was the initial depiction of pose-based image generation in a two-stage architecture; the first stage generated coarse images given a pose condition, while the second stage generated the detailed images through adversarial methods. This method inspired much of the future pose-guided generation work.
- EverybodyDanceNow [27] animates a static target subject, so they follow the movement of another subject, composed to be either a receptionist signing or a dancer with a softer partner, and the form of choreography is more common. The EverybodyDanceNow model was developed for dance generation but has also been shown to adapt to sign language avatars. It retains the identity and realism of the avatars.
- TexturePose [28] improved image fidelity by learning part-based textures using attention, so that folds in clothing and overlap between hands, etc., are represented in detail.

Using these GAN architectures, we can produce video (frames) that preserve the identity of the signer (e.g., clothing style), and of course background, while being consistent with the skeletal output.

8.4.3   Diffusion and flow-based video synthesis

While GANs can take care of the generation of static frames, maintaining temporal coherence between frames is challenging. Coping with this challenge has resulted in the introduction of diffusion-based models, and flow-based guided models have been introduced:

- VideoFusion [29] proposed to take a diffusion-based approach for generating video where temporal noise transitions across frames are modeled. The denoising backbone allows temporal noise, giving a greater sense of continuity between frames, so the motion dynamics stay fluid without observable seams and flickers.
- FlowFace [30] employed optical flow as the guidance to produce temporally coherent sequences of faces. Of course, the same process can be extended to hand and human bodies, and discards frame-to-frame inconsistencies by warping features in the flow of motion.
- Image animation via keypoint transfer [31] also used motion vectors, learned flow fields to animate a source image with the guided motion of keypoints. This source image animation (via occlusion reasoning) and modular flow estimation are still useful as a framework for rendering sign language gestures.

By integrating motion priors from optical flow predictions or denoising transitions in the diffusion space, these methods significantly increase the temporal realism and fluidity of signer-based videos.

8.4.4   Face and hand detail enhancement

In sign languages, facial expressions (non-manual markers) and finger nuances have significant grammatical and semantic information. Thus, clarifying these features is important to ensure that the generated signer not only visually looks realistic but also communicatively.

- GANimation [32] allows facial expressions to be controlled at a nuanced level by conditioning image generation on facial action units. This is important to gain emotional nuance and also maintain linguistically precise expressions.
- HiFiFace [33] generates high-resolution faces from sparse inputs like landmarks. By aligning features using pyramidal structures, the generated signer can have eye, lip, and eyebrow dynamics that are important to capturing expressivity in sign language.
- Few-shot talking head synthesis [34] also provides an efficient way to animate faces with a series of driving pose sequences and describes keypoint deformation aware of occlusions when animating.

Altogether, these methods will ensure the synthesized signer video is communicatively clear and represents emotional fidelity, especially for educational and broadcast contexts where expressivity is relevant.

8.5   Summary

In this chapter, an overview of methodologies to build an automated sign language generation and video synthesizing bimodal system was provided. We began from gloss representation, ended with a realistic video output, and explored various segments of symbolic input, pose estimation, and photorealistic video generation.

Multiple approaches for pose generation based on different architectures, including transformer-based, latent variable modeling, and skeleton/3D regression-based models, were discussed. A few exemplary methods of interest were highlighted, including conditional variational autoencoders and diffusion-based generators, which preserve semantic coherence when generating a realistic, expressive, signer-specific gesture. We also explored cutting-edge strategies such as NeRF-based and avatar-based methods, which can be utilized in multilingual or signer-independent settings.

The chapter then addressed pose-to-video translation models, such as GANs, flow-guided synthesis, and diffusion methods, which help to increase both temporal coherence and spatial realism. Irrespective of the modeling, valuable insights were provided into the refinement of fine articulators, like facial expressions and hand movements, through the models such as HiFiFace and GANimation, that enhanced the non-manual cues that are critical to the linguistic understanding of meaning.

This chapter provided a synthesis of multiple approaches to contribute toward producing real-time, scalable, and linguistically accurate sign language generation systems with significant potential implications on accessibility, education, and human–computer interaction.

Exercises

(I) **Multiple choice questions**
1. Which model uses a latent variable to capture stylistic variation in sign language synthesis?
   (a) SkeletonFormer
   (b) GlossCVAE
   (c) GANimation
   (d) PoseGPT

2. What does NeRF in NeRF-gestures stand for?
   (a) Neural expression recurrent flow
   (b) Nonlinear encoder for rendered frames
   (c) Neural radiance fields
   (d) Normalized embedding for realistic frames

3. Which technique is primarily used to enhance temporal consistency in sign video synthesis?
   (a) HiFiFace
   (b) Kalman filter
   (c) MoCoGAN-HD
   (d) SignAvatars

4. The main function of GANimation is to:
   (a) Animate skeletal poses into dance sequences
   (b) Convert glosses into text
   (c) Control facial expressions via action units
   (d) Track keypoints in real-time

5. Which model is commonly used for pose-to-video synthesis using keypoint-based driving frames?
   (a) VideoFusion
   (b) TexturePose
   (c) First-order motion model (FOMM)
   (d) GANformer

(II) **Short answer questions**
1. Differentiate between GAN-based and diffusion-based methods in sign language video synthesis.
2. Explain the role of temporal smoothing techniques in gesture refinement.
3. What are the advantages of using avatar-based models like SignAvatars in multilingual sign generation?
4. How do pose generation models like SkeletonFormer or PoseGPT contribute to sign synthesis?

5. What challenges arise in translating skeletal poses into high-fidelity sign language videos?

(III) **Discussion questions**
1. What are the comparative advantages and challenges of using diffusion-based models versus GANs for sign language video synthesis?
2. In what ways do avatar-based synthesis methods like SignAvatars support signer-independence and multilingual capabilities?
3. How do facial articulation models (e.g., HiFiFace, GANimation) enhance the expressiveness and grammatical correctness of generated sign language videos?

(IV) **Practical / Hands-on exercises**
1. Implement a basic pose-to-video pipeline using FOMM and MediaPipe skeleton input. Animate a signer performing basic signs.
2. Using a diffusion model library (e.g., hugging face diffusers), try generating a sequence of 3D human poses from gloss text input.
3. Evaluate two synthesized sign videos using FID and a simple human rating scale. Compare the results and discuss the implications.

References

[1] Saunders, B., Camgoz, N. C., and Bowden, R. (2020). Everybody sign now: translating spoken language to photo realistic sign language video. *arXiv preprint arXiv:2011.09846.* https://arxiv.org/abs/2011.09846

[2] Xie, P., Zhang, Q., Taiying, P., Tang, H., Du, Y., and Li, Z. (2024, March). G2P-DDM: generating sign pose sequence from gloss sequence with discrete diffusion model. *In Proceedings of the AAAI Conference on Artificial Intelligence* (Vol. 38, No. 6, pp. 6234–6242). AAAI Press.

[3] Tang, S., Xue, F., Wu, J., Wang, S., and Hong, R. (2025). Gloss-driven conditional diffusion models for sign language production. *ACM Transactions on Multimedia Computing, Communications and Applications, 21*(4), 1–17.

[4] Loper, M., Mahmood, N., Romero, J., Pons-Moll, G., and Black, M. J. (2023). SMPL: a skinned multi-person linear model. *In Seminal Graphics Papers: Pushing the Boundaries* (Vol. 2, pp. 851–866).

[5] Eunice, J., Sei, Y., and Hemanth, D. J. (2023). Sign2Pose: a pose-based approach for gloss prediction using a transformer model. *Sensors, 23*(5), 2853.

[6] Lee, T., Nam, H., Moon, G., and Lee, K. M. (2025). GLOS: sign language generation with temporally aligned gloss-level conditioning. *arXiv preprint arXiv:2506.07460.* https://arxiv.org/abs/2506.07460

[7] Tang, S., He, J., Guo, D., Wei, Y., Li, F., and Hong, R. (2025, April). Sign-IDD: iconicity disentangled diffusion for sign language production. *In Proceedings of the AAAI Conference on Artificial Intelligence* (Vol. 39, No. 7, pp. 7266–7274). AAAI Press.

[8] Liu, B., Duan, F., and Zhao, J. (2024, May). SkeletonFormer: point cloud completion with dynamic selective skeleton points. *In Proceedings of the 2024 International Conference on Multimedia Retrieval (ICMR)* (pp. 897–905). ACM: New York, USA.

[9]   Chatziagapi, A., Chaudhuri, B., Kumar, A., Ranjan, R., Samaras, D., and Sarafianos, N. (2024, September). TalkinNeRF: animatable neural fields for full-body talking humans. *In European Conference on Computer Vision* (pp. 148–166). Cham: Springer Nature Switzerland.

[10]   Yu, Z., Huang, S., Cheng, Y., and Birdal, T. (2024, September). Signavatars: a large-scale 3d sign language holistic motion dataset and benchmark. *In European Conference on Computer Vision* (pp. 1–19). Cham: Springer Nature Switzerland.

[11]   Zheng, C., Zhu, S., Mendieta, M., Yang, T., Chen, C., and Ding, Z. (2021). 3D human pose estimation with spatial and temporal transformers. *In Proceedings of the IEEE/CVF International Conference on Computer Vision (ICCV)* (pp. 11656–11665). IEEE.

[12]   Zhu, W., Ma, X., Liu, Z., Liu, L., Wu, W., and Wang, Y. (2023). Motion-BERT: a unified perspective on learning human motion representations. *In Proceedings of the IEEE/CVF International Conference on Computer Vision (ICCV)* (pp. 15085–15099). IEEE.

[13]   Yu, H., Fan, X., Hou, Y., *et al.* (2023). Toward realistic 3D human motion prediction with a spatio-temporal cross-transformer approach. *IEEE Transactions on Circuits and Systems for Video Technology, 33*(10), 5707–5720.

[14]   Tevet, G., Raab, S., Gordon, B., Shafir, Y., Cohen-Or, D., and Bermano, A. H. (2022). Human motion diffusion model. *arXiv preprint arXiv:2209. 14916.* https://arxiv.org/abs/2209.14916

[15]   Tevet, G., Gordon, B., Hertz, A., Bermano, A. H., and Cohen-Or, D. (2022, October). Motionclip: exposing human motion generation to clip space. *In European Conference on Computer Vision* (pp. 358–374). Cham: Springer Nature Switzerland.

[16]   Zhao, M., Liu, M., Ren, B., Dai, S., and Sebe, N. (2023). Modiff: action-conditioned 3D motion generation with denoising diffusion probabilistic models. *arXiv preprint arXiv:2301.03949.* https://arxiv.org/abs/2301.03949

[17]   Wang, Q., Zhang, K., and Asghar, M. A. (2022). Skeleton-based ST-GCN for human action recognition with extended skeleton graph and partitioning strategy. *IEEE Access, 10*, 41403–41410.

[18]   Li, C., Huang, Q., Mao, Y., Li, X., and Wu, J. (2024). Multi-granular spatial-temporal synchronous graph convolutional network for robust action recognition. *Expert Systems with Applications, 257*, 124980.

[19]   Chen, Y., Zhang, Z., Yuan, C., Li, B., Deng, Y., and Hu, W. (2021). Channel-wise topology refinement graph convolution for skeleton-based action recognition. *In Proceedings of the IEEE/CVF International Conference on Computer Vision (ICCV)* (pp. 13359–13368). IEEE.

[20]   Zhang, J., Zhang, Y., Cun, X., *et al.* (2023). Generating human motion from textual descriptions with discrete representations. *In Proceedings of the IEEE/CVF Conference on Computer Vision and Pattern recognition (CVPR)* (pp. 14730–14740) IEEE.

[21]   Lucas, T., Baradel, F., Weinzaepfel, P., and Rogez, G. (2022, October). PoseGPT: quantization-based 3D human motion generation and forecasting.

In European Conference on Computer Vision (pp. 417–435). Cham: Springer Nature Switzerland.

[22] Delmas, G., Weinzaepfel, P., Moreno-Noguer, F., and Rogez, G. (2023). Pose-fix: correcting 3D human poses with natural language. *In Proceedings of the IEEE/CVF International Conference on Computer Vision (ICCV)* (pp. 15018–15028). IEEE.

[23] Welch, G., and Bishop, G. (1995). *An Introduction to the Kalman Filter*.

[24] Qu, H., Xu, L., Cai, Y., Foo, L. G., and Liu, J. (2022). Heatmap distribution matching for human pose estimation. *Advances in Neural Information Processing Systems*, *35*, 24327–24339. Curran Associates, Inc.

[25] Lea, C., Flynn, M. D., Vidal, R., Reiter, A., and Hager, G. D. (2017). Temporal convolutional networks for action segmentation and detection. *In Proceedings of the IEEE Conference on Computer Vision and Pattern Recognition (CVPR)* (pp. 156–165). IEEE.

[26] Liu, K., Li, Q., and Qiu, G. (2020). PoseGAN: a pose-to-image translation framework for camera localization. *ISPRS Journal of Photogrammetry and Remote Sensing*, *166*, 308–315.

[27] Chan, C., Ginosar, S., Zhou, T., and Efros, A. A. (2019). Everybody dance now. *In Proceedings of the IEEE/CVF International Conference on Computer Vision (ICCV)* (pp. 5933–5942). IEEE.

[28] Pavlakos, G., Kolotouros, N., and Daniilidis, K. (2019). TexturePose: supervising human mesh estimation with texture consistency. *In Proceedings of the IEEE/CVF International Conference on Computer Vision (ICCV)* (pp. 803–812). IEEE.

[29] Luo, Z., Chen, D., Zhang, Y., *et al.* (2023). VideoFusion: decomposed diffusion models for high-quality video generation. arXiv preprint arXiv:2303.08320. https://arxiv.org/abs/2303.08320

[30] Zeng, H., Zhang, W., Fan, C., *et al.* (2023, June). FlowFace: semantic flow-guided shape-aware face swapping. *In Proceedings of the AAAI conference on artificial intelligence* (Vol. 37, No. 3, pp. 3367–3375). AAAI Press.

[31] Siarohin, A., Lathuilière, S., Tulyakov, S., Ricci, E., and Sebe, N. (2019). Animating arbitrary objects via deep motion transfer. *In Proceedings of the IEEE/CVF Conference on Computer Vision and Pattern Recognition (CVPR)* (pp. 2377–2386). IEEE.

[32] Pumarola, A., Agudo, A., Martinez, A. M., Sanfeliu, A., and Moreno-Noguer, F. (2018). Ganimation: anatomically-aware facial animation from a single image. *In Proceedings of the European Conference on Computer Vision (ECCV)* (pp. 818–833). Cham: Springer.

[33] Wang, Y., Chen, X., Zhu, J., *et al.* (2021). Hififace: 3D shape and semantic prior guided high fidelity face swapping. *arXiv preprint arXiv:2106.09965.* https://arxiv.org/abs/2106.09965

[34] Meshry, M., Suri, S., Davis, L. S., and Shrivastava, A. (2021). Learned spatial representations for few-shot talking-head synthesis. *In Proceedings of the IEEE/CVF International Conference on Computer Vision (ICCV)* (pp. 13829–13838). IEEE.

Chapter 9

Evaluation metrics and benchmarking in sign language recognition, translation, and generation

9.1 Introduction

Assessment of sign language technologies, including recognition, translation, and generation, involves specific challenges. Given the multimodal, spatiotemporal, and inherently visual-linguistic nature of sign languages, evaluating the performance of these systems is not the same as assessing spoken or written language technologies. Sign language processing involves complicated hand movements, body posture, facial expression, and timing that must be represented, interpreted, or generated.

In sign language recognition (SLR), the goal is to translate visual modalities (video or pose sequences) into glosses or texts. Identifying metrics for evaluation – to measure classification, temporal alignment, and robustness – is a challenge since different signers can have variations in how they produce signs.

Sign language translation (SLT) is a natural progression from SLR – translating the recognized gloss or raw sign video into grammatically accurate, semantically equivalent sentences in a spoken language. Evaluating SLT requires treating the output as multi-lingually accurate and fluent – and utilizing metrics used in sets of evaluations of natural language processing – we recommend those metrics that will accommodate glosses in a systematic way.

Finally, sign language generation (SLG) involves generating human-like sign videos from texts or speech. Evaluating SLG implies assessing the output for its factual accuracy and fluency, of course, but also for its naturalness and continuity, or visual realism. This implies developing assessments that utilize a combination of automatic perceptual metrics, pose similarity scores, and human evaluations.

Additionally, the current lack of benchmarks that are detailed or standardized with a set of resources, and the ever-widening regional diversity of sign languages, makes it difficult to compare degrees of other sign language models. As a point of importance to ensure fairness and reproducibility in AI technologies, benchmarks and publicly sourced datasets with evaluation scripts that clearly aid reproducibility are important.

This chapter offers a single framework to assess SLR, SLT, and SLG systems by organizing their existing metrics, exposing gaps, and proposing available dataset timing to facilitate direct comparisons. In addition, it outlines the limitations of the currently used metrics and indicates directions for developing a more holistic and signer-aware approach to evaluation.

9.2 Evaluation metrics for sign language recognition

In evaluating sign language systems across recognition, translation, and generation tasks, there is a large range of numerical metrics available that characterize various aspects of system performance in an objective fashion. These metrics are measured and computed using accuracy metrics, linguistic fidelity metrics, perceptual realism metrics, and structural fidelity metrics. In this section, the different evaluation metrics for sign language systems will be organized according to the task: SLR, SLT, and SLG. Each metric is discussed in terms of the purpose of the metric, its mathematical expression, and relevance to the sign language research field.

9.2.1 Metrics for sign language recognition

In SLR, the objective is to classify or identify gloss labels or sentences from visual inputs such as videos or pose sequences.

(a) **Classification metrics**

As such, classification and sequence alignment metrics are primarily used. Accuracy, precision, recall, and F1-score are standard classification metrics employed in SLR to assess the correctness and completeness of predicted glosses [1]. Given true positives (TP), false positives (FP), false negatives (FN), and true negatives (TN), these metrics are defined as:

$$Accuracy = \frac{TP + TN}{TP + TN + FP + FN} \tag{9.1}$$

$$Precision = \frac{TP}{TP + FP} \tag{9.2}$$

$$Recall = \frac{TP}{TP + FN} \tag{9.3}$$

$$F1Score = \frac{2 \, X \, Precsion \, X \, Recall}{Precision + Recall} \tag{9.4}$$

In multi-class gloss classification tasks, Top-K accuracy is often reported, especially in datasets with large vocabularies.

(b) **Frame-level accuracy**

This metric assesses the proportion of individual frames in a sign video that are correctly classified with respect to their associated gloss labels. It is particularly relevant in continuous SLR systems [2] that use frame-wise classification models or frame-level intermediate supervision.

$$Frame - Level \, Accuracy = \frac{Correct \, Frame \, Predictions}{Total \, Frames} \tag{9.5}$$

(c) **Levenshtein distance**

Another crucial metric is the edit distance (also known as Levenshtein distance), which measures the minimum number of insertions, deletions, and substitutions required to align the predicted gloss sequence with the ground truth. This metric is particularly useful in continuous sign recognition scenarios [3]. The edit distance between two sequences A and B of lengths m and n, respectively, is defined recursively as:

$$D(i,j) = \begin{cases} i & i = 0 \\ j & j = 0 \\ \min \begin{cases} D(i-1,j) + 1 \\ D(i,j-1) + 1 \\ D(i-1,j-1) + \delta \end{cases} & \text{otherwise} \end{cases} \tag{9.6}$$

where $\delta = 0$ if $A_i = B_j$ and $\delta = 1$ otherwise, $D(i,j)$ denotes the edit distance between the first i characters of A and the first j characters of B.

(d) **Gloss-level edit distance**

Gloss-level edit distance (GED) is a variation of the Levenshtein distance computed over gloss token sequences rather than character or word sequences. It is well suited for evaluating the alignment between predicted gloss sequences and ground truth in continuous SLR datasets [4].

$$GED = \frac{S + D + I}{L} \tag{9.7}$$

Where S is the number of substitutions, D is the deletions, I is the insertions, and L is the length of the reference gloss sequence.

(e) **Mean per joint position error**

When keypoint-based recognition is involved, pose estimation accuracy is quantified using mean per joint position error (MPJPE), which computes the average Euclidean distance between predicted and ground-truth joint coordinates [5]. Formally, it is given by

$$MPJPE = \frac{1}{N} \sum_{i=1}^{N} \left\| P_i^{pred} - P_i^{gt} \right\|_2 \tag{9.8}$$

where N is the number of keypoints. For each joint i, denote the ground-truth coordinate as $P_i^{gt} \in \mathbb{R}^d$ and the predicted coordinate as $P_i^{pred} \in \mathbb{R}^d$, where d $\in \{2,3\}$ depending on whether the data is 2D or 3D.

9.2.2   *Metrics for sign language translation*

SLT systems transform gloss sequences or sign videos into spoken or written language. Evaluation of such systems requires linguistic fidelity metrics borrowed from natural language processing.

(a) **BLEU**

Bilingual evaluation understudy (BLEU) measures the overlap of n-grams between the candidate and reference translations [6]. It is computed as

$$BLEU = BP.\exp\left(\sum_{n=1}^{N} w_n \log p_n\right) \quad (9.9)$$

where p_n is the modified n-gram precision, w_n is the weight (typically uniform), and BP is a brevity penalty applied if the candidate is shorter than the reference.

(b) **ChrF**

ChrF is a character-level F-score [7] metric that evaluates the harmonic mean of character n-gram precision and recall. It is especially useful for morphologically rich or low-resource languages where word-level metrics like BLEU underperform.

$$ChrF_\beta = \frac{(1 + \beta^2) \cdot Precision \cdot Recall}{\beta^2 \cdot Precision + Recall} \quad (9.10)$$

(c) **BLEURT**

BLEURT is a learning-based metric that uses fine-tuned BERT embeddings to predict human judgments of translation quality [8]. It captures contextual and semantic alignment more effectively than surface n-gram-based metrics.

$$BLEURT = f_\theta([BERT \text{ features of candidate, reference}]) \quad (9.11)$$

where f_θ is a learned regression function trained on human-annotated corpora.

(d) **METEOR**

METEOR improves upon BLEU by incorporating stemming, synonym matching, and paraphrase recognition, resulting in better alignment with human judgment [9]. It is calculated as:

$$METEOR = F_{mean}(1 - Penalty) \quad (9.12)$$

where

$$F_{mean} = \frac{10PR}{R + 9P} \quad (9.13)$$

(e) **ROUGE-N**

ROUGE-N [10] measures the recall of overlapping n-grams between the candidate output and the reference translation. The general formula for ROUGE-N is:

$$ROUGE - N = \frac{\sum_{gram_n \in Ref} \min\left(Count_{cand}(gram_n), Count_{ref}(gram_n)\right)}{\sum_{gram_n \in Ref} Count_{ref}(gram_n)}$$

$$(9.14)$$

where $ggram_n$ is an n-gram (typically unigram or bigram), $Count_{cand}$ and $Count_{ref}$ are the number of occurrences in the candidate and reference texts, respectively. This metric focuses on recall, i.e., how much of the reference is recovered by the candidate.

(f) **BERTScore**

BERTScore [11] computes the semantic similarity between a candidate and reference sentence by comparing their contextual embeddings using cosine similarity. Let $X = \{x_1, x_2, \ldots, x_m\}$ and $Y = \{y_1, y_2, \ldots, y_n\}$ be the sets of tokens in the candidate and reference sentences, and let $E(x_i)$ denote the embedding of token x_i from a pre-trained BERT model. The precision and recall components are defined as

$$P = \frac{1}{|X|} \sum_{x \in X} \max_{y \in Y} \cos\left(E(x), E(y)\right)$$ (9.15)

$$R = \frac{1}{|Y|} \sum_{y \in Y} \max_{x \in X} \cos\left(E(y), E(x)\right)$$ (9.16)

Then, the F1-score of BERTScore is

$$BERTScore_{F1} = \frac{2PR}{P + R}$$ (9.17)

This formulation allows BERTScore to capture semantic equivalence beyond surface-level n-gram overlap, making it especially suitable for evaluating paraphrased or restructured translations.

(g) **Word error rate**

In terms of error analysis, word error rate (WER) is commonly adopted to count the number of substitutions (S), deletions (D), and insertions (I) needed to match the system output to the reference [12]. It is defined as

$$WER = \frac{S + D + I}{P + R}$$ (9.18)

where N is the number of words in the reference sentence.

(h) **Translation edit rate**

Translation edit rate (TER) is an automatic evaluation metric [13] that quantifies the number of edits required to convert a system-generated sentence into one of the reference translations. It is particularly well-suited for evaluating translation outputs where acceptable variations in word order or phrasing are possible. Unlike WER, TER accounts for block shifts, allowing the movement of phrases as a single edit operation in addition to insertions, deletions, and substitutions.

The TER is formally defined as

$$TER = \frac{E}{R}$$ (9.19)

where E is the minimum number of edits (including insertions, deletions, substitutions, and shifts) needed to transform the hypothesis (generated sentence) into the closest matching reference, and R is the average number of words in the reference translation(s). Each edit is counted as one unit, regardless of the type (including block shifts). The use of shifts enables TER to better reflect human editing effort, especially in cases where reordering is necessary, but the content remains semantically accurate.

For example, if the candidate sentence *"the cat sits on mat"* needs to be transformed into the reference *"the cat sits on the mat,"* the TER would account for a single insertion of the word *"the,"* resulting in

$$TER = \frac{1}{5} = 0.2 \tag{9.20}$$

Assuming the reference has five words. TER values range from 0 (perfect match) to 1 (every word needs to be edited), and higher values indicate poorer alignment with the reference.

(i) **COMET**

COMET [14] is another learned evaluation metric, trained using multilingual encoders such as XLM-R and regression objectives aligned with human quality ratings. It excels at cross-lingual and semantically complex translations.

$$COMET = MLP(f_{XLM-R}([source, candidate, reference])) \tag{9.21}$$

where f_{XLM-R} is the encoder that extracts contextual embeddings, and MLP is the multi-layer perceptron trained to predict translation quality.

9.2.3 Metrics for sign language generation

SLG systems synthesize sign language videos from text or gloss inputs. Their evaluation requires a combination of visual fidelity and perceptual quality metrics.

(a) **Fréchet video distance**

Fréchet video distance (FVD) measures the distance between the distributions of features extracted from real and generated video sequences [15]. These features are typically obtained from a pre-trained deep video model, such as I3D (Inflated 3D ConvNet). The metric compares the multivariate Gaussian distributions estimated from both sets of embeddings. The formula is given as

$$FVD = \left\|\mu_r - \mu_g\right\|^2 + Tr\left(\Sigma_r + \Sigma_g - 2\left(\Sigma_r\Sigma_g\right)^{\frac{1}{2}}\right) \tag{9.22}$$

where μ_r and μ_g are the mean vectors of real and generated video embeddings, respectively, Σ_r and Σ_g are the corresponding covariance matrices, $Tr(\cdot)$ denotes the matrix trace operation, and $\left(\Sigma_r\Sigma_g\right)^{\frac{1}{2}}$ is the matrix square root. FVD is a multivariate extension of the Fréchet inception distance (FID) used for images, adapted to temporal video data.

(b) **Structural similarity index**

Structural similarity index (SSIM) evaluates the visual similarity between a pair of images or video frames based on structural information, luminance, and contrast [16]. Given two images x and y, SSIM is computed as

$$SSIM(x,y) = \frac{\left(2\mu_x\mu_y + c_1\right)\left(2\sigma_{xy} + c_2\right)}{\left(\mu_x^2 + \mu_y^2 + c_1\right)\left(\sigma_x^2 + \sigma_y^2 + c_2\right)} \tag{9.23}$$

where μ_x and μ_y are the means of x and y, σ_x^2 and σ_y^2 are their variances, σ_{xy} is the covariance between x and y, c_1 and c_2 are constants to stabilize the division when denominators are close to zero. SSIM values range from -1 to 1, with 1 indicating perfect structural similarity.

(c) **Learned perceptual image patch similarity**

Learned perceptual image patch similarity (LPIPS) is a perceptual similarity metric that compares image patches using deep features extracted from pre-trained convolutional neural networks (e.g., AlexNet, VGG) [17]. It is more aligned with human visual perception than pixel-wise metrics. The LPIPS between two images x and y is computed as

$$LPIPS(x,y) = \sum_t \frac{1}{H_t W_t} \sum_{h=1}^{H_t} \sum_{w=1}^{W_t} \left\| w_t \odot \left(\widehat{x}_{hw}^t - \widehat{y}_{hw}^t\right) \right\|_2^2 \tag{9.24}$$

where t indexes a layer of the CNN, $\widehat{x}_{hw}^t - \widehat{y}_{hw}^t$ are the normalized feature maps of x and y at layer t, H_t, W_t are the height and width of the feature maps at layer t, W_t is a learned per-channel weighting vector, $\odot$ denotes element-wise multiplication. LPIPS is typically computed over multiple layers and averaged.

(d) **Peak signal-to-noise ratio**

Peak signal-to-noise ratio (PSNR) is a simple and widely used metric that quantifies the ratio between the maximum possible pixel value and the error between corresponding pixels in the predicted and reference frames [18]. It is defined as

$$PSNR = 10.\log_{10}\left(\frac{MAX_I^2}{MSE}\right) \tag{9.25}$$

where MAX_I^2 is the maximum possible pixel intensity value (e.g., 255 for 8-bit images) and MSE is the mean squared error between the predicted and reference images. While PSNR is easy to compute and interpret, it often correlates poorly with human perception and is generally used as a supporting metric.

(e) **Temporal consistency metric**

Temporal consistency metric (TCM) assesses how smoothly pose or appearance changes across frames in a generated sign language video [19]. It is essential to ensure natural motion, especially for articulators like hands and face.

$$TCM = \frac{1}{T-1} \sum_{t=1}^{T-1} \|P_t - P_{t+1}\|_2 \tag{9.26}$$

where P_t is the pose vector at frame t and T is the total frames.

(f) **Pose structure score**

Pose structure score (PSS) evaluates whether the generated pose skeletons conform to anatomically valid structures [20]. It can be computed by training a binary classifier or generative adversarial networks (GAN) discriminator that distinguishes real from generated poses.

$$PSS = DiscriminatorScore(J) \tag{9.27}$$

where J is the joint configuration vector.

(g) **Percentage of correct keypoints:**

Percentage of correct keypoints (PCK) measures the proportion of keypoints that fall within a specified threshold distance from the ground truth, normalized by image size or bounding box size [21].

$$PCK@a = \frac{Number\ of\ keypoints\ with\ distance \leq a}{Total\ keypoints} \tag{9.28}$$

where a is a normalized distance threshold. It defines how close a predicted keypoint must be to the ground truth keypoint (in pixels) relative to a reference length (e.g., torso size, head size, image size, or bounding box size). A keypoint is considered correctly predicted if

$$distance\left(P_{pred}, P_{gt}\right) \leq a.L \tag{9.29}$$

where P_{pred} and P_{gt} are predicted and ground truth keypoint coordinates and L is the reference length (e.g., upper-body length or image diagonal).

(h) **Multi-modal diversity score**

Multi-modal diversity score (MDS) captures how diverse the outputs of a generative model are when conditioned on the same input. This is important in SLG to ensure the model is not deterministic or mode-collapsing.

$$MDS = \frac{2}{N(N-1)} \sum_{i<j} Dissimilarity(x_i, x_j) \tag{9.30}$$

where x_i and x_j are generated videos, and dissimilarity can be LPIPS or cosine distance.

(i) **Sign comprehensibility score**

Sign comprehensibility score (SCS) is the human-rated score that reflects how comprehensible or acceptable the generated sign sequence is when viewed by fluent signers [22]. It often uses a Likert scale and aggregates judgments from multiple raters.

$$SCS = \frac{1}{n} \sum_{i=1}^{n} Rating_i \tag{9.31}$$

where n is the number of signers and $Rating_i \in \{1, 2, \ldots, 5\}$ or $\{1 - 10\}$.

9.3 Comparative analysis of evaluation metrics

This section presents a comparative review of evaluation metrics for SLR, SLT, and SLG. Although these tasks are all designed to aid accessibility and understanding of sign languages, they utilize different types of input data, transform data into different types of output, and have different goals and uses; hence, they will have different evaluation aims.

The comparison is organized into three distinct tables, each corresponding to one task. Tables 9.1–9.3 summarize the comparative analysis of SLR, SLT, and SLG, respectively. Metrics are evaluated along the following parameters:

- Metric name: The name of the metric that was used to evaluate.
- Task type: The task type for which the measurement was primarily made, e.g., classification, sequence alignment, and generation.
- Output format: The output format that the model is expected to produce, e.g., gloss labels, sentences of written text, and videos.
- Interpretability: The level of understanding a human evaluator will have to explain the outputs from the metric.
- Sensitive to imbalance: The behavior of the metric in imbalanced datasets (e.g., more instances for some signs).
- Temporal sensitivity: The extent to which it reflects change over time, which is particularly relevant for dynamically articulated gestures, or when considering a sequence of frames.
- Pose sensitivity: The extent to which it reflects the spatial correctness of where the predicted joint/keypoint locations were.
- Granularity: The level of evaluation that is capturing, e.g., frame, gloss, sequence, or pixel.

9.4 Human evaluation protocols

While automatic metrics are very scalable and objective, human evaluation is still important for evaluating perceptual, semantic, and linguistic factors that cannot be readily assessed by an algorithm. At the same time, in the case of SLR, SLT, and SLG, human judgments still provide one of the most valuable baseline sources for ensuring that the system output is aligned with what fluent signers and users expect. This discusses human evaluation protocols and scoring methods that have been commonly used.

Table 9.1 Comparative analysis of SLR evaluation metrics

Metric name	Task type	Output format	Interpretability	Sensitivity			Granularity
				Imbalance	Temporal	Pose	
Accuracy	Classification	Single-label	High	High	✗	✗	Gloss-level
Precision	Classification	Single-label	Medium	High	✗	✗	Gloss-level
Recall	Classification	Single-label	Medium	Low	✗	✗	Gloss-level
F1-score	Classification	Single-label	Medium	Medium	✗	✗	Gloss-level
Top-K accuracy	Classification	Multi-class	Medium	High	✗	✗	Gloss-level
Edit distance	Sequence alignment	Gloss sequence	Medium	Low	✓	✗	Sequence-level
Gloss edit distance (GED)	Sequence alignment	Gloss sequence	Medium	Low	✓	✗	Sequence-level
Frame-level accuracy	Frame-wise classification	Frame labels	High	High	✓	✗	Frame-level
Mean per joint position error (MPJPE)	Pose estimation	3D keypoint	Low	N/A	✓	✓	Joint-level

Table 9.2   Comparative analysis of SLT evaluation metrics

Metric name	Task type	Output format	Interpretability	Sensitivity			Granularity
				Imbalance	Temporal	Pose	
BLEU	Sequence-to-text	Text	Medium	Low	✗	✗	n-gram level
METEOR	Sequence-to-text	Text	High	Low	✗	✗	Word/Phrase level
ROUGE-N	Sequence-to-text	Text	Medium	Medium	✗	✗	n-gram level
BERTScore	Sequence-to-text	Text	Low	High	✗	✗	Semantic embedding level
Word error rate (WER)	Sequence alignment	Text	High	Medium	✓	✗	Word level
Translation edit rate (TER)	Sequence alignment	Text	Medium	Medium	✓	✗	Phrase level
COMET	Regression-based Scoring	Text	Low	High	✓	✗	Sentence level

Table 9.3   Comparative analysis of SLG evaluation metrics

Metric name	Task type	Output format	Interpretability	Sensitivity			Granularity
				Imbalance	Temporal	Pose	
FVD	Generation	Video sequences	Medium	Low	✓	✓	Sequence-level
SSIM	Frame-level comparison	Image frames	High	Low	✗	✗	Frame-level
LPIPS	Frame-level comparison	Image patches	High	Low	✗	✗	Patch-level
PSNR	Frame-level comparison	Image frames	High	Low	✗	✗	Pixel-level
TCM	Generation	Pose sequences	Medium	N/A	✓	✓	Sequence-level
PSS	Pose validation	Pose vectors	Low	N/A	✓	✓	Pose-level
PCK	Keypoint estimation	2D/3D coordinates	Medium	N/A	✗	✓	Joint-level
MDS	Diversity analysis	Generated sequences	Low	N/A	✓	✗	Sequence-level
SCS	Human evaluation	Generated videos	High	N/A	✓	✓	Sequence-level

9.4.1   Naturalness and fluency judgments

Naturalness and fluency judgments [23,24] assess the extent to which the sign outputs generated or predicted resembled a natural human sign output in terms of motion fluidity, expressiveness, and articulatory coherence. Naturalness and fluency are critical judgments in SLG and SLT, where linguistic and visual accuracy are paramount. Evaluators might assess an output for the smoothness between signs, consistency of handshapes, and non-manual markers (e.g., facial expressions), and the appropriate signing space. Ratings are usually collected using a Likert measure [saints from 1 (very unnatural) to 5 (perfectly natural and fluent)].

9.4.2   Comprehensibility assessment

Comprehensibility refers to the clarity and understandability of the predicted/generated content [25]. In SLT and SLG systems, comprehensibility is an essential component of comprehensibility assessment because it allows researchers to verify that the intended meaning is successfully transmitted to human viewers, especially when the semantic content is mongrel or intricate. Assessment protocols involve presenting signers with system output and asking them to identify or reinterpret the intended message, or they may be asked to rate the comprehensibility using a scale. The scale could be binary (e.g., understandable/not understandable) or ordinal (e.g., 1–5, in which a score of 1 indicates poor comprehension and a score of 5 indicates full comprehension).

9.4.3   Mean opinion score

The mean opinion score (MOS) is a widely used subjective measure of assessment used to determine the overall perceived quality of generated outcomes [26,27]. Originally created for speech and multimedia systems, MOS is often used to assess the perceived quality of sign language videos, primarily in SLG. The MOS rating is defined as the arithmetic mean of the ratings given by several human evaluators:

$$MoS = \frac{1}{N} \sum_{i=1}^{N} Rating_i \tag{9.32}$$

where N is the number of evaluators and $Rating_i$ is the individual score provided by the ith evaluator. Common rating scales range from 1 (bad quality) to 5 (excellent quality).

9.4.4   Ethical considerations and annotator consistency

Human judgments of sign language data in research contexts must be carried out in a rigorous ethical and methodological manner [24]. This means that if deaf participants or fluent signers are involved, we must make certain that informed consent was provided, that participants receive reasonable remuneration, and that any interaction embodies cultural considerations. If evaluation tasks are developed in collaboration with the deaf community, participants will be more likely to view the evaluation tasks as inclusive, culturally relevant, and acceptable.

The consistency of Shuman judgments is gauged using inter-annotator agreement (IAA), with measures including Cohen's Kappa, Fleiss' Kappa, or Krippendorff's Alpha [28,29]. High IAA scores indicate that the judgments made by different evaluators are reliable and can be reproduced consistently. Many evaluation protocols, such as those referenced in the previous chapter, emphasize reliability because evaluation can often be subjective. To enhance reliability, the use of anchor samples that were scored, calibrated as a group iteration before beginning the annotation process, and using blind double-annotation and a reconciliation phase afterwards are some of the strategies used to help improve or maintain reliability for IAA.

9.5 Summary

This chapter covered an extensive review of evaluation methods for sign language technology across three primary tasks: SLR, SLT, and SLG. It began by identifying task-related metrics, with specific metric examples that included classification-type metrics (e.g., accuracy, F1-score) in SLR, alignments (e.g., BLEU, ROUGE, METEOR) and text generation (to simulate SLR) in SLT, and visual quality metrics with FVD, SSIM, and LPIPS for SLG, and tables with defined metrics provided side-by-side comparisons regarding their application in different tasks, interpretation of results, sensitivity, and granularity.

Next, the chapter summarized methods of human evaluations, which included, but were not limited to, measures of naturalness, fluency, comprehensibility, and MOS. As some metrics included perceptions that may be abstracted by the automated metrics, evaluation methods that establish human ratings are more qualitative in nature and grounded in subjective aspects.

Ethical considerations regarding the role of differential cultural and language representation, annotator reliability and evaluator consistency, and the process of fair and accurate evaluations were highlighted in the accompanying section. These considerations intersect with the later discussion of respect and the impacts on benchmarking quality in evaluations.

Using the above combination of approaches creates a robust manual for benchmarks of sign language systems to aggregate data on both performance and user-defined perceptual quality while adhering to some baseline of second-language accuracy, user expectations, and accessibility considerations.

Exercises

(I) **Multiple choice questions**
   1. Which of the following metrics is primarily used to evaluate pose accuracy in keypoint-based sign recognition systems?
       (a) BLEU
       (b) MPJPE
       (c) METEOR
       (d) SSIM

2. Which metric accounts for block shifts and is an extension of WER?
   (a) ROUGE-L
   (b) METEOR
   (c) TER
   (d) BLEU

3. What does the FVD metric evaluate in sign language generation?
   (a) Gloss alignment
   (b) Visual quality of video sequences
   (c) Text translation accuracy
   (d) Audio clarity

4. Which metric is best suited to assess the structural integrity of pose skeletons in SLG?
   (a) PCK
   (b) LPIPS
   (c) PSS
   (d) SSIM

5. What is a typical use of the mean opinion score (MOS) in sign language evaluation?
   (a) Analyzing grammatical structure
   (b) Measuring inter-annotator agreement
   (c) Assessing perceived video quality
   (d) Computing token frequency

(II) **Short answer questions**
1. How is gloss-level edit distance (GED) used to evaluate sign language recognition systems?
2. What makes COMET more suitable for evaluating sign language translation compared to BLEU or METEOR?
3. Describe how Fréchet video distance (FVD) measures the quality of generated sign language videos.
4. What is the significance of the temporal consistency metric (TCM) in sign language generation tasks?
5. Why is human evaluation essential in sign language research despite the availability of automatic metrics?

(III) **Discussion questions**
1. Why are both automatic and human evaluation methods important in sign language systems?
2. How does metric sensitivity to temporal and pose information affect SLG evaluation?
3. Discuss the ethical considerations that must be followed when involving deaf participants in human evaluations.
4. Compare the use of BLEU and METEOR in assessing SLT outputs. Which one is more aligned with human judgment and why?

(IV)   **Practical / Hands-on exercises**

1. Implement a function in Python to compute BLEU and ROUGE scores for a sample SLT dataset using NLTK or HuggingFace libraries.
2. Given a set of predicted and ground-truth joint coordinates, calculate the MPJPE in 2D space.
3. Design a Likert-based human evaluation survey form to rate sign language video generation outputs on fluency and comprehensibility.
4. Extract features using a pre-trained I3D model and compute FVD between real and generated sign language videos using a deep learning framework like PyTorch or TensorFlow.
5. Analyze annotator agreement using Cohen's Kappa for three human raters scoring sign comprehensibility on a 5-point scale.

References

[1]   Koller, O., Forster, J., and Ney, H. (2015). Continuous sign language recognition: towards large vocabulary statistical recognition systems handling multiple signers. *Computer Vision and Image Understanding*, *141*, 108–125.

[2]   Koller, O., Zargaran, S., Ney, H., and Bowden, R. (2018). Deep sign: enabling robust statistical continuous sign language recognition via hybrid CNN-HMMs. *International Journal of Computer Vision*, *126*, 1311–1325.

[3]   Assan, M., and Grobel, K. (1997). Video-based sign language recognition using hidden Markov models. In: Wachsmuth, I., Fröhlich, M., (eds.). *International Gesture Workshop* (pp. 97–109). Berlin, Heidelberg: Springer Berlin Heidelberg.

[4]   Forster, J., Schmidt, C., Koller, O., Bellgardt, M., and Ney, H. (2014). Extensions of the sign language recognition and translation corpus RWTH-PHOENIX-Weather. *In Proceedings of the Ninth International Conference on Language Resources and Evaluation (LREC 2014). (pp. 1911–1916). European Language Resources Association (ELRA)*.

[5]   Martinez, J., Hossain, R., Romero, J., and Little, J. J. (2017). A simple yet effective baseline for 3D human pose estimation. In *Proceedings of the IEEE International Conference on Computer Vision (ICCV)* (pp. 2640–2649). IEEE.

[6]   Papineni, K., Roukos, S., Ward, T., and Zhu, W. J. (2002). Bleu: a method for automatic evaluation of machine translation. In *Proceedings of the 40th annual meeting of the Association for Computational Linguistics (ACL)* (pp. 311–318).

[7]   Popović, M. (2015). ChrF: character n-gram F-score for automatic MT evaluation. In *Proceedings of the Tenth Workshop on Statistical Machine Translation (WMT)* (pp. 392–395). Association for Computational Linguistics.

[8]   Sellam, T., Das, D., and Parikh, A. P. (2020). BLEURT: learning robust metrics for text generation. *arXiv preprint arXiv:2004.04696*. https://arxiv.org/abs/2004.04696

[9]   Banerjee, S., and Lavie, A. (2005). METEOR: an automatic metric for MT evaluation with improved correlation with human judgments. In *Proceedings*

of the ACL Workshop on Intrinsic and Extrinsic Evaluation Measures for Machine Translation and/or Summarization* (pp. 65–72). Association for Computational Linguistics.

[10]   Lin, C. Y. (2004). Rouge: a package for automatic evaluation of summaries. *In Text Summarization Branches Out: Proceedings of the ACL-04 Workshop* (pp. 74–81). Association for Computational Linguistics.

[11]   Zhang, T., Kishore, V., Wu, F., Weinberger, K. Q., and Artzi, Y. (2019). Bertscore: evaluating text generation with Bert. *arXiv preprint arXiv:1904. 09675.* https://arxiv.org/abs/1904.09675

[12]   Goldwater, S., Jurafsky, D., and Manning, C. D. (2010). Which words are hard to recognize? Prosodic, lexical, and disfluency factors that increase speech recognition error rates. *Speech Communication, 52*(3), 181–200.

[13]   Snover, M., Dorr, B., Schwartz, R., Micciulla, L., and Makhoul, J. (2006). A study of translation edit rate with targeted human annotation. In *Proceedings of the 7th Conference of the Association for Machine Translation in the Americas: Technical Papers (AMTA 2006)* (pp. 223–231).

[14]   Rei, R., Stewart, C., Farinha, A. C., and Lavie, A. (2020). COMET: a neural framework for MT evaluation. *arXiv preprint arXiv:2009.09025.* https:// arxiv.org/abs/2009.09025

[15]   Unterthiner, T., Van Steenkiste, S., Kurach, K., Marinier, R., Michalski, M., and Gelly, S. (2018). Towards accurate generative models of video: a new metric and challenges. *arXiv preprint arXiv:1812.01717.* https://arxiv.org/ abs/1812.01717

[16]   Wang, Z., Bovik, A. C., Sheikh, H. R., and Simoncelli, E. P. (2004). Image quality assessment: from error visibility to structural similarity. *IEEE Transactions on Image Processing, 13*(4), 600–612.

[17]   Zhang, R., Isola, P., Efros, A. A., Shechtman, E., and Wang, O. (2018). The unreasonable effectiveness of deep features as a perceptual metric. In *Proceedings of the IEEE Conference on Computer Vision and Pattern Recognition (CVPR)* (pp. 586–595). IEEE.

[18]   Huynh-Thu, Q., and Ghanbari, M. (2008). Scope of validity of PSNR in image/video quality assessment. *Electronics Letters, 44*(13), 800–801.

[19]   Tulyakov, S., Liu, M. Y., Yang, X., and Kautz, J. (2018). Mocogan: decomposing motion and content for video generation. In *Proceedings of the IEEE Conference on Computer Vision and Pattern Recognition (CVPR)* (pp. 1526–1535). IEEE.

[20]   Yang, C., Wang, Z., Zhu, X., Huang, C., Shi, J., and Lin, D. (2018). Pose guided human video generation. In *Proceedings of the European Conference on Computer Vision (ECCV)* (pp. 201–216). Cham: Springer.

[21]   Andriluka, M., Pishchulin, L., Gehler, P., and Schiele, B. (2014). 2D Human pose estimation: new benchmark and state of the art analysis. In *Proceedings of the IEEE Conference on Computer Vision and Pattern Recognition (CVPR)* (pp. 3686–3693). IEEE.

[22]   Quandt, L. C., Willis, A., Schwenk, M., Weeks, K., and Ferster, R. (2022). Attitudes toward signing avatars vary depending on hearing status, age of

signed language acquisition, and avatar type. *Frontiers in Psychology*, *13*, 730917.

[23] Huenerfauth, M., and Lu, P. (2010). Accurate and accessible motion-capture glove calibration for sign language data collection. *ACM Transactions on Accessible Computing (TACCESS)*, *3*(1), 1–32.

[24] Bragg, D., Koller, O., Bellard, M., *et al.* (2019). Sign language recognition, generation, and translation: an interdisciplinary perspective. In *Proceedings of the 21st International ACM SIGACCESS Conference on Computers and Accessibility (ASSETS)* (pp. 16–31). ACM: New York, USA.

[25] Camgoz, N. C., Hadfield, S., Koller, O., Ney, H., and Bowden, R. (2018). Neural sign language translation. In *Proceedings of the IEEE Conference on Computer Vision and Pattern Recognition (CVPR)* (pp. 7784–7793). IEEE.

[26] Athitsos, V., Neidle, C., Sclaroff, S., *et al.* (2008). The American sign language lexicon video dataset. In *2008 IEEE Computer Society Conference on Computer Vision and Pattern Recognition Workshops (CVPRW)* (pp. 1–8). IEEE.

[27] Berke, L., Huenerfauth, M., and Patel, K. (2019). Design and psychometric evaluation of American sign language translations of usability questionnaires. *ACM Transactions on Accessible Computing (TACCESS)*, *12*(2), 1–43.

[28] Sartinas, E. G., Psarakis, E. Z., and Kosmopoulos, D. I. (2023). Motion-based sign language video summarization using curvature and torsion. *arXiv preprint arXiv:2305.16801*. https://arxiv.org/abs/2305.16801

[29] Zadeh, A., Chen, M., Poria, S., Cambria, E., and Morency, L. P. (2017). Tensor fusion network for multimodal sentiment analysis. *arXiv preprint arXiv:1707.07250*. https://arxiv.org/abs/1707.07250

Chapter 10

Human-centered design and accessibility in sign language systems

10.1 Introduction

Human-centered design (HCD) is a design philosophy and approach that centers the lived experiences, preferences, and contextual needs of end users throughout the development process. With the emergence of sign language technologies, especially those addressing the needs of deaf and hard-of-hearing (DHH) consumers, HCD is an invaluable framework for addressing accessibility at the design stage, rather than as an add-on later in development.

10.1.1 Fundamentals of inclusion and empathy

The POUR principle provides one of the most basic accessibility frameworks in HCD – perceivable, operable, understandable, and robust (POUR) as shown in Figure 10.1. The POUR principles established and advanced by the web content accessibility guidelines (WCAG) ask developers if users can perceive the digital interface (e.g., visual quality), operate using convenient mechanisms, understand by following a familiar pattern or structure, and be robust across assistive resources [1].

The WCAG principles and principles of inclusive and universal design expand accessibility in technology from the disability context toward a wider diversity of user abilities, languages, and cultural contexts. Customizable font sizes, functioning to promote visual clarity, and multimodal input/output channels for a wider range of users can be achieved using the early design process for inclusive design [2].

Using participatory design and co-creation approaches is necessary to ensure authenticity and outcomes. Deaf people are often placed merely as testers or users in consumption pipelines of technology, which creates discrepancies in how tools operate and what the user expects [3]. They offer consideration of equitable engagement – confronting power imbalances, enabling deaf leadership, and avoiding façade consultation.

The emergence of human-centered AI (HCAI) expands into AI agents that integrate and operationalize the principles identified. New systems of sign language generation, particularly in systems that use a transformer architecture, have incorporated customizable, editable user interfaces in which the user can intervene and make corrections to system output. For example, editable speech-to-sign transformer [4] and a prototype [5] enable deaf users to manipulate sign output through

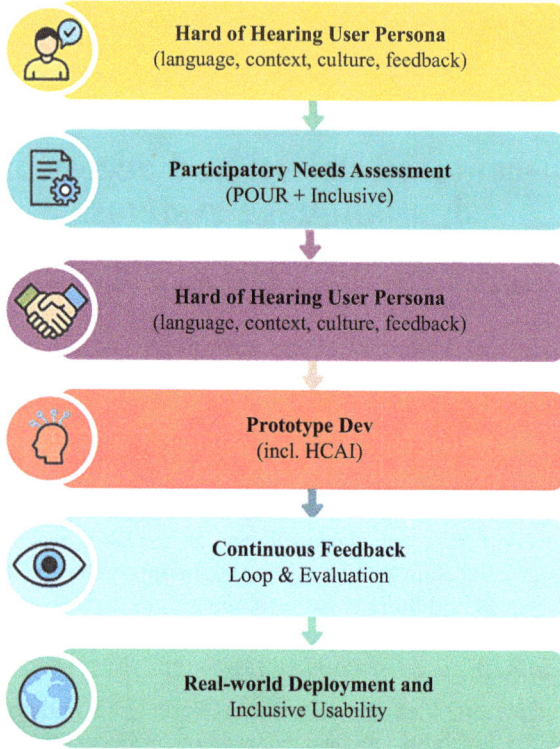

Figure 10.1   A human-centered design framework tailored for sign language systems

JSON-editable layers, generating more natural and contextualized signing outputs aligned to user feedback.

10.1.2   The importance of POUR principles

The principles of design above are not simply ideals; they are critical to the linguistic and cultural fidelity required for sign language interfaces. Sign languages are inherently rich, combining both hand gestures (manual) and facial expression and body posture (non-manual). Systems that do not accommodate these two modalities, often produce outputs that lack flexibility and ambiguity [3]. Further, because technologies that are co-designed with deaf professionals help build community engagement, trust, and ultimately longevity are increased. As Wired [5] reminds us involving deaf professionals as leaders during the design process develops tools that respond to actual communication needs rather than enforced limitations.

Lastly, when systems that are designed with accessibility in mind become widely adopted, they will likely have added value for more than one population. Features that augment real-time signing, pacing, or caption alignment enhance not only the use of DHH individuals, but also language learners, children developing language use, and those using tools in noisy spaces – emphasizing the equity and worth of inclusive/inclusive design.

10.2 Core usability principles for sign language interfaces

To design successful interfaces for sign language technologies, it is necessary to ground yourself in usability principles and adapt them to take account of DHH users' linguistic, cultural, and sensory specificities. This section describes how general usability principles (the POUR framework and some of Nielsen's heuristics) can be interpreted in the context of sign language applications. Figure 10.2 is a hierarchical representation of usability principles tailored for sign language interfaces. The model is structured across four tiers: (1) foundational accessibility principles (POUR: perceivable, operable, understandable, robust), (2) adapted usability heuristics (e.g., system status feedback, consistency, error prevention), (3) sign-accessible UX evaluation methods (e.g., video-based surveys, Wizard-of-Oz testing), and (4) input modalities supporting non-verbal interaction. The layered design emphasizes the importance of inclusive and iterative development informed by deaf user feedback.

10.2.1 Applications of the POUR framework

The four POUR principles of perceivable, operable, understandable, and robust are core to the design of accessible digital interfaces [6]. The principles do require adjustments in relation to DHH domain specificities in the context of sign language tools, as follows:

(a) Perceivable has some specificities in terms of technologies that have all visuals designed to be comprehensible including (1) having a selection to

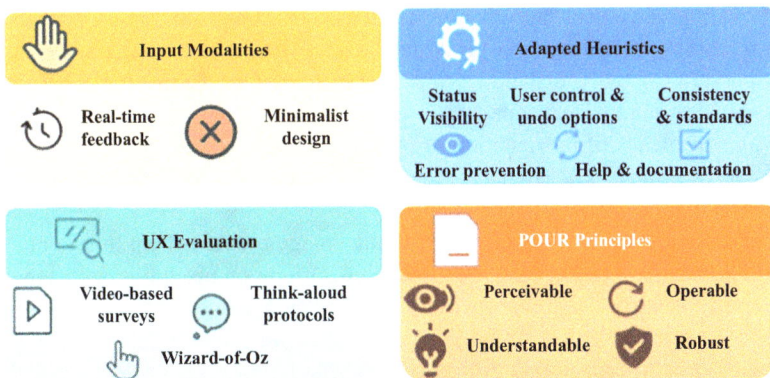

Figure 10.2 Usability design framework for sign language interfaces

ensure enough contrast exists, (2) consideration of the background (solid colors to avoid distractions, intersections such at depth on the sign as to avoid confusion whilst also attempting comprehensible adequate contrasts), and (3) the clarity of resolution. The considerations should allow all aspects of manual (which we know) and non-manual signing (do we really know?) recognition [7].

(b)   Operable should also ensure that different functions on systems are able to take place with varied input options. For example, signing with gestures/ sign and thumb-based or keyboard controls; and providing users the option to toggle between one key and a signed function is a form of empowerment and autonomy [8].

(c)   Understandable sign interfaces need to ensure consistent spatial layout and location of sign-aligned iconography and spatial layout across various pages. Also including gloss-level references aids navigation for cognitive accessibility for diverse DHH users [6]. It would be best design practice to incorporate both functionality and usability when designing for DHH users.

(d)   Robust should ensure the system allows for integration across access tech-nologies and environments. For example, captioning tools, embedded sign interpreters, and device browser extensions that consider usability across technological advances which is essential for enduring usability [6].

10.2.2   *Adaptation of usability heuristics*

The usability heuristics provided by Nielsen have been modified for sign language users [9]. Key modifications in usability heuristics for sign language include:

- Real-time feedback for sign output and verification of system utilization.
- Mapping the system conventions with real-world sign usages, including local sign variants and the sign language's spatial grammar.
- Providing easy user control means, including the ability to pause, replay, or modify sign output.
- Providing consistent presentation, feedback, and feedback representation.
- Sometimes presenting errors is better than preventing them, such as displaying a preview of the translation prior to sign output or asking for confirmation about sign output decisions.
- Minimal means of presentation to reduce cognitive demands or presenting the most relevant sign language input, by removing high-background noise distractions.
- Provides context-sensitive help as sign language provides help through tutorial information by embedding video demonstrations or providing sign language step or instructional cue sequencing (e.g., adding numbers in order).
- These usability heuristics have been adapted and ensure that sign language interfaces can be not only accessible, but moreover, usable intuitively by their respective communities.

10.2.3   User experience evaluation in sign language usability

Standard UX evaluation methods can pose challenges for DHH participants due to the reliance on text. Earlier studies have shown how powerful the use of video-based questionnaires, sign language think-aloud protocols, and multimedia semantic differential scales was for gathering meaningful feedback from DHH users [10]. Also, Wizard-of-Oz testing is effective for prototyping ASL-based interfaces for smart home applications, allowing researchers to assess usability early in the design process, without a back-end system being in place, highlighting interactive bottlenecks [11].

10.2.4   Accommodating multiple input modalities

Given the expressed nature of sign language use, interfaces had to accept inputs that were not exclusively based on written text content or syntax, like hand gestures, touch, and voice-to-sign pipelines. Camera-based recognition systems are still needed to estimate the grammatical accuracy of the full body space grammar used in sign language gestures and consider markers (non-manual) relating to body language. Also, hybrid systems can now accommodate tactile and visual modalities in smart environments, which can result in improved accuracy and significantly reduce cognitive load [12,13].

10.3   Understanding the user experience in deaf and hard-of-hearing communities

Designing for sign language technologies requires a deep understanding of the experience, culture, and behavior of DHH users. This section highlights current research on UX (user experience) evaluation methods and gesture-based interaction, forming an evidence-based rationale for future HCDs. Figure 10.3 shows a layered summary of core considerations in designing user-centered sign language systems. The model highlights three domains: (1) sign language UX Evaluation using video-based surveys, Wizard-of-Oz testing, and signer-centric interfaces;

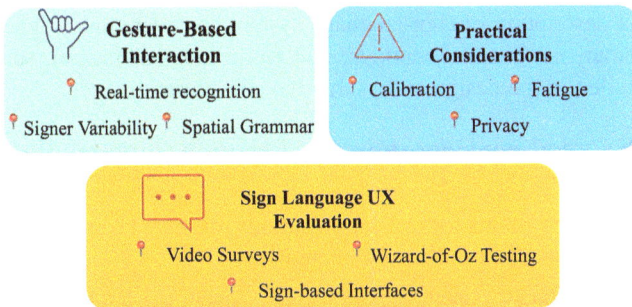

Figure 10.3   User experience in DHH communities

(2) gesture-based Interaction emphasizing real-time recognition, spatial grammar, and signer variability; and (3) practical considerations including calibration, physical fatigue, and privacy. This framework ensures inclusive, feedback-driven design aligned with the lived experiences of DHH users.

10.3.1   Sign language-centered user experience evaluations

Traditional UX methods – such as questionnaires or text surveys – are often inaccessible to deaf signers as they rely on written language. Researchers have made ASL-centric survey tools, such as SL surveys, that provide open-ended responses in sign language video form. A think-aloud study of deaf participants showed that modifying text-based tools into sign language means awkward and unintuitive interfaces and frustrated users [14].

To avoid these complications, design researchers and practitioners have explored alternative immersive methods (such as video surveys, sign-language think-aloud protocols, and Wizard-of-Oz testing). Wizard-of-Oz testing involves asking participants to believe they are interacting with automated systems, while, in fact, their responses are being controlled manually. Their interaction can be recorded and reviewed without designing the full technological solution. Researchers used deaf users' smart-home assistants to discover that replicating ASL input was superior, particularly in scenarios such as cooking where participants had dirty hands. Participants expressed substantially higher ASL usage for smart-home assistants indicating potential for widespread use. These approaches allowed facilitation of evaluations in a way that cared for specific deaf linguistic and cultural experiences, while providing more genuine, authentic, and reliable evaluations.

10.3.2   Gesture-based interaction and spatial grammar

Gesture recognition technology is crucial for sign-language systems. A hybrid Transformer–CNN model [15] incorporates information from both hand-region and whole-frame features. The presented system exhibited high accuracy and low latency, which are both crucial for performing ASL in real-time. The study surveyed [16] the literature within gesture recognition research, creating a description of technique developments from the previous five years. Underlying this procedural review was a description of sign-language system considerations: signer variance, spatial grammar, non-manual markers, and environmental factors, such as light, must be included in the design and evaluative considerations.

10.3.3   Practical considerations: calibration, fatigue, and privacy

Also, using gesture systems for real-world actions presented some of the users with experience problems that needed to be noted:

- Calibration: In the primary design, an interaction is simple with a very fine recognition hand gesture recognition, but normally a personal calibration will be needed to adapt to the size of the signer. Additionally, lighting conditions will also be signaled for calibration – automatic autoencoder pre-processing can make good enough mapping for recognition under low-light or high variance environments [17].

- Physical Fatigue: Signing that uses extended signing and requires a significant amount of expression can always result in fatigue. Hybrid introductory models are also working toward developing gesture, touch, and voice-to-sign interactions that could reduce the amount of embodied effort required to use the gesture [16].
- Privacy issues: And finally, most gesture systems using cameras invade personal space – voice-driven translation (video-based dictionaries) systems require a thoughtful design process to deal with timeline lags, so each part doesn't become frustrating to the user but also creates the challenge to consider a user's data privacy [18].

10.4   Interface design for translation tools

The interface is the platform of interaction for users of sign language translation (SLT) systems, and the interface design is a key factor in the accessibility, fluency, and usability of the translation tools for the DHH communities. This section will explore how avatar- versus video-based systems function, design for visual customization, interaction design, awareness of device-specific limitations, and a case study using a real translation tool experience based on contemporary design and research descriptions and reflections.

10.4.1   Avatar-based versus video-based translation interfaces

Two common paradigms exist for representing the sign language input for digital translation tools: animated avatars and recorded or live video of human interpreters. Avatar-based systems are flexible and scalable, allowing for relative control over elements like the speed of the avatar, the orientation relative to the translation, or even some control of the gloss-level structure of the signing. The downside of avatar systems is the inability to replicate the rich non-manual markers such as facial expression and posture. In studies [19,20], users rated sign fluent in an avatar setting only at 72% (in comparison to the human signing rate of 93%). There is a perceptual gap for expressiveness to avatars.

On the flip side, video-based translation (recorded or live video interpreted) provides a better naturalistic signing fidelity. For video systems, users typically prefer the experience of authentic and emotionally accurate signing. There are still the problems of performance in video-based systems that are commonly reported, such as latency, misaligned lip-sync, background distractions, and less adaptability of output to device-specified options [21]. The most recent advancements in hybrid systems that utilize avatars for productive output and fall back to video in expressive, or domain-sensitive, contexts, show a considerable middle ground [22].

10.4.2   Visual customizability and timing controls

A key characteristic of effective SLT tools is the extent to which the user can customize the visual output to their own linguistic and perceptual preferences. For example, many systems can dynamically resize the signing window, which is advantageous for users who have visual impairments or educators who must sign in broader contexts. Also, in Ref. [23], the value of variable rates of avatar animation is cited and noted that users often preferred slow signing rates for long, intricate sentences or for glosses they were unfamiliar with.

Furthermore, since avatars cannot provide a fully natural facial expression, alternate visuals have been used as adjuncts. These include overlays to provide markups for eyebrow movement, pauses to simulate phrasing, or color-coded grammar markers. These additions seek to augment the communication bandwidth of avatars and provide more complete comprehension where expressive detail may fall short.

10.4.3   Interactive feedback and editing control

Modern systems have more interactive user feedback and greater scope for preview editing of the translation. This includes revisions of glosses before sign rendering; an example would be a user replacing "STORE FUTURE" with a more natural gloss, "WILL GO STORE." Many systems incorporate preview-confirm work-flows, where the user can see the generated sign language before they finalize the system. The SignEase app is an example of this and allows users to intuitively replay, adjust speed, and edit the final product [24]. These features demonstrate an increasing emphasis from passive consumption to active contribution to the translation process and probably contribute to user agency and satisfaction.

10.4.4   Context-specific interface variants

Platform and deployment context influence interface structure and control mechanisms. Desktop applications provide expansive layouts suitable for multi-pane translation interfaces, whereas mobile systems require compact, gesture-driven toggles and readability controls. Public installations – such as kiosks – demand privacy filters and trigger-based playback, reflecting research that illustrates layout and control priorities across user environments. Table 10.1 highlights how interface components must be adapted based on device capabilities and usage environments, reinforcing the principle of context-aware design in SLT systems.

10.5   Case studies in sign language translation Interfaces

This section categorizes recent SLT tools by design modality, linguistic scope, and interaction style. The organization reflects both technological diversity and global inclusivity, with systems ranging from avatar-based renderers to gesture-driven recognition platforms.

Table 10.1   Context-specific interface across devices

Parameter	Desktop/web	Mobile devices	Public kiosks
Display real estate	Full multi-panel layout with gloss and video panes	Compact screen; swipe/toggle layouts needed	Fixed-size UI; simplified layout for legibility
Input modalities	Keyboard, mouse, optional gesture control	Touch, voice, on-screen gestures	Motion sensors, minimal touch interaction
Privacy requirements	Medium – typically used in personal settings	High – personal devices used in public	Very high – used in public; must guard visual data
Network dependence	Stable, high-bandwidth connections	Variable; offline mode beneficial	Often restricted; local processing preferred
Customization options	Extensive – users can adjust gloss, speed, avatar	Moderate – avatar speed and gloss settings available	Minimal – preset output configurations only
Interactivity level	Full editing, preview, and confirmation supported	Partial editing and limited preview options	Low – automated playback with limited control
Latency sensitivity	Low latency; real-time rendering feasible	Moderate; may delay rendering in poor networks	High – prebuffering and instant feedback critical
Cognitive load	Manageable due to visual space and keyboard input	Moderate; requires optimized visual hierarchy	Low – highly simplified UI reduces overload
Environmental noise	Minimal; used in quiet, controlled environments	Moderate; depends on the user's physical environment	High – interfaces must compete with ambient noise

10.5.1   Avatar-based translation systems

Avatar-based interfaces use animated characters such as 2D and 3D animated characters that allow a sign language to be derived from a text or spoken form of communication. Avatar-based systems allow for scalability and interactive control of a sign language in ways such as speed of speed and clarification of signs. However, the expressive fidelity of the avatar translation, particularly non-manual components (e.g., facial expression, bodily posture), is often limited.

(a) **Hand Talk (Brazil: Libras, English → ASL)**

Hand Talk [25] uses "Hugo" as the avatar character to translate Portuguese – and recently English – to Brazilian sign language (Libras) and American sign language (ASL). Hand Talk has seen widespread application in Brazilian media, education, and public services. Studies show deaf users rated hand talk highly for usability, while the researchers recognized some expressive intensity and grammar fidelity mismatches.

(b) **VLibras (Brazil: Portuguese → Libras)**
VLibras [26] was developed to provide access to Brazilian government and other institutional content on the web. Text-to-sign technologies using avatars developed into VLibras. The UI has been recently evaluated for effectiveness and comparative performance, with outputs showing considerable customization such as avatar features and playback speed, while engaging users and promoting user understanding.

(c) **SignGemma (USA: ASL)**
SignGemma announced in 2025 [27] by Google is an on-device generative AI model for ASL translation. SignGemma processes sign motion by detecting signs using a smartphone camera, with potential benefits of privacy (process sign information on the device) and near real time. Initial reports and previews of SignGemma indicate that users report the app has a high interpretative accuracy of ASL.

(d) **SignMeet (Signapse) (UK: BSL, ASL)**
Signapse's SignStudio and SignStream [28] platforms deploy broadcast-quality avatars to render signs in British sign language (BSL) and ASL. Available in UK transportation systems and on streaming channels, the sign avatars focus on realism and dialect inclusion, with updates continuously driven by deaf community input.

(e) **SignAvatar (global research: ASL)**
SignAvatar [29] is a transformer-conditional variational autoencoder (CVAE) model that generates realistic 3D motion in ASL from text input. SignAvatar used the ASL3DWord dataset and a CVAE model to substantially improve the fluency of motion and expressivity of the signer.

10.5.2   Vision-based translation systems

Vision-based sign language technologies utilize computer vision to understand actions through RGB or depth cameras. These technologies emphasize interaction and precise gesture recognition while accommodating user input preferences. They present opportunities for facilitating dynamic communication. In contrast, to character-driven platforms vision centric systems enable the conversion of gestures into text or speech frequently empowering deaf individuals to communicate directly with those who do not know sign language.

(a) **KinTrans (ArSL + ASL)**
KinTrans is a technology that recognizes sign language using depth sensors and is tailored for use in settings such as businesses and public spaces like airports and banks. It can interpret sign language (ArSL) and ASL converting real-time gestures into either text or spoken words. Successful trials have taken place in Dubai and several cities in the United States including pilot programs at Emirates NBD banks showing the system's potential for providing accessibility on the frontline. A cloud-based analysis dashboard aids in enhancement and customization to meet client needs [30,31].

(b) **Signs by NVIDIA (USA:ASL)**
The Signs platform was developed in partnership with the American Society for Deaf Children. Hello Monday/DEPT® to assist in learning ASL using regular webcams powered by AI technology. Its unique feature includes providing visual feedback by comparing user gestures with verified 3D models in real time. The platform currently includes around 100 signs in its database and offers educational activities to help users practice accurately and improve their fluency [32,33].

(c) **PJM Kinect recognition (Poland)**
A recent 2025 study presented a deep neural network model that recognizes Polish sign language (PJM) static signs using RGB webcam input. By analyzing distances between hand, elbow, and shoulder landmarks, the model achieved 96.45% accuracy, 96.15% recall, and 96.66% precision across two public PJM datasets [34].

(d) **BSL real-time recognition (UK)**
Researchers, in Britain have developed a system that utilizes a combination of technology to interpret sign language (BSl) in real time. By integrating OpenCV for capture and MediaPipe landmarks with LSTM classification techniques, they have successfully achieved an accuracy rate of 94% in fingerspelling and around 99% for six frequently used signs. This showcases the system's practicality and dependability in real-world scenarios according to a recent study conducted [35].

(e) **MediaPipe-based ISL recognition (India)**
This educational model utilizes Googles MediaPipe Holistic to identify points for hand movements and facial expressions in both still and moving gestures within the context of Indian sign language (ISL). Through a comparison of CNN and LSTM approaches in the project's framework, the system accomplished over 99% accuracy in recognizing gestures. This success showcases its resilience in lighting conditions and camera settings suggesting its potential for practical use in educational settings [36].

10.5.3 *Dictionary and lexical tools for sign language systems*

Lexical resources and digital dictionaries serve as foundational components for sign language learning, translation, and annotation. These tools bridge the gap between written/spoken languages and sign languages, especially in low-resource settings. The following platforms offer diverse features such as multimodal search, example glosses, avatar support, and community contributions. A growing number of lexical databases and dictionary tools have been developed to support both linguistic research and public engagement with sign languages across different regions.

As summarized in Table 10.2, platforms such as Spread the Sign and Dicta-Sign Lexicon span multiple sign languages and are instrumental for multilingual

Table 10.2   Comparative overview of multilingual sign language lexicons and dictionary platforms

Project/re-source name	Languages covered	Type of resource	Annotation features	Modality
Spread the Sign [37]	40+ (SSL, PJM, ISL, LSF)	Multilingual dictionary	Gloss, video example	Video
SignBank+ [38]	ASL, BSL, DGS, LSF, PJM	Multilingual dataset	Gloss, POS, iconicity, lemma	Text, Video
Dicta-Sign-LSF-v2 [39]	LSF	Corpus	Gloss, POS, non-manuals	Video
SwissSLi [40]	DSGS, LSF, DGS, French, German	Corpus	Gloss, parallel translations	Multimodal (Video, Text)
ISL Dictionary [41]	ISL, Hindi, English	Dictionary (Official)	Gloss, bilingual labels	Video, Text
Swiss–German SL annotation [42]	DSGS	Annotation tool	Gloss, continuous data, timestamps	Video
SignON [43]	ISL, BSL, LSF, DGS, GSL	Multimodal MT platform	Gloss, phonology, POS, multilingual alignments	Multimodal (Text, avatar, video)
BSL-DGS lexical database [44]	BSL, DGS	Lexical database	Iconicity, POS, concreteness	Text
Swiss DSGS annotator [42]	DSGS	Annotation framework	Timestamped multi-level labels	Video
JSL web dictionary [45]	JSL	Web diction-ary	Glosses, region-based variants	Video

alignment and educational outreach [46,47]. Language-specific resources, including ASL Signbank (2025) and BSL SignBank (2024), offer morphological and phonological tagging features essential for computational modeling. National initiatives, such as the ISL Dictionary in India [41] and PJM SignLex in Poland [48], demonstrate how digital lexicons contribute to language revitalization, corpus development, and policy-aligned dissemination of sign resources.

10.5.4   *Embodied and robotic sign interaction*

Recent advances in embodied AI have produced humanoid and social robots capable of performing sign language, designed for interactive communication, instruction, and social support for DHH communities. These platforms blend gesture comprehension, motor control, and linguistic alignment to engage users more naturally.

A variety of embodied and robotic systems have been developed to facilitate sign language interaction across different modalities, user groups, and application domains. Table 10.3 provides a high-level functional comparison of prominent sign language robots and agents covering supported languages, autonomy levels, and

Table 10.3 Functional overview of sign language robotic interfaces

Tool	Language	Platform/ type	Key features	Sign direction	Level of autonomy	Application domain
SignBot [49]	Chinese sign language (CSL)	Humanoid robot	Bi-directional; Real-time sign generation; Joint-level control; NLP integration	Bi-directional	Fully autonomous	Public Service
Tactile SL arm [50]	Tactile sign language (t-SL)	Robotic arm	Tactile feedback; scripted tactile sign output for deaf–blind	Output-only	Scripted	Healthcare
Pepper SLR system [51]	American sign language (ASL)	Humanoid robot	Speech-to-Sign pipeline; LLM integration; Pepper robot with SL output	Bi-directional	Semi-autonomous	Education
Real-time SL translator [52]	Korean sign language (KSL)	Desktop + webcam system	Real-time SL generation; deep learning translation; Korean corpus based	Bi-directional	Fully autonomous	Education
NAO for CSL [53]	Colombian sign language (LSC)	NAO humanoid robot	Gloss learning; NAO robot interaction; teacher-guided learning	Output-only	Semi-autonomous	Education
Teo robot [54]	Spanish sign language (LSE)	Teo humanoid robot	User study; Physical execution of signs; Vocabulary sign accuracy	Output-only	Scripted	Public awareness
Social imitation agent [55]	American sign language (ASL)	Simulated agent	Imitation learning; motion modeling from video; Interactive avatar	Input-only	Semi-autonomous	Research

intended domains of use. Table 10.4 complements this by detailing the technical aspects, user interaction capabilities, and accessibility features of these tools. These comparisons highlight ongoing efforts in integrating multimodal perception, imitation learning, and human-robot interaction frameworks to support diverse sign

Table 10.4 Technical and accessibility-oriented features of sign language robots

Tool	Perception capabilities	User interaction mode	Sign Type supported	Dataset/training source	Evaluation metrics used	Accessibility features
SignBot [49]	Vision + speech	Voice + vision	Gloss + Fingerspelling	Custom corpus + imitation	User comprehension, motion accuracy	Real-time visual output
Tactile SL arm [50]	Tactile only	Tactile interaction	Tactile signs	Hand-designed patterns	MOS, user feedback	Tactile output for deaf–blind
Pepper SLR system [51]	Vision + speech	Voice command	Gloss + phrases	ASL datasets + LLM	Accuracy %, fluency	Multilingual input
Realtime SL translator [52]	Vision + speech	Voice + gesture	Gloss signs	Custom training	User study, system latency	On-device translator
NAO for CSL [53]	Vision	Scripted dialogue	Gloss signs	Custom NAO training	User feedback	Child-friendly interface
Teo robot [54]	None	Pre-programmed	Gloss signs	Scripted	User satisfaction	Interactive demo
Social imitation agent [55]	Vision	Gesture input	Gloss imitation	Imitation learning	Imitation accuracy	Flexible learning modes

languages, including CSL, ASL, KSL, LSC, LSE, and tactile signing for deaf–blind users [49–55].

10.6 Summary

This chapter discussed the recent innovations in sign language technology, particularly on embodied sign interaction systems and multilingual translation frameworks. Embodied platforms such as SignBot, Pepper-based SLR systems, and NAO humanoids are examples of humanoid robots that can generate, recognize, or imitate sign language gestures effectively, which currently includes applications in public service, educational, and healthcare applications. Each of these systems is different in terms of autonomy, sign directionality, and perception. Each system has varying levels of perceived tactile feedback for communication with deaf–blind, and others utilize large language models or imitate gestures to improve fidelity to users' intent while signing.

The chapter also examined multilingual sign language systems, such as SignON. These systems support SL-to-SL and SL-to-text translations of ISL, BSL, DGS, LSE, and LSF. Examples include inclusive design principles illustrated by Google's Live Transcribe and the level of communication support provided in multilingual and mixed-modality contexts. Through comparative analysis tables, we have identified some variables that differ across systems, including but not limited to, the languages supported, where the datasets were from, the application domain, and the evaluation metrics. Together, these efforts highlight a real emphasis on cross-lingual accessibility, robotic embodiment, and user-centered design that offers promise for the future of intelligent agents, capable of providing inclusive and naturalistic sign language communication in real-world contexts.

Exercises

(I) **Multiple choice questions**
   1. Which robot uses imitation learning from video-based sign data?
      (a) SignBot
      (b) NAO for CSL
      (c) Social Imitation Agent
      (d) Tactile SL Arm

   2. What modality is primarily used by the Tactile SL Arm to communicate?
      (a) Audio
      (b) Vision
      (c) Tactile
      (d) Gesture

   3. Which project supports multilingual SL-to-SL translation across five European sign languages?
      (a) NAO for CSL
      (b) SignON
      (c) SignBot
      (d) Teo Robot

   4. What type of sign directionality is supported by the Pepper SLR System?
      (a) Input-only
      (b) Output-only
      (c) Bi-directional
      (d) Scripted

5. Which system integrates speech, NLP, and joint-level motion planning for sign output?
   (a) NAO for CSL
   (b) SignBot
   (c) Realtime SL Translator
   (d) DigiRob

(II) **Short Answer Questions**
   1. What is the primary purpose of using humanoid robots like NAO and Pepper in sign language systems?
   2. Explain how tactile sign language systems help deaf–blind individuals.
   3. What are the key features of the SignON project that make it suitable for cross-lingual SL communication?

(III) **Discussion questions**
   1. Discuss the ethical and practical implications of deploying humanoid robots for sign language education in public settings.
   2. Compare the levels of autonomy across different sign language robots and discuss how this affects user interaction and accessibility.
   3. What are the challenges in designing multilingual sign language translation systems, and how does SignON address them?

(IV) **Practical/Hands-on exercises**
   1. Explore the SignON project documentation and write a summary of its core components and multilingual pipeline.
   2. Simulate a sign recognition model using MediaPipe or OpenPose for any one hand gesture and explain how the skeleton keypoints can be used for classification.
   3. Design a basic flowchart for a real-time SL-to-text translation system using webcam input, outlining the major modules and their data flow.

References

[1] US Web Design System. (n.d.). *Accessibility.* https://designsystem.digital. gov/documentation/accessibility/.
[2] Inclusive Design Research Centre. (n.d.). *Definition of inclusive design.* OCAD University. https://en.wikipedia.org/wiki/Inclusive_Design_Research_Centre.
[3] De Meulder, M., Van Landuyt, D., and Omardeen, R. (2024). Lessons in co-creation: the inconvenient truths of inclusive sign language technology development. *arXiv preprint arXiv:2408.13171.* https://arxiv.org/abs/2408. 13171.
[4] Li, Y. (2025). Design an editable speech-to-sign-language transformer system: a human-centered AI approach. *arXiv preprint arXiv:2506.14677.* https://arxiv.org/abs/2506.14677.

[5]   Hill, S. (2025). *Silence Speaks: How AI is Learning Sign Language – From the Deaf Themselves*. WIRED. https://www.wired.com/story/silence-speaks-deaf-ai-signing.

[6]   W3C. (2025). *Web Content Accessibility Guidelines (WCAG) 2.1.*https://www.w3.org/TR/2025/REC-WCAG21-20250506.

[7]   WAI. (n.d.). *Accessibility Principles. Web Accessibility Initiative*. https://www.w3.org/WAI/fundamentals/accessibility-principles.

[8]   Boudreault, P., Abubakar, M., Duran, A., Lam, B., Liu, Z., Vogler, C., and Kushalnagar, R. (2024, July). Closed sign language interpreting: a usability study. In *International Conference on Computers Helping People with Special Needs* (pp. 42–49). Cham: Springer Nature Switzerland.

[9]   Nielsen, J. (2024). *10 Usability Heuristics for User Interface Design*. Nielsen Norman Group. https://www.nngroup.com/articles/ten-usability-heuristics.

[10]   Pečnik, K., Juvan, Ž., Dolinar, G., and Pogačnik, M. (2025). User experience questionnaire in sign language for native users of Slovenian sign language. *Scientific reports*, *15*(1), 5802.

[11]   Alkhudaidi, K., Burke, T., Boll, R., Mahajan, S., Solovey, E. T., and Reis, J. (2025). Perceptions and preferences: deaf ASL-signing users' insights on video elements, styles and layouts. In *Proceedings of the 2025 CHI Conference on Human Factors in Computing Systems* (pp. 1–20). ACM. https://doi.org/10.1145/3706598.3714296.

[12]   Tran, N., DeVries, P. S., Seita, M., Kushalnagar, R., Glasser, A., and Vogler, C. (2024). Assessment of sign language-based versus touch-based input for deaf users interacting with intelligent personal assistants. In *Proceedings of the 2024 CHI Conference on Human Factors in Computing Systems* (pp. 1–15). ACM. https://doi.org/10.1145/3613904.3642094.

[13]   Wang, J., Ivrissimtzis, I., Li, Z., Zhou, Y., and Shi, L. (2023). User-defined hand gesture interface to improve user experience of learning American sign language. In *International Conference on Intelligent Tutoring Systems* (pp. 479–490). Cham: Springer Nature Switzerland.

[14]   Boll, R., Mahajan, S., Burke, T., *et al.* (2023). User perceptions and preferences for online surveys in american sign language: an exploratory study. In *Proceedings of the 25th International ACM SIGACCESS Conference on Computers and Accessibility* (pp. 1–17). ACM. https://doi.org/10.1145/3597638.3608444.

[15]   Aly, M., and Fathi, I. S. (2025). Recognizing American sign language gestures efficiently and accurately using a hybrid transformer model. *Scientific Reports*, *15*(1), 1–27.

[16]   Zhang, Y., and Jiang, X. (2024). Recent advances on deep learning for sign language recognition. *CMES-Computer Modeling in Engineering & Sciences*, *139*(3), 2399–2450.

[17]   Rastgoo, R., Kiani, K., Escalera, S., and Sabokrou, M. (2024). Multi-modal zero-shot dynamic hand gesture recognition. *Expert Systems with Applications*, *247*, 123349.

[18] Hassan, S., Bohacek, M., Kim, C., and Crochet, D. (2025). Towards an AI-driven video-based american sign language dictionary: exploring design and usage experience with learners. *arXiv preprint arXiv:2504.05857.* https://arxiv.org/abs/2504.05857.

[19] Wolfe, R., McDonald, J. C., Hanke, T., *et al.* (2022). Sign language avatars: a question of representation. *Information, 13*(4), 206.

[20] Soudi, A., Hakkaoui, M. E., and Van Laerhoven, K. (2023). Do predictability factors towards signing avatars hold across cultures?. *arXiv preprint arXiv:2307.02103.* https://arxiv.org/abs/2307.02103.

[21] Rivas Velarde, M., Jagoe, C., and Cuculick, J. (2022). Video relay interpretation and overcoming barriers in health care for deaf users: scoping review. *Journal of Medical Internet Research, 24*(6), e32439.

[22] Sinlapanuntakul, P., and Zachry, M. (2025, June). Perception in pixels: effects of avatar representation in video-mediated collaborative interactions. In *Proceedings of the 4th Annual Symposium on Human-Computer Interaction for Work* (pp. 1–16).

[23] Chen, S., Cheng, H., Su, S., Patterson, S., Kushalnagar, R., Huang, Y., and Wang, Q. (2025). Customizing generated signs and voices of AI avatars: deaf-centric mixed-reality design for deaf-hearing communication. *Proceedings of the ACM on Human-Computer Interaction, 9*(2), 1–31.

[24] Sadaf, A., Bahadure, V., Mondal, A., and Rindhe, A. (2025). SignEase: intuitive sign language translation with enhanced features. In *International Conference on Advances and Applications in Artificial Intelligence (ICAAAI 2025)* (pp. 860–872). Atlantis Press.

[25] Google Cloud Platform Podcast. (2023). Hand Talk with Thadeu Luz [Podcast episode]. GCP Podcast. https://www.gcppodcast.com/post/episode-132-hand-talk-with-thadeu-luz/.

[26] Agência Brasil. (2021). *VLibras Increases Number of Signs by More Than 30% in 2 Years.* https://agenciabrasil.ebc.com.br/en/geral/noticia/2021-12/vilibras-increases-number-signs-more-30-2-years.

[27] Multilingual. (2024). *Google's SignGemma Brings ASL Translation to Mobile.* https://multilingual.com/google-signgemma-on-device-asl-translation/.

[28] Signapse. (2024). *AI-Driven Sign Language Avatars for Transport and Media.* https://signapse.ai/.

[29] Dong, L., Chaudhary, L., Xu, F., Wang, X., Lary, M., and Nwogu, I. (2024). Signavatar: sign language 3d motion reconstruction and generation. In *2024 IEEE 18th International Conference on Automatic Face and Gesture Recognition (FG)* (pp. 1–10). IEEE.

[30] Sakelaris, Nicholas (2018). *KinTrans Movement Tech Turns Motion Into Voice, Text – And Translates Sign Language.* Retrieved from https://dallasinnovates.com/kintrans-sign-language-tech-translates-movements-text-voice/.

[31] Bentley, Catherine (2017). *KinTrans & Microsoft – Hands Can Talk. Microsoft New England and KinTrans Partnership.* Retrieved from https://blogs.microsoft.com/newengland/2017/07/14/kintrans-microsoft-hands-can-talk/.

[32] Boone, M. (2025). *It's a Sign: AI Platform for Teaching American Sign Language Aims to Bridge Communication Gaps*. NVIDIA Blog. Retrieved from https://blogs.nvidia.com/blog/ai-sign-language/.

[33] Inês Saraiva (2025). Hello Monday/DEPT® collaborates with NVIDIA to launch Signs Platform for ASL learning and community engagement. *DEPT®*. Retrieved from https://www.deptagency.com/insight/hello-monday-dept-collaborates-with-nvidia-to-launch-signs-platform-for-asl-learning-and-community-engagement/.

[34] Barańczyk, W., and Duch, P. (2025). Deep neural network based algorithm for recognition of static signs of Polish Sign Language. In *Proceedings of the 17th International Conference on Agents and Artificial Intelligence (ICAART 2025)* (Vol. 3, pp. 201–208). ScitePress. https://doi.org/10.5220/0013112400003890.

[35] Isiaq, S. O., and Stephen, S. (2025). Developing an intelligent recognition system for British sign language: a step towards inclusive communication. *Journal of Intelligent Communication*, 4(1), 42–57.

[36] Goyal, K. (2023). Indian sign language recognition using mediapipe holistic. *arXiv preprint arXiv:2304.10256*. https://arxiv.org/abs/2304.10256.

[37] Hilzensauer, M., and Krammer, K. (2015). A multilingual dictionary for sign languages: "spreadthesign". In *ICERI2015 Proceedings* (pp. 7826–7834). IATED.

[38] Moryossef, A., and Jiang, Z. (2023). Signbank+: preparing a multilingual sign language dataset for machine translation using large language models. *arXiv preprint arXiv:2309.11566*. https://arxiv.org/abs/2309.11566.

[39] Belissen, V., Braffort, A., and Gouiffès, M. (2020). Dicta-Sign-LSF-v2: remake of a continuous French sign language dialogue corpus and a first baseline for automatic sign language processing. In *LREC 2020, 12th Conference on Language Resources and Evaluation*. (pp. 6040–6048). European Language Resources Association (ELRA), Marseille, France.

[40] Jiang, Z., Göhring, A., Moryossef, A., Sennrich, R., and Ebling, S. (2024). SwissSLi: the multi-parallel sign language corpus for Switzerland. In *Proceedings of the 2024 Joint International Conference on Computational Linguistics, Language Resources and Evaluation (LREC-COLING 2024)* (pp. 15448–15456). ELRA.

[41] Indian Sign Language Research and Training Centre (ISLRTC). (2024). *The Indian Sign Language–English–Hindi Dictionary* [Mobile app & website]. Retrieved from https://www.islrtc.nic.in.

[42] Battisti, A., Tissi, K., Sidler-Miserez, S., and Ebling, S. (2024). Advancing annotation for continuous data in Swiss German sign language. In *Proceedings of the LREC-COLING 2024 11th Workshop on the Representation and Processing of Sign Languages: Evaluation of Sign Language Resources* (pp. 1–12).

[43] Saggion, H., Shterionov, D., Labaka, G., Van de Cruys, T., Vandeghinste, V., and Blat, J. (2021). SignON: bridging the gap between sign and spoken languages. In *SEPLN (Projects and Demonstrations)* (pp. 21–24).

[44] Ortega, G., Schiefner, A., Lazarus, N., and Perniss, P. (2025). A lexical database of British Sign language (BSL) and German sign language (DGS): iconicity ratings, iconic strategies, and concreteness norms. *Behavior Research Methods, 57*(5), 139.

[45] Suzuki, E., Suzuki, T., and Kakihana, K. (2006). On the web trilingual sign language dictionary to learn the foreign sign language without learning a target spoken language. In *LREC* (pp. 2307–2310). ELRA, Genoa, Italy.

[46] Dicta-Sign Project Consortium. (2013). *DICTA-SIGN Final Report: Sign Language Recognition, Generation, and Modelling with Application in Deaf Communication* (FP7-ICT Project No. 231135). Retrieved from https://www. ilsp.gr/wp-content/uploads/2020/05/DICTA-SIGN_final_report.pdf.

[47] European Union of the Deaf (2025). *Annual Report on Sign Language Rights and Accessibility in the EU*. Brussels: EUD. Retrieved from https://eud.eu/ wp-content/uploads/2025/06/D2.4-Report-on-the-implementation-of-the-European-Accessibility-Act.pdf.

[48] Kuder, A., Wójcicka, J., Mostowski, P., Rutkowski, P. (2022). Open repository of the Polish sign language corpus: Publication project of the Polish sign language corpus. In *Proceedings of LREC 2022 Workshop on Sign Languages* (pp. 118–123).

[49] Qiao, G., Lin, S., Wu, R. Z. Z., Jia, K., and Liu, G. (2025). SignBot: learning human-to-humanoid sign language interaction. *arXiv preprint arXiv:2505. 24266.* https://arxiv.org/abs/2505.24266.

[50] Johnson, S. T. (2021). *Robotic Arm Signing Tactile Sign Language (t-SL) to Aid Deaf-Blind (DB) Communication* (Master's thesis, Northeastern University).

[51] Lim, J., Sa, I., MacDonald, B., and Ahn, H. S. (2023). A sign language recognition system with pepper, lightweight-transformer, and LLM. *arXiv preprint arXiv:2309.16898.* https://arxiv.org/abs/2309.16898.

[52] Lee, D. U., Kim, M. S., Kim, N. H., and Choi, G. M. (2023). Implementation of real-time sign language AI translation program. 디지털콘텐츠학회논문지 *(J. DCS), 24*(10), 2585–2591.

[53] Mora-Zarate, J. E., Garzón-Castro, C. L., and Rivillas, J. A. C. (2024). Learning signs with NAO: humanoid robot as a tool for helping to learn Colombian Sign Language. *Frontiers in Robotics and AI, 11*, 1475069.

[54] Gago, J. J., Victores, J. G., and Balaguer, C. (2019). Sign language representation by teo humanoid robot: end-user interest, comprehension and satisfaction. *Electronics, 8*(1), 57.

[55] Tavella, F., Galata, A., and Cangelosi, A. (2024). Bridging the communication gap: artificial agents learning sign language through imitation. In *International Conference on Social Robotics* (pp. 460–474). Singapore: Springer Nature Singapore.

Chapter 11

Responsible futures: ethics and emerging directions in sign language AI

11.1 Introduction

The emergence of sign language systems utilizing generative AI is a landmark development in expanding access and inclusion within communication. These systems range across the full pipeline from gesture and pose recognition to linguistic translation and expressive sign generation. There are several exciting advancements, especially concretely focused on bringing swiftly piloted creations from research projects to commercial-level applications employing generative adversarial network (GAN)-based gloss generation or transformer-driven sign synthesis. Advancements are underway, but in the spirit of these technical developments, we need to consider the ethical implications, societal consequences, and trajectories.

Sign language systems engage directly with human identity – encoding gestures, expressions, and context-embedded cultural signs. Bob Kohn was adamant in placing responsible design as the foundational principle of his work. Processes producing visual gestures engage a deeper form of both personal and communal expression. From this perspective, developing generative architectures with methodologies such as diffusion-based, and multimodal encoders places creators of sign language sign generation material on a landing station directly affiliated with dataset bias replication, cultural exclusion, or compromising individual privacy.

Recent responsible AI research and publications, often examining the natural language processing domain, are moving away from mere performance benchmarks to human-aligned development that integrates fairness, transparency, and social context as a part of model design [1]. The concerns of these concerns are not just auxiliary; over permutations in multimodality and grammar, our sign context imposes a greater duty of care, and it can be illustrated as follows: except for textual natural language processing systems, sign language processors must encode both linguistic structure and embodied, visual expressions, and as such, we must act professionally and with thoughtfulness and care.

In time, as contemporary research activities coalesce toward real-time, cross-lingual translation, and avatar generation of sign language (and sign) content, the field will need to incorporate ethical principles at every stage of the research lifecycle. This concluding chapter serves as a stepping stone to consider what the field

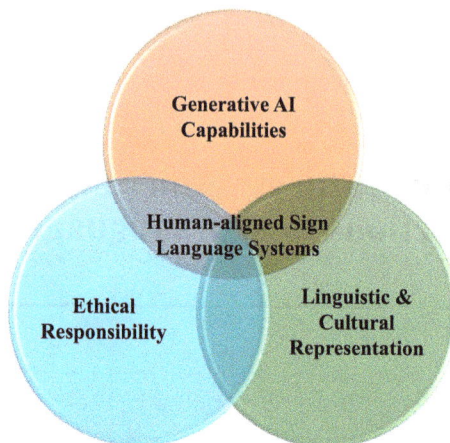

Figure 11.1   Convergence of ethics, technology, and culture in responsible sign language systems

has accomplished, and what there remains to be addressed – both the ethical challenges researchers will grapple with and the emergent areas of research.

In doing so, we take a cue from the growing consensus on trustworthy AI [2,3], while situating our discourse within the novel expectations of gesture-driven, multimodal communication systems.

> "Technologies that shape language shape culture. In building AI for sign, we're not just building tools – we're building bridges."
> – Dr. Naomi Caselli, BU NSF SLR Project, 2023 [4]

As shown in Figure 11.1, building responsible sign language systems requires an intersectional approach that integrates generative AI capabilities, ethical responsibility, and linguistic-cultural representation. True alignment occurs at the center – where technological progress is guided by ethical values and inclusive design.

11.2   Ethical issues related to sign language systems

The design and operation of sign language systems are increasingly informed by generative, data-driven approaches and, therefore, they have unique ethical concerns associated with both artificial intelligence and human communication. These systems are not simply making gestures or movements; they encode a typified social, cultural, and linguistic representation of communities that were designed and constructed with limited access and historically limited communities. As such, ethics by design are crucial to monitor in their development, deployment, and assessment. Figure 11.2 illustrates that the development of sign language systems must account for critical ethical dimensions – ranging from dataset bias and privacy

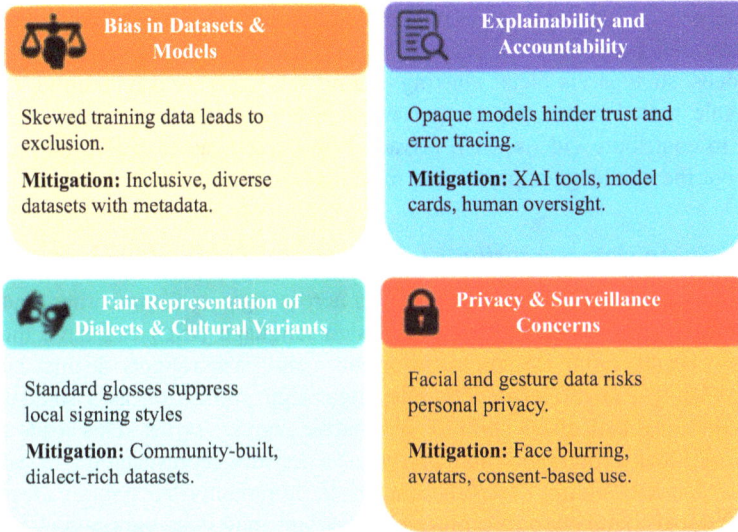

Figure 11.2   Key ethical issues and mitigation strategies in sign language systems

risks to the fair representation of dialects and explainability of generative models. Each concern demands tailored mitigation strategies, including inclusive data practices, privacy-preserving preprocessing, community co-creation, and interpretable AI techniques.

11.2.1   Bias in datasets and models

Bias in training datasets is perhaps one of the most concerning barriers to creating equitable sign language systems. For example, many publicly available datasets designed for sign language recognition include a dominant demographic or use a single sign language. Taking RWTH-PHOENIX-Weather 2014T and American sign language lexicon video dataset (ASLLVD) as examples, the example data in these datasets are almost exclusively dominated by white adult signers. As a result, these systems might have limited generalizability when considering different dialects, age groups, gender, regions of the World and other local, indigenous signing variants.

A recent study reviewing 101 sign language AI papers revealed systemic bias: datasets often underrepresent Deaf communities and certain signing variations, and the field is driven primarily by hearing researchers' agendas [5]. Other research using American sign language (ASL) Citizen showed demographic-specific model discrepancies and applied bias mitigation methods to reduce these disparities [6].

11.2.2   Privacy and surveillance concerns

Unlike text-based systems, sign language systems capture and process rich visual information including facial expressions, hand movements, and body posture. This makes them inherently more susceptible to privacy violations, especially when real-time systems are deployed in public or surveillance-heavy environments (e.g., transit stations, hospitals). The work at Ref. [7] discussed anonymizing large-scale sign videos, such as via facial blurring, during self-supervised pretraining to limit identifiable data leakage [8]. Earlier work also revealed that signers are more willing to contribute videos when privacy filters like avatars or blurred faces are used – but the challenge is preserving meaning while protecting identity.

11.2.3   Fair representation of dialects and cultural variants

Sign languages are not universal; they differ across regions, communities, and even contexts. A single language like Indian sign language (ISL) can have multiple dialects – urban, rural, classroom, informal – and each reflects distinct cultural nuances. Many generative models today treat sign production as a standardized output, ignoring dialectical shifts or alternative signing styles. This leads to the erasure of local expressions and promotes a narrow representation of what is deemed "correct" signing. Experts emphasize community-led dataset creation – such as Global Signbank – to capture local variants and document regional usage, although AI models rarely adopt these inclusive practices yet [8,9].

11.2.4   Explainability and accountability in sign models

As generative models (e.g., GANs, diffusion transformers) become central to sign synthesis and recognition, their black-box nature makes it difficult to explain why a model failed – or worse, why it signed something offensive or inappropriate.

Explainable AI (XAI) in vision-based SL systems remains nascent. Existing attempts, like keypoint saliency mapping or temporal attention visualizations, are limited and rarely used in deployment. This opacity hinders error attribution, user trust, and system debugging, especially when models are used in sensitive domains like education or healthcare.

In multi-stage pipelines – for example, recognition → translation → generation – errors can propagate silently. Without accountability mechanisms or traceable logs, it becomes difficult to determine whether a mistake was due to poor hand detection, incorrect gloss mapping, or translation bias.

The AI community has recommended model cards [1] and datasheets for datasets [10] to support transparency. These practices must be adopted in the SL system pipelines to ensure responsible development.

11.3   Designing responsible sign language systems

Designing responsible sign language systems goes beyond algorithmic improve-ments. It requires co-creation with the deaf community, transparent documentation, and robust safeguards across development stages. Figure 11.3 shows the pipeline of designing responsible sign language systems involves a multi-stage framework beginning with deaf-led co-creation, followed by participatory interface

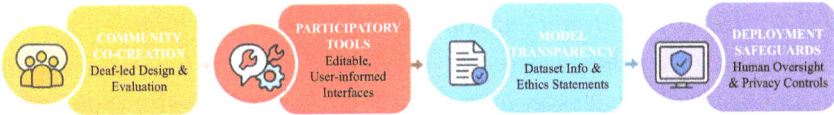

Figure 11.3   Responsible design pipeline for sign language systems

development, transparent documentation practices, and secure, human-supervised deployment. Each stage represents an essential ethical checkpoint to ensure that technological advancements align with community needs and values.

11.3.1   Community-driven development

Engaging deaf communities as collaborators, rather than mere participants, is essential to ensuring cultural and linguistic relevance. A recent study [11] critically examines two major EU projects – EASIER and SignON – highlighting that despite superficial claims of inclusive design, power imbalances and limited Deaf leadership persisted. The authors argue for a deliberate restructuring of project governance, advocating not only for truthful co-creation but also for expanded Deaf research representation. Their analysis offers seven practical guidelines – such as acknowledging Deaf collaborators' labour and fostering genuine decision-making authority – forming a blueprint for future responsible design.

"Deaf participants reported higher trust in Deaf researchers than hearing ones," illustrating the value of genuine representation [12].

11.3.2   Participatory design and evaluation

Recent auditory-to-sign generation frameworks integrate human-in-the-loop editing tools, placing control directly in the hands of Deaf users. A speech-to-sign system is introduced [13] based on a conformer–transformer architecture, enriched with JSON-based intermediate representations that users can inspect and modify. In controlled trials with 20 Deaf signers and five professional interpreters, the system yielded statistically significant improvements in usability (mean SUS +13 points) and reduction in cognitive load ($p < .001$. This paradigm exemplifies how participatory evaluation can materially enhance both system performance and user trust.

11.3.3   Transparency in documentation and release

While studies [11] have called for the infusion of DEI into transparency, many sign language systems lack critical documentation, such as the source of the datasets, demographic information about the signers involved, and limitations of the models [14]. It is essential to take principles from model cards and datasheets to document the sign language context. Documentation provides transparency into who the system is intended to serve, how the data was collected, and where the ethical lines are drawn, so that responsible reuse and accountability can be facilitated.

11.3.4   Deployment mechanisms and human-in-the-loop

When deploying sign language systems into domains that are high-stakes (healthcare, education, legal proceedings), there must be enough safeguards, human oversight, or intervention. Recent work has indicated that tools deployed without human intervention may perpetuate misinterpretation and degradation of linguistic norms [15]. In addition, "on-device" model implementations, such as Google's SignGemma [16], are interesting because they allow for translation in a mostly local context without individuals being commercially monetized for their privacy. However, in the recommendations made for this study of on-device sign language systems, we recommend always providing confidence scores, alert systems for the user, and audit logs, to appropriate levels of accountability or remediation.

11.4   Future research directions in sign language systems

The landscape of sign language technology is expanding rapidly, yet several challenges remain unresolved. Future advancements must not only enhance performance and generalization but also preserve equity, inclusivity, and linguistic authenticity across emerging contexts. Below are the most interesting and current research trajectories and Figure 11.4 summarizes key emerging research trajectories in sign language systems, including real-time cross-lingual translation, zero- and few-shot learning, brain–computer interface (BCI) integration, large language model (LLM)-based understanding, domain-specific deployments, multimodal generation, privacy-preserving training, and ethical considerations.

11.4.1   Real-time, cross-lingual sign-to-sign translation

Cross-lingual translation between sign languages (i.e., ASL to British sign language (BSL) or ASL to ISL) has additional requirements other than grammar and lexical alignment, primarily addressing visual morphology and cultural space. A thorough evaluation was performed [17] of zero-shot and MT-based approaches to multilingual

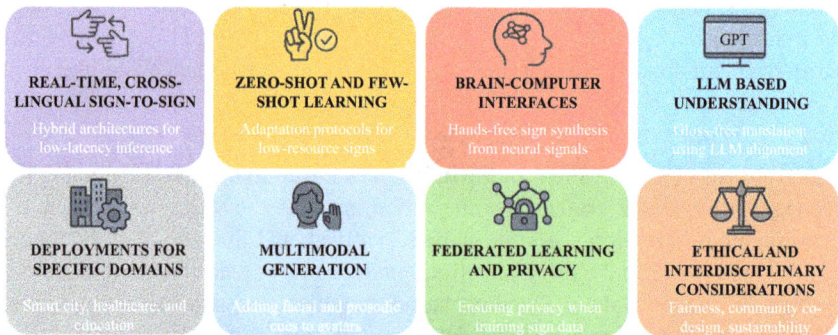

REAL-TIME, CROSS-LINGUAL SIGN-TO-SIGN	ZERO-SHOT AND FEW-SHOT LEARNING	BRAIN-COMPUTER INTERFACES	LLM BASED UNDERSTANDING
Hybrid architectures for low-latency inference	Adaptation protocols for low-resource signs	Hands-free sign synthesis from neural signals	Gloss-free translation using LLM alignment
DEPLOYMENTS FOR SPECIFIC DOMAINS	MULTIMODAL GENERATION	FEDERATED LEARNING AND PRIVACY	ETHICAL AND INTERDISCIPLINARY CONSIDERATIONS
Smart city, healthcare, and education	Adding facial and prosodic cues to avatars	Ensuring privacy when training sign data	Fairness, community co-design, sustainability

Figure 11.4   Future research directions in sign language systems

question-answering. Both approaches were found to be viable; nonetheless, zero-shot transfer consistently produced better performance in the presence of lexical gaps while MT-based approaches struggled due to task-specific modeling limitations [18,19].

The results from their study suggest that some sort of hybrid architecture that combines zero-shot transfer with a gloss-level pivot approach may offer better outcomes if the focus is on translation fidelity across varying sign languages, particularly when designed for real-time and on-device inference. However, addressing low-latency still needs to be an important consideration and requires further exploration of simplified model architectures, as well as the methods for deploying models for on-device multilingual sign communication.

11.4.2 Zero-shot and few-shot learning for low-resource sign languages

One significant bottleneck for scaling sign language systems to underrepresented languages (e.g., Ghanaian sign language, Indigenous sign systems) is the lack of large-annotated datasets. A potential solution is to build on vision-language pre-training and contrastive learning frameworks, which would allow sign language models to generalize to never-before-seen signs without task-specific training.

An example of such a framework is SignCLIP [20], a contrastive learning model based on CLIP structured for sign language video data. SignCLIP was trained on Spreadthesign – a dictionary of $\sim$500,000 video-annotation pairs in 44 sign languages – and demonstrated strong text-to-video and video-to-text retrieval, as well as few-shot recognition capabilities over unseen signers and domains.

Importantly, vision-language models such as BLIP-2 [21] also demonstrated exceptional zero-shot cross-modal capabilities in image-text tasks and would provide a scalable embedding backbone to generate sign video embeddings.

Using the pre-trained embeddings in a contrastive learning framework, researchers demonstrated up to 76% top-5 retrieval accuracy for unseen glosses, an important benchmark for low-resource adaptation.

These models offer a pathway to few-shot adaptation across demographic groups and dialects, with minimal manual annotation labour. Future work should consider how visual pretraining could be combined with minimal-lived fine-tuning, dialect clustering, and meta-learning to improve generalization across distinct local signing populations.

11.4.3 Brain–computer interfaces for hands-free sign generation

BCIs represent a cutting-edge frontier for sign generation without physical gesture. EEG2TEXT [22], a model leveraging multi-view transformers and EEG pretraining to decode open-vocabulary text from EEG signals; it demonstrated a notable improvement of up to 5% points in BLEU and ROUGE scores compared to previous state-of-the-art baselines.

Complementing this work, CET-MAE [23] is a pre-trained contrastive EEG-text masked autoencoder paired with EEG-to-text decoding via BART. Their system, E2T-PTR, achieved 32% higher BLEU-4 and 8% higher ROUGE-1 scores on the ZuCo dataset.

These findings suggest that combining continuous neural decoding with gloss-level translation modules may yield hands-free sign synthesis. Nonetheless, developing practical BCI-to-sign pipelines necessitates careful attention to neuro-privacy, informed consent, and the interpretative authority of neural-generated content.

11.4.4   *Large-language-model-based sign understanding*

Efforts to leverage LLMs for gloss-free sign translation are gaining momentum. Sign2GPT [24], which aligns sign video representations with LLM embeddings using lightweight adapters. Evaluated on RWTH-PHOENIX-Weather 2014T and CSL-Daily, the model achieved stronger gloss-free translation performance, outperforming prior state-of-the-art methods.

Another notable method, SignLLM [25], utilizes vector-quantized visual tokens combined with optimal-transport alignment to bridge sign videos and LLM input. This approach demonstrated improved semantic alignment for gloss-free translation tasks. Scaling these embedding-based architectures will require new evaluation benchmarks, community-driven validation, and safeguards to ensure that the outputs reflect authentic sign-language content.

11.4.5   *Deployments for specific domains: smart cities,*
healthcare, and education

The deployment of sign language technologies in certain application domains is accelerating, especially in terms of human–machine interaction and accessibility.

A sign language translation system relevant from an accessibility and interfaces point of view is sign.mt: an offline capable, open-source spoken to sign language translation system that uses photorealistic avatars for spoken and signing outputs. As a result, users can easily conduct bidirectional communication in virtual, public contexts with low connectability. It was awarded the Outstanding Demo Paper Award at EMNLP 2024 for its deployability in low-resource contexts [26].

In classroom and clinical scenarios, multi-view gesture recognition systems are proving to be effective. A large-scale, multi-angle dataset is introduced [27] and demonstrated that models trained using ten synchronized camera views significantly outperformed those trained on single-view data – achieving up to 19.8% improvement in sign recognition accuracy, particularly for occluded and overlapping gestures.

There are some potential advantages of using on-device SL systems for consumer-facing deployments (e.g., interactive kiosks, home automation systems, learning platforms) with respect to latency, memory and bandwidth consumption, privacy, and autonomy (especially since these are public deployments with no edge dependency). For example, Google has SignGemma, a real-time low-latency ASL translation model for smartphones that minimizes memory and bandwidth usage with a focus on privacy and responsiveness [16].

SignEdgeLVM [28] enables the quantized low-rank adaptation for compressed sign language transformer models for real-time mobile inferences for (e.g., home or wearable) devices that produced a 99.2% parametric storage reduction per attention head without loss of accuracy.

Ultimately, both finding a domain where the sign language technology can have value to human–computer interactions and the specific tailoring (e.g., realism of actors, multi-view input fusion on camera inputs, or edge-dependant) of deployment will be necessary to ensure the usability and inclusion of sign language technologies in rich real-world environments.

11.4.6   Multimodal sign language generation with emotion and context awareness

Natural sign language is inherently multimodal, combining manual signs with facial expressions, head movements, and gaze to convey emotional and grammatical cues. Most current models overlook these non-manual signals, limiting expressiveness and naturalness in generated outputs.

Recent approaches integrate sentiment and semantic features into facial synthesis, achieving improved expressivity and evaluation metrics such as Frechet expression distance [29]. Morph-target-based facial pipelines aligned with linguistic formalisms (e.g., AZee) have enhanced synchronization between facial and manual components [30]. Broader reviews emphasize the need for culturally accurate affective modeling and ethical safeguards [31].

Future research should focus on multimodal transformers that jointly model gloss, punctuation, and emotional signals, as well as synchronized generation of pose and facial dynamics for realistic avatar rendering.

11.4.7   Federated and privacy-preserving learning for sign data

Sign language datasets often contain sensitive visual information, including facial features and body movement, making privacy a key concern – especially in domains like healthcare and education. Traditional centralized training exposes users to potential data misuse.

Recent methods employ federated learning to train gesture recognition models across edge devices without transmitting raw videos, mitigating privacy risks while maintaining accuracy [32,33]. Complementary techniques using differential privacy – such as noise injection during model updates – have shown minimal performance trade-offs on sign datasets [34].

Emerging directions include signer-personalized federated updates, encrypted inference using homomorphic encryption, and consent-aware protocols that log and restrict data access based on user preferences.

11.4.8   Ethical and interdisciplinary considerations

As sign language systems make strides toward real-world applications, ethically embedding principles and responsibilities are crucial. Performing well is one thing, but there are deeper engagements these systems have with linguistic identity, cultural expression, and personal privacy, which need robust ethical considerations beyond technical performance.

(a) **Neuroprivacy and informed consent**
   BCIs and systems that capture facial expression render sensitive biometric data [35]. Ethical scholarship has made clear that privacy is an ethical concern, and we are often reminded of the importance of informed consent, especially in cases where a user may find themselves in a vulnerable state (for instance, locked-in syndrome). It is especially essential to have a clear outlining for neuroprivacy practices, and through the lens of ethics we should include a feedback loop on ongoing consent, data ownership, and securely storing private data in relation to BCIs. The processes we use to verify consent and understand user autonomy must be upheld in the neuroethics space.

(b) **Representation and fairness**
   To address demographic bias and ensure equitable sign systems, recent studies have leveraged demographic metadata in ASL datasets, revealing performance disparities across gender, age, and signing fluency. They successfully reduced such disparities through data re-sampling and bias mitigation techniques [5,6,36].

(c) **Community engagement**
   Ethically deploying a system requires co-design with Deaf communities and signing communities where cultural perspective represented is evident within all parts of the design process from the dataset to the model evaluation to interface design. Multidisciplinary partnerships with technologists, linguists, and Deaf-centered scholars serve to create systems that are authentic and have cultural fidelity [11].

(d) **Sustainability and access**
   From an ethical perspective, sustainability [37] needs to be incorporated into the framework using energy-efficient architecture and edge deployment models within specific contexts, such as socially vulnerable communities. Bringing together federated learning with devices equipped with on-device inference can be valuable in reducing energy consumption while continuing to support privacy.

11.5   Summary

This chapter explored the ethical imperatives and future pathways shaping sign language systems. We emphasized that fairness, privacy, and inclusivity are not optional add-ons but foundational to building trustworthy communication tools. Ethical considerations such as neuroprivacy, dialectal representation, and community-led design must guide system development – especially as we integrate advanced modalities like emotion-aware generation, BCIs, and cross-lingual sign translation.

Looking forward, promising research avenues include few-shot learning for under-resourced sign languages, multimodal fusion with speech and emotion cues, federated learning for privacy-aware training, and scalable deployment in education, healthcare, and smart cities. The field is moving toward holistic, culturally grounded, and human-aligned sign language systems – demanding not only technical innovation but also interdisciplinary stewardship.

Exercises

(I) **Multiple choice questions**

1. Which research area focuses on adapting models for low-resource sign languages without large annotated datasets?
    (a) Brain–computer interfaces
    (b) Zero-shot and few-shot learning
    (c) Domain-specific deployment
    (d) Multimodal sign generation

2. What does the term "neuroprivacy" relate to in the context of sign language systems?
    (a) Data storage format
    (b) Facial landmark detection
    (c) Ethical handling of brain-signal data
    (d) Training of gloss models

3. Which system enables real-time low-latency ASL translation on smartphones?
    (a) SignLLM
    (b) SignGemma
    (c) SignCLIP
    (d) Sign2GPT

4. What type of architecture is Sign2GPT based on?
    (a) Visual-only CNN
    (b) BERT transformer
    (c) LLM embedding alignment
    (d) Homomorphic encryption

5. Which ethical factor emphasizes community participation in the design of sign language systems?
    (a) Federated adaptation
    (b) Community engagement
    (c) Low-rank quantization
    (d) Zero-shot glossing

(II)   **Short answer questions**
1.   What is the advantage of using multimodal generation in sign language avatars?
2.   Why is federated learning important in sign language applications?
3.   How do brain–computer interfaces contribute to sign generation?

(III)   **Discussion questions**
1.   What are the ethical concerns related to synthesizing sign language using avatars and deep learning techniques?
2.   Discuss the limitations of current evaluation metrics in capturing the linguistic accuracy of sign language generation.
3.   How can models be adapted for low-resource sign languages while maintaining output quality?

(IV)   **Practical / Hands-on exercises**
1.   Train a SignCLIP-based contrastive model on a small-scale custom dataset and test its retrieval accuracy.
2.   Simulate a federated learning setup using at least three edge devices with privacy constraints on sign gesture data.
3.   Build a gloss-to-sign avatar using MediaPipe pose landmarks and generate signs for ten predefined glosses.

References

[1]   Mitchell, M., Wu, S., Zaldivar, A., *et al.* (2019). Model cards for model reporting. *In Proceedings of the Conference on Fairness, Accountability, and Transparency* (pp. 220–229). ACM. https://doi.org/10.1145/3287560.3287596.

[2]   Cannarsa, M. (2021). Ethics guidelines for trustworthy AI. In DiMatteo, L., Greenstein, A. H., and Poncibò, C., (eds.). *The Cambridge Handbook of Lawyering in the Digital Age Part V: Legal Ethics and Societal Values Confront Technology*, Cambridge University Press, 283–297 https://doi.org/10.1017/9781108939901.023.

[3]   James Manyika, and Demis Hassabis. (2025). *Responsible AI: Our 2024 Report and Ongoing Work. Google Research.* https://blog.google/technology/ai/responsible-ai-2024-report-ongoing-work/.

[4]   Cook, J., and Tumer, K. (2022). Fitness shaping for multiple teams. In *Proceedings of the Genetic and Evolutionary Computation Conference* (pp. 332–340). ACM. https://doi.org/10.1145/3512290.3528829.

[5]   Desai, A., De Meulder, M., Hochgesang, J. A., Kocab, A., and Lu, A. X. (2024). Systemic biases in sign language AI research: a deaf-led call to reevaluate research agendas. *arXiv preprint arXiv:2403.02563.* https://arxiv.org/abs/2403.02563.

[6] Atwell, K., Bragg, D., and Alikhani, M. (2024). Studying and mitigating biases in sign language understanding models. *arXiv preprint arXiv:2410. 05206*. https://arxiv.org/abs/2410.05206.

[7] Rust, P., Shi, B., Wang, S., Camgöz, N. C., and Maillard, J. (2024). Towards privacy-aware sign language translation at scale. *arXiv preprint arXiv:2402. 09611*. https://arxiv.org/abs/2402.09611.

[8] Bragg, D., Koller, O., Caselli, N., and Thies, W. (2020). Exploring collection of sign language datasets: privacy, participation, and model performance. In *Proceedings of the 22nd International ACM SIGACCESS Conference on Computers and Accessibility* (pp. 1–14).https://doi.org/10.1145/3373625. 3417024.

[9] Duarte, A., Palaskar, S., Ventura, L., *et al.* (2021). How2sign: a large-scale multimodal dataset for continuous American sign language. In *Proceedings of the IEEE/CVF Conference on Computer Vision and Pattern Recognition* (pp. 2735–2744). IEEE.

[10] Gebru, T., Morgenstern, J., Vecchione, B., *et al.* (2021). Datasheets for datasets. *Communications of the ACM*, *64*(12), 86–92.

[11] De Meulder, M., Van Landuyt, D., and Omardeen, R. (2024). Lessons in co-creation: the inconvenient truths of inclusive sign language technology development. *arXiv preprint arXiv:2408.13171*. https://arxiv.org/abs/2408. 13171.

[12] O'Boyle, S., Mathews, E., Brosens, C., *et al.* (2024). A deaf-centred art-science approach to community engagement with sign language technologies. *Journal of Science Communication*, *23*(5), N04.

[13] Li, Y. (2025). Design an editable speech-to-sign-language transformer system: a human-centered AI approach. *arXiv preprint arXiv:2506.14677*. https://www.arxiv.org/abs/2506.14677.

[14] De Meulder, M. (2025). Deaf in AI: AI language technologies and the erosion of linguistic rights. *arXiv preprint arXiv:2505.02519*. https://arxiv.org/ abs/2505.02519.

[15] Marcolino, M. S., Oliveira, L. F. R., Valle, L. R., *et al.* (2025). Sign Language recognition system for deaf patients: protocol for a systematic review. *JMIR Research Protocols*, *14*(1), e55427.

[16] Multilingual. (2025). *Google Unveils On-Device Sign Language Model for Translators and LSPs*. Retrieved from https://multilingual.com/google-sign-gemma-on-device-asl-translation.

[17] Ebrahimi, A., and Wense, K. (2024). Zero-shot vs. translation-based cross-lingual transfer: the case of lexical gaps. In *Proceedings of the 2024 Conference of the North American Chapter of the Association for Computational Linguistics: Human Language Technologies* (*Volume 2: Short Papers*) (pp. 443–458).

[18] Cheng, X., Zhu, Z., Yang, B., Zhuang, X., Li, H., and Zou, Y. (2024). Cyclical contrastive learning based on geodesic for zero-shot cross-lingual spoken language understanding. *In Findings of the Association for Computational Linguistics ACL 2024* (pp. 1806–1816).

[19]   Zhang, B., Tanzer, G., and Firat, O. (2024). Scaling sign language transla-
        tion. *arXiv preprint arXiv:2407.11855.* https://arxiv.org/abs/2407.11855.

[20]   Jiang, Z., Sant, G., Moryossef, A., Müller, M., Sennrich, R., and Ebling, S.
        (2024). SignCLIP: connecting text and sign language by contrastive learning.
        In EMNLP 2024 (Main), pp. 9171–9193. *arXiv preprint arXiv:2407.01264.*
        https://aclanthology.org/2024.emnlp-main.518/.

[21]   Li, J., Li, D., Savarese, S., and Hoi, S. (2023). Blip-2: bootstrapping
        language-image pre-training with frozen image encoders and large language
        models. In *International Conference on Machine Learning* (pp. 19730–
        19742). PMLR.

[22]   Liu, H., Hajialigol, D., Antony, B., Han, A., and Wang, X. (2024). EEG2-
        TEXT: open vocabulary EEG-to-text decoding with EEG pre-training and
        multi-view transformer. *arXiv preprint arXiv:2405.02165.* https://arxiv.org/
        abs/2405.04164.

[23]   Wang, J., Song, Z., Ma, Z., Qiu, X., Zhang, M., and Zhang, Z. (2024).
        Enhancing EEG-to-text decoding through transferable representations from
        pre-trained contrastive EEG-text masked autoencoder. In ACL 2024 (Long
        Papers), pp. 7278–7292. https://doi.org/10.18653/v1/2024.acl-long.393.

[24]   Wong, R., Camgoz, N. C., and Bowden, R. (2024). Sign2GPT: leveraging
        large language models for gloss-free sign language translation. *arXiv pre-
        print arXiv:2405.04164.* https://arxiv.org/abs/2402.17433.

[25]   Gong, J., Foo, L. G., He, Y., Rahmani, H., and Liu, J. (2024). LLMs are good
        sign language translators. In *Proceedings of the IEEE/CVF Conference on
        Computer Vision and Pattern Recognition* (pp. 18362–18372).

[26]   Moryossef, A. (2023). sign.mt: real-time multilingual sign language trans-
        lation application. *arXiv preprint arXiv:2310.05064.* https://arxiv.org/abs/
        2310.05064.

[27]   Dinh, N. S., Nguyen, T. D., Tran, D. T., *et al.* (2025). Sign language
        recognition: a large-scale multi-view dataset and comprehensive evaluation.
        In *2025 IEEE/CVF Winter Conference on Applications of Computer Vision
        (WACV)* (pp. 7887–7897). IEEE.

[28]   Damdoo, R., and Kumar, P. (2025). SignEdgeLVM transformer model for
        enhanced sign language translation on edge devices. *Discover Computing, 28*
        (1), 15.

[29]   Azevedo, R. V., Coutinho, T. M., Ferreira, J. P., Gomes, T. L., and
        Nascimento, E. R. (2024). Empowering sign language communication:
        integrating sentiment and semantics for facial expression synthesis. *Compu-
        ters & Graphics, 124,* 104065.

[30]   Sharma, P., Challant, C., and Filhol, M. (2024). Facial expressions for sign
        language synthesis using FACSHuman and AZee. In *11th Workshop on the
        Representation and Processing of Sign Languages: Evaluation of Sign Lan-
        guage Resources.*

[31]   Wang, Y., Yan, S., Liu, Y., *et al.* (2024). A Survey on facial expression
        recognition of static and dynamic emotions. *arXiv preprint arXiv:2408.
        15777.* https://arxiv.org/abs/2408.15777.

[32] Maragatham, R. S., Baker El-Ebiary, Y. A., Sridharan, K., Rao, V. S., and Godla, S. R. (2024). Enhancing HCI through real-time gesture recognition with federated CNNs: improving performance and responsiveness. *International Journal of Advanced Computer Science & Applications*, *15*(4), 859–867.

[33] Diba, B. S., Plabon, J. D., Rahman, M. M., Mistry, D., Saha, A. K., and Mridha, M. F. (2024). Explainable federated learning for privacy-preserving Bangla sign language detection. *Engineering Applications of Artificial Intelligence*, *134*, 108657.

[34] Alzu'bi, A., Al-Hadhrami, T., Albashayreh, A., and Younis, L. B. (2025). A federated learning-based virtual interpreter for Arabic sign language recognition in smart cities. *Nafath*, *10*(28), 1–10.

[35] Livanis, E., Voultsos, P., Vadikolias, K., Pantazakos, P., Tsaroucha, A., and Tsaroucha, A. (2024). Understanding the ethical issues of brain-computer interfaces (BCIs): a blessing or the beginning of a dystopian future? *Cureus*, *16*(4), e57757. https://www.cureus.com/articles/232122-understanding-the-ethical-issues-of-brain-computer-interfaces-bcis-a-blessing-or-the-beginning-of-a-dystopian-future.

[36] Li, Y., Wang, H., Hossain, E., *et al.* (2025). Leveraging usefulness and autonomy: designing AI-mediated ASL communication between hearing parents and deaf children. *In Proceedings of the 24th Interaction Design and Children* (pp. 512–526).

[37] Iacob, A., Gusmão, P. P., Lane, N. D., *et al.* (2023). Privacy in multimodal federated human activity recognition. *arXiv preprint arXiv:2305.12134*.

Appendix A

Chapter-wise supplementary code listings and implementation guide

This supplementary material accompanies the book **"Generative AI for Sign Language Translation"** and provides **chapter-wise code implementations**, detailed explanations, and corresponding GitHub repository links.

Each chapter focuses on key techniques and datasets related to generative AI applications in sign language research, with step-by-step Python code snippets and placeholders for result visualizations (e.g., plots, heatmaps, outputs).

🗀 **Complete Code Repository**: https://github.com/Elakkiya16/IETGenAI-SLT

Chapter 3: Sign language datasets

GitHub Folder: https://github.com/Elakkiya16/IETGenAI-SLT/tree/main/Chapter%203
  Sections:

(a) 3.1 Dataset preprocessing and gloss analysis
(b) 3.2 Video augmentation demo
(c) 3.3 Keypoint extraction using MediaPipe
(d) 3.4 Signer style analysis
(e) 3.5 Gloss noise flagging

Chapter 4: Generative AI techniques for SLT

GitHub Folder: https://github.com/Elakkiya16/IETGenAI-SLT/tree/main/Chapter%204
  Sections:

(a) 4.1 Data preprocessing pipelines
(b) 4.2 Transformer-based sentence embeddings
(c) 4.3 Synonym replacement for augmentation
(d) 4.4 Back-translation
(e) 4.5 Embedding visualization using t-SNE and PCA
(f) 4.6 Text-to-gloss generation using Flan-T5

Chapter 5: Speech-to-sign language translation

GitHub Folder: https://github.com/Elakkiya16/IETGenAI-SLT/tree/main/Chapter
%205
Sections:

(a) 5.1 Speech-to-text transcription using Whisper
(b) 5.2 Text-to-gloss generation using few-shot prompting
(c) 5.3 T5 Fine-tuned gloss generation
(d) 5.4 Gloss evaluation using BLEU, WER, ROUGE

Chapter 6: Generative architectures and evaluation extensions for SLT

GitHub Folder: https://github.com/Elakkiya16/IETGenAI-SLT/tree/main/Chapter
%206
Sections:

(a) 6.1 Transformer variants comparison and embedding visualization
(b) 6.2 Simulated diffusion-based denoising on sign keypoints
(c) 6.3 Multimodal prompting with BLIP-2 on sign frames
(d) 6.4 Model comparison dashboard and visual analysis

Chapter 7: Vision-based sign recognition and pose-based modeling

GitHub Folder: https://github.com/Elakkiya16/IETGenAI-SLT/tree/main/Chapter
%207
Sections:

(a) 7.1 Visualization of 2D and 3D skeletal poses
(b) 7.2 Pose-based temporal encoders (GCN, TCN, transformer)
(c) 7.3 Advanced temporal models with evaluation (LSTM, TCN, transformer)
(d) 7.4 Pose denoising and visualization

Chapter 8: Sign language generation and video synthesis

GitHub Folder: https://github.com/Elakkiya16/IETGenAI-SLT/tree/main/Chapter
%208
Sections:

(a) 8.1 Video synthesis from pose/gloss frames
(b) 8.2 Pose-based video synthesis from keypoints

Chapter 3: Sign language datasets

This section provides the complete supplementary code and explanations for Chapter 4, which emphasizes preprocessing, keypoint extraction, and signer motion analysis using the ISL_CLSRT dataset and a few selected videos. Each notebook demonstrates foundational components necessary for generative model readiness.

All code notebooks and relevant files are hosted at:

🗁 **Chapter 3 GitHub Folder:** https://github.com/Elakkiya16/IETGenAI-SLT/tree/main/Chapter%203

(a) **Dataset preprocessing and gloss analysis**

This notebook performs thorough preprocessing on the ISL_CLSRT metadata. It removes duplicates, handles missing values, computes gloss and sentence lengths, and visualizes distributions. It also analyzes signer-level variation in sentence and gloss lengths, extracts the full gloss vocabulary, exports it to a text file, and prints a few random sentence–gloss pairs to evaluate alignment. Additional plots include sentence vs. gloss length scatter, gloss distribution by signer, and top gloss frequencies.

Notebook Link: 3.4_preprocessing_enhanced.ipynb

Code Snippet:

```python
# Clean data and compute basic lengths
df = df.drop_duplicates().dropna(subset=['Sentences',
'gloss_sequence']).reset_index(drop=True)
df['sentence_len'] = df['Sentences'].apply(lambda x: len(str(x).split()))
df['gloss_len'] = df['gloss_sequence'].apply(lambda x: len(str(x).split()))

# Gloss vocabulary extraction and export
all_glosses = ' '.join(df['gloss_sequence'].dropna()).split()
vocab = Counter(all_glosses)
with open('gloss_vocab.txt', 'w') as f:
    for token in sorted(vocab):
        f.write(f"{token}\n")

# Sentence-gloss sample preview
sample = df.sample(5, random_state=42)
for _, row in sample.iterrows():
    print(f"Sentence: {row['Sentences']}\nGloss: {row['gloss_sequence']}\n---
")

# Scatter and box plots
sns.scatterplot(x='sentence_len', y='gloss_len', data=df)
sns.boxplot(x='signer_id', y='gloss_len', data=df)

# Top 20 glosses
common_glosses = vocab.most_common(20)
glosses, counts = zip(*common_glosses)
sns.barplot(x=list(counts), y=list(glosses))
```

Sample Outputs:

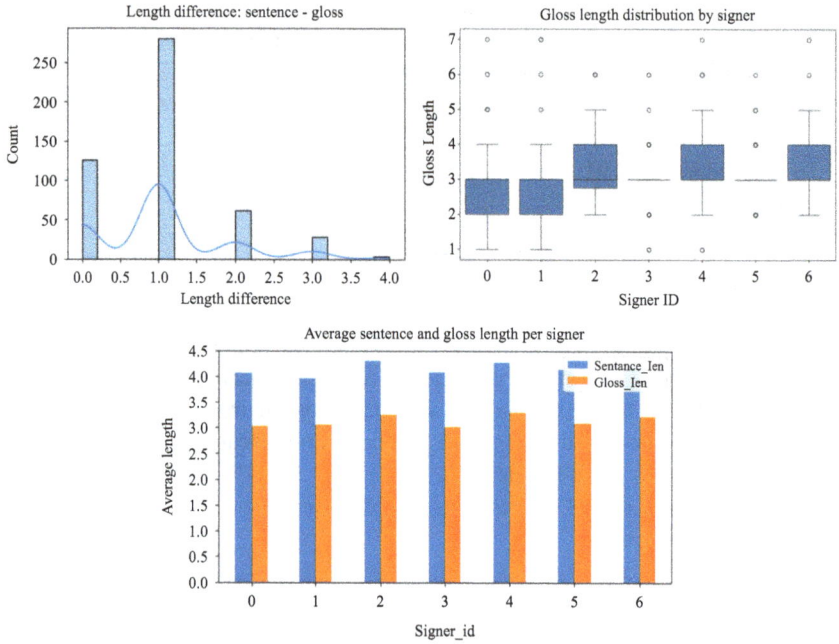

(b) **Video augmentation demo**

This notebook demonstrates frame-level data augmentation on sign language videos using OpenCV. It includes horizontal flipping, center cropping, frame skipping, and upper-body cropping to simulate signer variation and spatial shift, making training data more robust.

    Notebook Link: 3.5_video_augmentation_demo.ipynb

    Code Snippet:

```python
# Load and flip frame
frame = cv2.flip(frame, 1)

# Skip and extract middle frame
cap.set(cv2.CAP_PROP_POS_FRAMES, 10)
ret, frame = cap.read()

# Apply center and upper-body crop
def center_crop(frame, crop_size=(200, 200)):
    h, w = frame.shape[:2]; ch, cw = crop_size
    return frame[h//2-ch//2:h//2+ch//2, w//2-cw//2:w//2+cw//2]

def upper_body_crop(frame, ratio=0.6):
    h = int(frame.shape[0] * ratio)
    return frame[:h, :]
```

Sample Outputs:

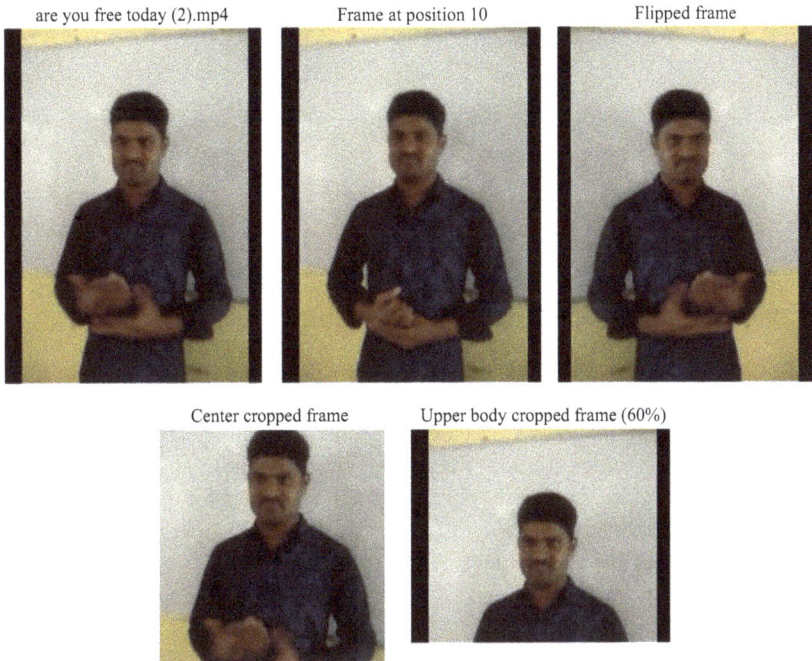

are you free today (2).mp4   Frame at position 10   Flipped frame

Center cropped frame   Upper body cropped frame (60%)

(c) **Keypoint extraction using MediaPipe**
This notebook uses MediaPipe Holistic to extract pose, left/right hand, and partial face keypoints from sign videos. It saves all keypoints frame-wise as . npy arrays for future gesture modeling. Additionally, one frame per video is overlaid with landmarks for qualitative validation.
  Notebook Link: 3.6_keypoint_extraction_mediapipe.ipynb
  Code Snippet:

```python
# Landmark extraction loop (pose, hands, face)
row = []

if results.pose_landmarks:
    for lm in results.pose_landmarks.landmark:
        row.extend([lm.x, lm.y, lm.z, lm.visibility])
else:
    row.extend([0]*132)
...
# Save each keypoint array
np.save(f"{video_name}_keypoints.npy", np.array(keypoint_data))

# Visualize one frame
mp_drawing.draw_landmarks(annotated, results.pose_landmarks,
mp_holistic.POSE_CONNECTIONS)
```

Sample Outputs:

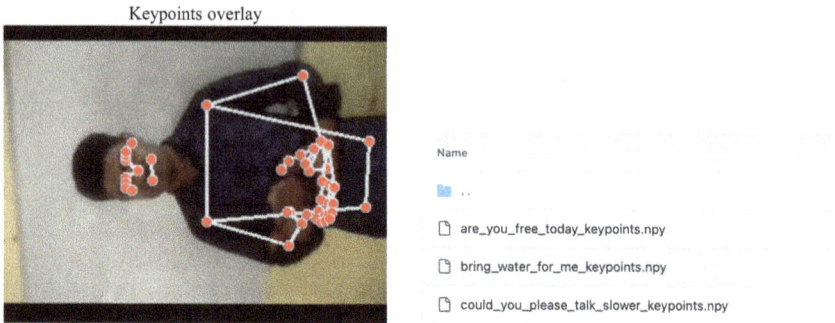

Keypoints overlay

(d) **Signer style analysis**

This notebook analyzes extracted keypoints to quantify signer-specific styles. It computes average motion, range, and speed for pose and hand parts. It also tracks wrist/index landmark trajectories across frames for qualitative inspection of gesture fluidity.

Notebook Link: 3.7_signer_style_analysis.ipynb

Code Snippet:

```python
# Compute motion between frames
def compute_motion(arr, part):
    start, end = get_part_range(part)
    return np.mean([np.linalg.norm(arr[i, start:end] - arr[i-1, start:end])
for i in range(1, len(arr))])

# Range and speed calculations
def calculate_range(arr, part):
    start, end = get_part_range(part)
    return np.max(arr[:, start:end]) - np.min(arr[:, start:end])

# Track trajectory of wrists/index tip
trajectory = keypoints_array[:, index:index+3]   # (x, y, z)
```

Sample Outputs:

Motion Magnitude Summary:

	video	pose_motion	left_hand_motion	right_hand_motion
0	are_you_free_today	0.013843	0.054376	0.161078
1	bring_water_for_me	0.024398	0.000000	0.119285
2	could_you_please_talk_slower	0.038955	0.204063	0.318941

Range of Motion Summary:

	video	pose_range	left_hand_range	right_hand_range
0	are_you_free_today	2.919573	0.992430	0.930633
1	bring_water_for_me	2.911127	0.000000	1.062696
2	could_you_please_talk_slower	3.032146	1.031865	0.987863

Speed of Motion Summary:

	video	pose_speed	left_hand_speed	right_hand_speed
0	are_you_free_today	0.013843	0.054376	0.161078
1	bring_water_for_me	0.024398	0.000000	0.119285
2	could_you_please_talk_slower	0.038955	0.204063	0.318941

Plotting trajectories for video: are_you_free_today

Landmark trajectories (Y vs X) for Video: 'are_you_free_today'

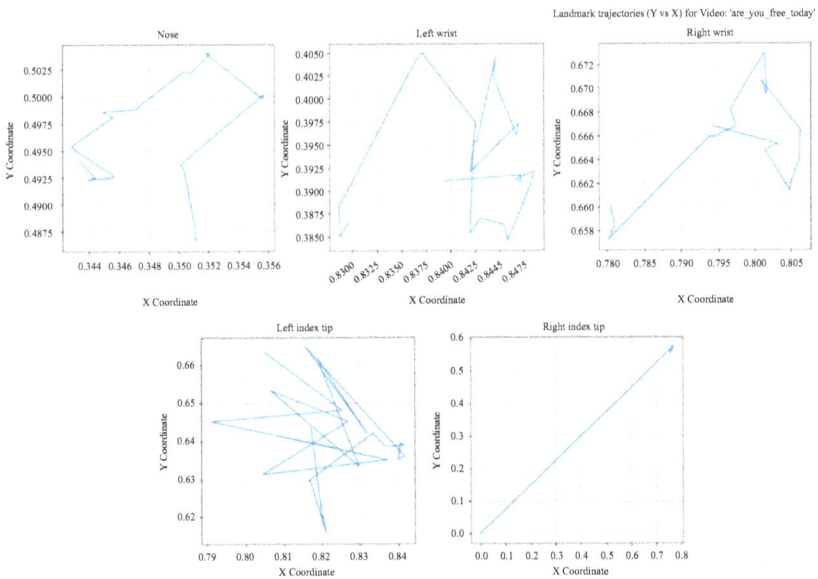

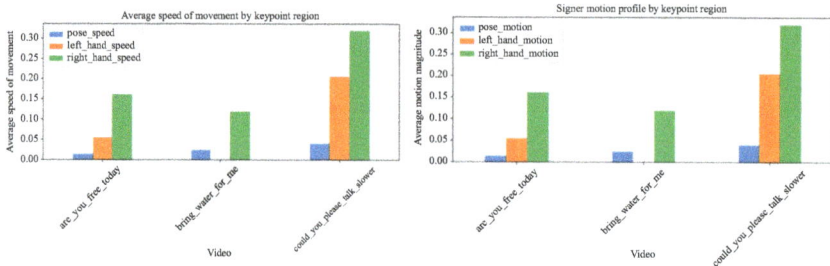

(e) **Gloss noise flagging**

This notebook performs gloss quality control using multiple heuristics—rare token count, sentence–gloss length mismatch, and keyword alignment issues. It visualizes their distribution and saves flagged entries for review.

Notebook Link: 3.8_gloss_noise_flagging.ipynb
Code Snippet:

```python
# Rare token detection
freq = Counter(' '.join(df['gloss_sequence']).split())
rare = {k for k, v in freq.items() if v == 1}
df['has_rare_token'] = df['gloss_sequence'].apply(lambda g: any(w in rare for
w in str(g).split()))

# Keyword mismatch flag
stop_words = {...}  # Large list omitted
df['keyword_mismatch'] = df.apply(lambda row:
check_keyword_mismatch(row['Sentences'], row['gloss_sequence']), axis=1)

# Visualization and export
plt.hist(df['length_diff'], bins=20)
df.to_csv('flagged_gloss_samples_updated.csv')
```

Sample Outputs:

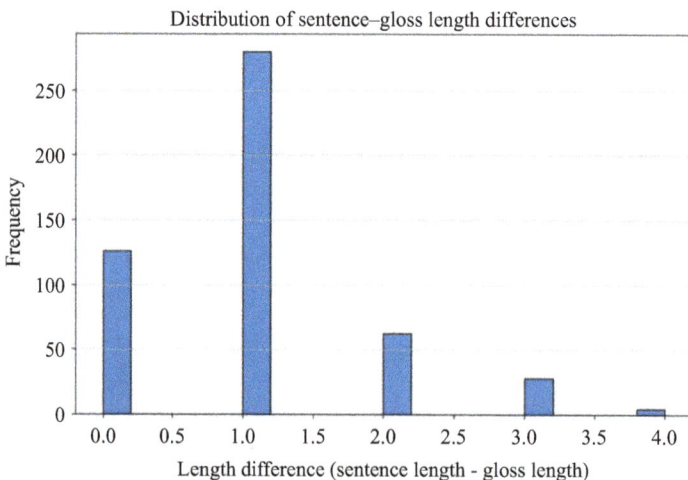

Distribution of samples with rare gloss tokens

Distribution of samples with large length mismatches

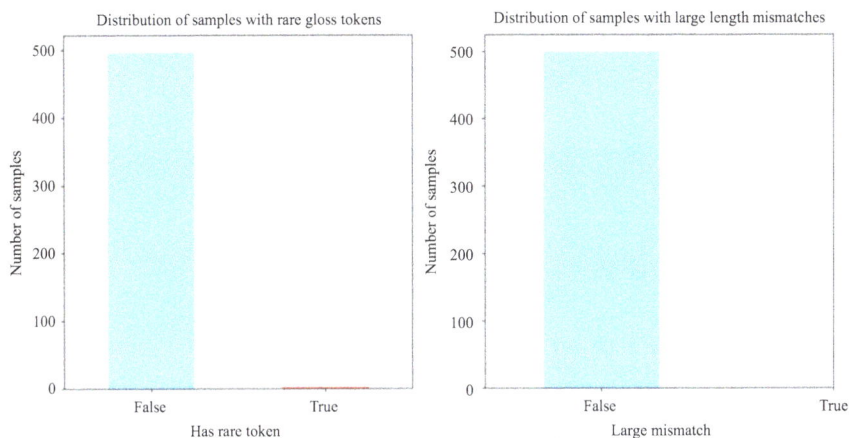

Chapter 4: Generative AI techniques for sign language translation

Overview

This section provides the complete supplementary code and explanations for Chapter 4, which focuses on applying Generative AI methods for text preprocessing, embedding generation, data augmentation, translation, and sequence generation in sign language translation (SLT).

The code covers essential generative techniques such as:

- Data preprocessing pipelines
- Transformer-based sentence embeddings
- Augmentation via synonym replacement
- Back-translation
- Embedding visualization using t-SNE and PCA
- Text-to-gloss generation using Flan-T5 (zero-shot prompting)

⬜ **Chapter 4 GitHub Folder:** https://github.com/Elakkiya16/IETGenAI-SLT/tree/main/Chapter%204

(a) **Data preprocessing pipelines**

This This notebook demonstrates preprocessing of raw sentences from ISL_CLSRT, including lowercasing, punctuation removal, optional stopword removal, and conversion to gloss-style uppercase sequences. These text cleaning steps are crucial for reducing noise and ensuring consistent input quality before applying downstream generative AI techniques such as embedding generation or sequence generation.

Notebook Link: 1_text_cleaning_isl_clsrt.ipynb

Code Snippet:

```python
import re
import nltk
from nltk.corpus import stopwords

nltk.download('stopwords')
stop_words = set(stopwords.words('english'))

def clean_text(sentence, remove_stopwords=True):
    sentence = sentence.lower()
    sentence = re.sub(r'[^\w\s]', '', sentence)
    sentence = re.sub(r'\s+', ' ', sentence).strip()
    tokens = sentence.split()
    if remove_stopwords:
        tokens = [word for word in tokens if word not in stop_words]
    gloss = ' '.join(tokens).upper()
    return gloss
```

Output:

Out [ ]:		Sentences	cleaned_gloss
	0	it does not make any difference to me	MAKE DIFFERENCE
	1	tell me truth	TELL TRUTH
	2	do me a favour	FAVOUR
	3	do not worry	WORRY
	4	do not abuse him	ABUSE

(b) **Transformer-based sentence embeddings**
This notebook demonstrates how to compute sentence embeddings using a pre-trained MiniLM model. It evaluates semantic similarity between cleaned gloss sentences via cosine similarity and visualizes them using heatmaps. This embedding-based similarity analysis is useful for analyzing gloss redundancy and aligning textual inputs in SLT systems.
   Notebook Link: 2_embedding_similarity_isl_clsrt.ipynb
   Code Snippet:

```python
from sentence_transformers import SentenceTransformer
from sklearn.metrics.pairwise import cosine_similarity

model = SentenceTransformer('sentence-transformers/all-MiniLM-L6-v2')
embeddings = model.encode(df['cleaned_gloss'].dropna().tolist())
similarity_matrix = cosine_similarity(embeddings)
```

Output:

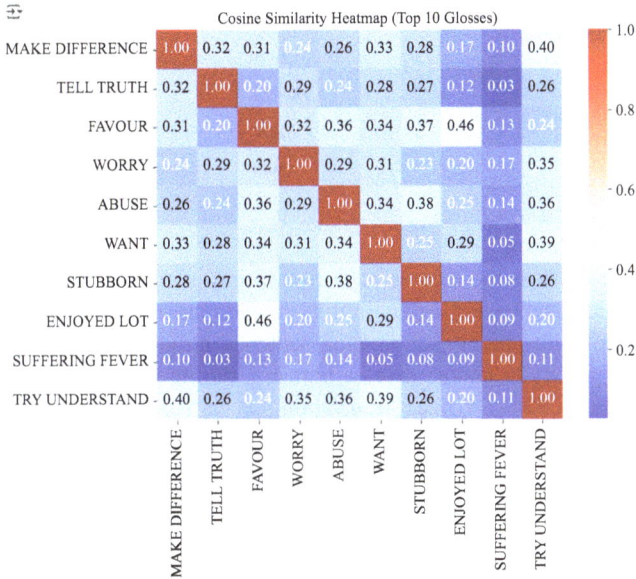

Cosine Similarity Heatmap (Top 10 Glosses)

(c) **Augmentation via synonym replacement and back-translation**

This notebook demonstrates data augmentation by performing synonym replacement using WordNet. This augmentation strategy increases the diversity of gloss representations, making generative models more robust to linguistic variations during training.

Notebook Link: 3_synonym_replacement_isl_clsrt.ipynb

Code Snippet:

```python
from nltk.corpus import wordnet as wn
from itertools import chain

def synonym_replacement(sentence, replacement_prob=0.3):
    tokens = sentence.split()
    new_tokens = []
    for word in tokens:
        if random.uniform(0, 1) < replacement_prob:
            synonyms = wn.synsets(word.lower())
            lemmas = set(chain.from_iterable([syn.lemma_names() for syn in
synonyms]))
            lemmas = [lemma.upper() for lemma in lemmas if lemma.upper() !=
word]
            if lemmas:
                word = random.choice(lemmas)
        new_tokens.append(word)
    return ' '.join(new_tokens)
```

Output:

Out [ ]:	cleaned_gloss	augmented_gloss
0	MAKE DIFFERENCE	MAKE DIVERGENCE
1	TELL TRUTH	TELL TRUTH
2	FAVOUR	FAVOUR
3	WORRY	WORRY
4	ABUSE	ABUSE

(d) **Back translation**

This notebook demonstrates back-translation using MarianMT models, translating gloss sentences from English to German and back to English. Back-translation introduces paraphrased sentence structures, enhancing generative models' ability to handle diverse phrasing during training and evaluation.

Notebook Link: 4_back_translation_isl_clsrt.ipynb

Code Snippet:

```python
from transformers import MarianMTModel, MarianTokenizer

src_model = MarianMTModel.from_pretrained('Helsinki-NLP/opus-mt-en-de')
src_tokenizer = MarianTokenizer.from_pretrained('Helsinki-NLP/opus-mt-en-de')
tgt_model = MarianMTModel.from_pretrained('Helsinki-NLP/opus-mt-de-en')
tgt_tokenizer = MarianTokenizer.from_pretrained('Helsinki-NLP/opus-mt-de-en')

def translate(text, tokenizer, model):
    inputs = tokenizer(text, return_tensors="pt")
    output = model.generate(**inputs)
    return tokenizer.decode(output[0], skip_special_tokens=True)
```

Output:

	cleaned_gloss	german	back_translated
361	GOOD	WAHRSCHEINLICHKEIT	LIKELIHOOD
73	NICE CHATTING	NICE CHATING	NICE CHATING
374	GOT HURT	GUT HURT	GOOD CURRENCY
155		Der Präsident	The President
104	CAME TRAIN	KAME TRAIN	KAME TRAIN
394	NEED MEDICINE TAKE ONE	NOTWENDIGES MEDIZIN ERWACHET	NEEDED MEDICALLY AWAKES
377	SPEAK SOFTLY	SPRACHEN SOFTLICH	LANGUAGES SOFTLY
124	CAME TRAIN	KAME TRAIN	KAME TRAIN
68		Der Präsident	The President
450	CAME TRAIN	KAME TRAIN	KAME TRAIN

(e) **Embedding visualization (PCA, t-SNE)**

This notebook applies dimensionality reduction techniques (PCA and t-SNE) on gloss sentence embeddings to visualize the underlying semantic distribution. These visualization techniques help qualitatively assess the separability and clustering tendencies in generative model embeddings.

Notebook Link: 5_tsne_pca_visualization_isl_clsrt.ipynb

Code Snippet:

```python
from sklearn.decomposition import PCA
from sklearn.manifold import TSNE

pca_result = PCA(n_components=2).fit_transform(embeddings)
tsne_result = TSNE(n_components=2).fit_transform(embeddings)
```

Output:

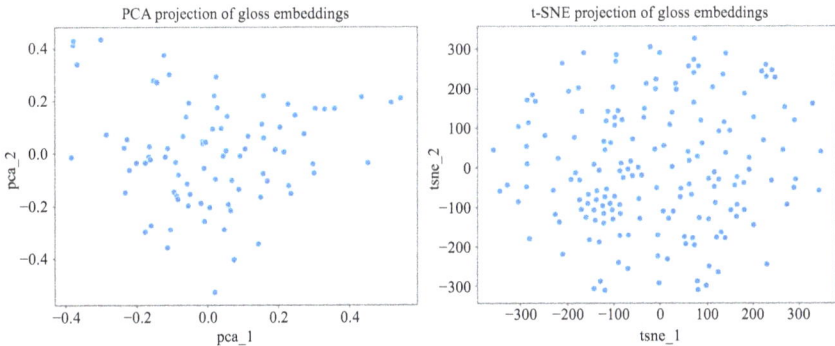

(f) **Text-to-gloss generation using Flan-T5**

This notebook demonstrates zero-shot text-to-gloss generation using Flan-T5 models via instruction prompting. This approach uses generative transformers to directly produce gloss sentences from input text, showcasing the effectiveness of instruction-tuned large language models for SLT tasks.

Notebook Link: 6_text_to_gloss_generation_isl_clsrt.ipynb

Code Snippet:

```python
from transformers import AutoTokenizer, AutoModelForSeq2SeqLM

model = AutoModelForSeq2SeqLM.from_pretrained('google/flan-t5-small')
tokenizer = AutoTokenizer.from_pretrained('google/flan-t5-small')

def generate_gloss(sentence):
    prompt = f"Convert the sentence to sign language gloss: {sentence}"
    inputs = tokenizer(prompt, return_tensors="pt")
    output = model.generate(**inputs, max_length=30)
    return tokenizer.decode(output[0], skip_special_tokens=True)
```

Output:

Out [6]:		Sentences	cleaned_gloss	generated_gloss
	361	you are good	GOOD	you are good
	73	it was nice chatting with you	NICE CHATTING	it was nice chatting with you
	374	i got hurt	GOT HURT	i got hurt
	155	you can do it	NaN	you can do it
	104	he came by train	CAME TRAIN	he came by train
	394	you need a medicine, take this one	NEED MEDICINE TAKE ONE	you need a medicine, take this one
	377	speak softly	SPEAK SOFTLY	speak softly
	124	he came by train	CAME TRAIN	he came by train
	68	we are all with you	NaN	we are all with you
	450	he came by train	CAME TRAIN	he came by train

Chapter 5: Speech-to-sign language translation

This section provides supplementary material includes code, detailed explanations, and Notebook Links for Chapter 5 of the book "Generative AI for Sign Language Translation." This chapter explores **speech-to-text transcription**, **text-to-gloss generation**, and **gloss-level evaluation**. The focus is on using Whisper for transcription, T5 for gloss generation, and evaluation pipelines to benchmark model outputs.

All code notebooks and relevant files are hosted at:

📂 **Chapter 5 GitHub Folder:** https://github.com/Elakkiya16/IETGenAI-SLT/tree/main/Chapter%205

(a) **Speech-to-text transcription using Whisper**

This notebook demonstrates end-to-end speech transcription using OpenAI's Whisper model. The pipeline loads a sample .mp3 audio file, converts it to .wav, plays back the audio, visualizes the waveform, and transcribes the speech into text. The transcription is then saved to a local file for downstream gloss prediction.

Notebook Link: 5_1_speech_to_text_whisper_updated.ipynb

Key Code Snippet:

```
#    Step 1: Mount Google Drive
drive.mount('/content/drive')


#    Step 2: Install required packages
#!pip install -q git+https://github.com/openai/whisper.git
#!pip install -q librosa torchaudio pydub
```

```
#      Step 3: Load and convert audio
from   pydub import AudioSegment
mp3_path = '/content/drive/MyDrive/IETGenAI-SLT/Chapter 5/could
_you_please_talk_slower.mp3'
wav_path = '/content/drive/MyDrive/IETGenAI-SLT/Chapter
5/could_you_please_talk_slower.wav'
audio = AudioSegment.from_mp3(mp3_path)
audio.export(wav_path, format= 'wav')


#      Step 4: Visualize waveform
y, sr = librosa.load(wav_path)
plt.plot(y); plt.title('Waveform of Audio')


#      Step 5: Load Whisper and transcribe
model = whisper.load_model('small')
result = model.transcribe(wav_path)
print("Transcription:", result['text'])


#      Step 6: Save transcription
with open ('/content/drive/MyDrive/IETGenAI-SLT/Chapter 5/transcription.txt',
'w') as f:
    f.write(result['text'])
```

Output:

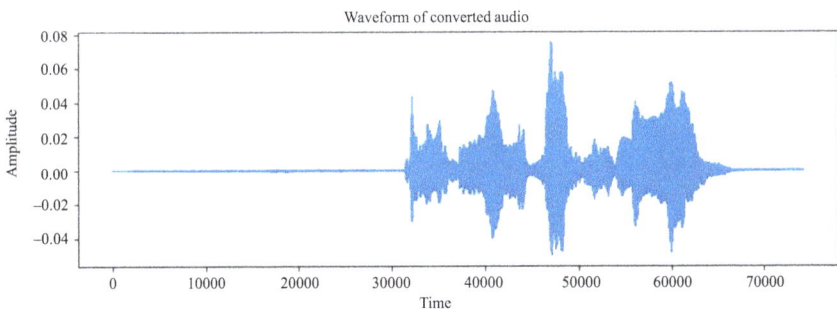

(b) **Text-to-gloss generation using few-shot prompting**

This This notebook uses the Flan-T5 model to convert transcribed spoken sentences into glosses using few-shot prompting. It provides three example pairs in the prompt and requests the model to generate the gloss for a fourth, unseen sentence. This approach demonstrates the generative capability of large language models without any fine-tuning. However, the generated glosses lacked fidelity and alignment with ground truth glosses—hence a fine-tuned model was developed in the next section.

Notebook Link: 5_2_text_to_gloss_generation_fewshot.ipynb

Key Code Snippet:

```python
#     Step 1: Mount Google Drive
from google.colab import drive
drive.mount('/content/drive')

#     Step 2: Install Transformers
#!pip install -q transformers

#     Step 3: Import Libraries
from transformers import AutoTokenizer, AutoModelForSeq2SeqLM
import torch

#     Step 4: Load Flan-T5 Model
model_name = "google/flan-t5-small"
tokenizer = AutoTokenizer.from_pretrained(model_name)
model = AutoModelForSeq2SeqLM.from_pretrained(model_name)

#     Step 5: Generate gloss using few-shot prompting
prompt = """Convert the sentence to sign language gloss:
Example 1:
Sentence: you are good
Gloss: YOU GOOD
Example 2:
Sentence: it was nice chatting with you
Gloss: YOU CHAT NICE
Example 3:
Sentence: Could you please talk slower?
Gloss:"""
inputs = tokenizer(prompt, return_tensors = "pt")
output = model.generate(** inputs, max_length = 30)
gloss = tokenizer.decode(output[0], skip_special_tokens = True)
print("Generated Gloss:", gloss)
```

Output:

```python
# ✅ Step 5: Generate gloss using few-shot prompting
prompt = """Convert the sentence to sign language gloss:
Example 1:
Sentence: you are good
Gloss: YOU GOOD
Example 2:
Sentence: it was nice chatting with you
Gloss: YOU CHAT NICE
Example 3:
Sentence: Could you please talk slower?
Gloss:"""
inputs = tokenizer(prompt, return_tensors="pt")
output = model.generate(**inputs, max_length=30)
gloss = tokenizer.decode(output[0], skip_special_tokens=True)
print("Generated Gloss:", gloss)

Generated Gloss: Could you please talk slower?
```

(c) **T5 Fine-tuned gloss generation**

This notebook demonstrates fine-tuning a T5 model (t5-small) on sentence-to-gloss pairs from the ISL_CLSRT dataset. It includes preprocessing, tokenization, training with HuggingFace's Trainer API, BLEU-based evaluation, and final inference. Generated glosses are stored and evaluated using the fine-tuned model.

Notebook Link: 5_3_t5_finetune_gloss_generation.ipynb

Key Code Snippet:

```python
#    Step 1: Mount Google Drive
drive.mount('/content/drive')

#    Step 2: Install dependencies
!pip install -q transformers datasets evaluate accelerate

#    Step 3: Import Libraries
from transformers import T5Tokenizer, T5ForConditionalGeneration,
TrainingArguments, Trainer, DataCollatorForSeq2Seq
from datasets import Dataset
import pandas as pd

#    Step 4: Prepare Dataset
df = pd.read_csv('/content/drive/MyDrive/IETGenAI-SLT/Chapter
4/isl_train_meta.csv')
df = df[['Sentences', 'gloss_sequence']].dropna().drop_duplicates()
df['input_text'] = 'translate English to gloss: ' + df['Sentences']
df = df.rename(columns={'gloss_sequence': 'target_text'})
dataset = Dataset.from_pandas(df[['input_text', 'target_text']])
dataset = dataset.train_test_split(test_size=0.1)

#    Step 5: Tokenization
tokenizer = T5Tokenizer.from_pretrained('t5-small')
def tokenize_function(example):
    model_inputs = tokenizer(example['input_text'], truncation=True,
padding='max_length', max_length=64)
    labels = tokenizer(example['target_text'], truncation=True,
padding='max_length', max_length=32)
    model_inputs['labels'] = labels['input_ids']
    return model_inputs

tokenized_datasets = dataset.map(tokenize_function, batched=True)

#    Step 6: Define Model & Training
model = T5ForConditionalGeneration.from_pretrained('t5-small')
args = TrainingArguments(
    output_dir='/content/t5-gloss-output-tuned',
    eval_strategy='epoch',
    learning_rate=1e-4,
    per_device_train_batch_size=4,
    per_device_eval_batch_size=4,
    num_train_epochs=10,
    weight_decay=0.01,
    save_strategy='epoch',
    metric_for_best_model='bleu'
)
data_collator = DataCollatorForSeq2Seq(tokenizer=tokenizer, model=model)
```

```
#    Step 7: Trainer Setup
trainer = Trainer(
    model=model,
    args=args,
    train_dataset=tokenized_datasets['train'],
    eval_dataset=tokenized_datasets['test'],
    tokenizer=tokenizer,
    data_collator=data_collator,
    compute_metrics=compute_metrics
)

#    Step 8: Train and Save
trainer.train()
model.save_pretrained('/content/drive/MyDrive/IETGenAI-SLT/Chapter 5/t5-
gloss-finetuned')
tokenizer.save_pretrained('/content/drive/MyDrive/IETGenAI-SLT/Chapter 5/t5-
gloss-finetuned')

#    Step 9: Inference
def generate_gloss(sentence):
    prompt = f"translate English to gloss: {sentence}"
    inputs = tokenizer(prompt, return_tensors="pt").to(model.device)
    outputs = model.generate(**inputs, max_length=32)
    return tokenizer.decode(outputs[0], skip_special_tokens=True)

df['generated_gloss'] = df['Sentences'].apply(generate_gloss)

#    Step 10: Save CSV
output_path = '/content/drive/MyDrive/IETGenAI-SLT/Chapter
5/isl_train_meta_with_generated_glosses.csv'
df.to_csv(output_path, index=False)
```

Output:

```
Generated Glosses:
English: Could you please talk slower?
Gloss: YOU PLEASE TALK SLOWER?
----------------------
English: I am going to the market.
Gloss: I GO TO THE MY MY MY MY.
----------------------
English: What is your name?
Gloss: HOW DO YOU WANT WHAT
----------------------
English: He is a good person.
Gloss: Er ist eine gute Person.
----------------------
```

	Sentences	target_text	input_text	generated_gloss
0	it does not make any difference to me	IT MAKE ANY DIFFERENCE ME DO NOT	translate English to gloss: it does not make a...	I CAN NOT DIFFERENCE
1	tell me truth	TELL TRUTH	translate English to gloss: tell me truth	I RÉAL
2	do me a favour	DO FAVOUR ME	translate English to gloss: do me a favour	DO MONEY FOUR
3	do not worry	DONOT WORRY	translate English to gloss: do not worry	DO NOT HELP ME
4	do not abuse him	HIM ABUSE DONOT	translate English to gloss: do not abuse him	YOU MISS him

(d) **Gloss evaluation using BLEU, WER, ROUGE**

This notebook evaluates the quality of the generated glosses by comparing them against reference gloss sequences. It uses popular NLP evaluation metrics like BLEU, Word Error Rate (WER), and ROUGE-L. The code computes metric scores for each row and summarizes them for global evaluation. The glosses being evaluated are those generated by the fine-tuned T5 model from Section 5.3.

Notebook Link: 5_4_gloss_evaluation.ipynb
Key Code Snippet:

```
# Install necessary libraries
!pip install -q jiwer evaluate rouge_score

import jiwer
import evaluate
import pandas as pd
from nltk import word_tokenize

# Load metrics
bleu = evaluate.load("bleu")
rouge = evaluate.load("rouge")

# Compute metrics for each row
bleu_scores = []
wer_scores = []
rougeL_scores = []

for index, row in df_merged.iterrows():
    generated_gloss = str(row['generated_gloss'])
    reference_gloss = str(row['gloss_sequence'])

    bleu_score = bleu.compute(predictions=[generated_gloss],
references=[[reference_gloss]])
    bleu_scores.append(bleu_score['bleu'])

    wer = jiwer.wer(reference_gloss, generated_gloss)
    wer_scores.append(wer)

    rouge_score = rouge.compute(predictions=[generated_gloss],
references=[[reference_gloss]])
    rougeL_scores.append(rouge_score['rougeL'])

# Store results
df_merged['bleu_score'] = bleu_scores
df_merged['wer_score'] = wer_scores
df_merged['rougeL_score'] = rougeL_scores

# Display metrics
display(df_merged.head())
print(df_merged[['bleu_score', 'wer_score', 'rougeL_score']].describe())
```

Output:

	Sentences	target_text	input_text	generated_gloss	gloss_sequence	levenshtein_distance	token_precision	token_recall	token_f1_score	jaccard_similarity	bleu_score	wer_score	rougeL_score
0	it does not make any difference to me	IT MAKE ANY DIFFERENCE ME DO NOT	translate English to gloss: it does not make a...	I CAN NOT DIFFERENCE	IT MAKE ANY DIFFERENCE ME DO NOT	19	0.5	0.285714	0.363636	0.222222	0.0	0.857143	0.181818
1	it does not make any difference to me	IT MAKE ANY DIFFERENCE ME DO NOT	translate English to gloss: it does not make a...	I CAN NOT DIFFERENCE	IT MAKE ANY DIFFERENCE ME DO NOT	19	0.5	0.285714	0.363636	0.222222	0.0	0.857143	0.181818
2	it does not make any difference to me	IT MAKE ANY DIFFERENCE ME DO NOT	translate English to gloss: it does not make a...	I CAN NOT DIFFERENCE	IT MAKE ANY DIFFERENCE ME DO NOT	19	0.5	0.285714	0.363636	0.222222	0.0	0.857143	0.181818
3	tell me truth	TELL TRUTH	translate English to gloss: tell me truth	I RÉAL	TELL TRUTH	8	0.0	0.000000	0.000000	0.000000	0.0	1.000000	0.000000
4	tell me truth	TELL TRUTH	translate English to gloss: tell me truth	I RÉAL	TELL TRUTH	8	0.0	0.000000	0.000000	0.000000	0.0	1.000000	0.000000

Chapter 6: Generative architectures and evaluation extensions for SLT

Overview
This section provides the complete supplementary code and explanations for Chapter 6, which explores advanced generative architectures, visualizations, and evaluation strategies for SLT. Each notebook aligns with a core section in the chapter, offering runnable demonstrations using ISL_CLSRT and supporting samples.

The code includes:

- Transformer-based inference and embedding visualizations
- Simulated diffusion pipelines with keypoint data
- Multimodal prompt-based generation using BLIP-2
- Model size, task, and feature comparison charts

📁 **Chapter 6 GitHub Folder:** https://github.com/Elakkiya16/IETGenAI-SLT/tree/main/Chapter%206

(a) Transformer variants comparison and embedding visualization
This section aims to compare the performance and output variation of different zero-shot transformer models on gloss-to-text generation. By using a few gloss samples from the ISL_CLSRT dataset, we evaluate model responses from BART and mBART under a shared prompt. The results are extended into a semantic embedding visualization using a t-SNE projection to understand how closely model outputs semantically align with the source gloss inputs.

Notebook File: 1_transformer_variants_comparison.ipynb
Dataset: IETGenAI-SLT/Chapter 4/isl_train_meta.csv

- Columns used: gloss_sequence, Sentences
- A random sample of five gloss-text pairs is selected.
    Models Compared:
- facebook/bart-base
- facebook/mbart-large-50-many-to-many-mmt
- *(Optional)* google/ul2—commented out due to resource constraints

Each model receives a gloss input with the prompt: "translate gloss to English:"

Code Snippets:
Output:

```
Out[3]:
```

	gloss_sequence	Sentences
0	I HELP NOT	i can not help you there
1	I REALLY GRATEFUL	i am really grateful
2	I VERY HAPPY	i am very happy
3	YOU TELL HIM WHAT	what did you tell him
4	I SOMEHOW GOT KNOW ABOUT IT	i somehow got to know about it

```
Out[6]:
```

	gloss_sequence	Sentences	BART-base_output	mBART-50_output
0	I HELP NOT	i can not help you there	translate gloss to English: I HELP NOT	Gloss auf Englisch übersetzen: Ich helfe nicht
1	I REALLY GRATEFUL	i am really grateful	translate gloss to English: I REALLY GRATEFUL	przetłumacz Gloss na polski: Bardzo Cieszę się
2	I VERY HAPPY	i am very happy	translate gloss to English: I VERY HAPPY	przetłumacz Gloss na angielski: Jestem bardzo ...
3	YOU TELL HIM WHAT	what did you tell him	translate gloss to English: YOU TELL HIM WHAT	你告诉他什么
4	I SOMEHOW GOT KNOW ABOUT IT	i somehow got to know about it	translate gloss to English: I SOMEHOW GOT KNOW...	Gloss ins Englische übersetzen: Ich habe es ir...

```
Gloss: I  HELP NOT
Expected: i can not help you there
BART-base Output: translate gloss to English: I  HELP NOT
mBART-50 Output: Gloss auf Englisch übersetzen: Ich helfe nicht
----------------------------------
Gloss: I REALLY GRATEFUL
Expected: i am really grateful
BART-base Output: translate gloss to English: I REALLY GRATEFUL
mBART-50 Output: przetłumacz Gloss na polski: Bardzo Cieszę się
----------------------------------
Gloss: I VERY HAPPY
Expected: i am very happy
BART-base Output: translate gloss to English: I VERY HAPPY
mBART-50 Output: przetłumacz Gloss na angielski: Jestem bardzo szczęśliwy
----------------------------------
Gloss:  YOU TELL HIM WHAT
Expected: what did you tell him
BART-base Output: translate gloss to English:  YOU TELL HIM WHAT
mBART-50 Output: 你告诉他什么
----------------------------------
Gloss: I SOMEHOW GOT KNOW ABOUT IT
Expected: i somehow got to know about it
BART-base Output: translate gloss to English: I SOMEHOW GOT KNOW ABOUT IT
mBART-50 Output: Gloss ins Englische übersetzen: Ich habe es irgendwie gewusst
----------------------------------
```

t-SNE Embedding Visualization:

We visualize embeddings of gloss sequences and model predictions using sentence-transformers/all-MiniLM-L6-v2:

```python
from transformers import AutoTokenizer, AutoModel
from sklearn.manifold import TSNE
import matplotlib.pyplot as plt
import seaborn as sns

embedding_model_name = "sentence-transformers/all-MiniLM-L6-v2"
tokenizer = AutoTokenizer.from_pretrained(embedding_model_name)
model = AutoModel.from_pretrained(embedding_model_name)

# Compute mean pooled embeddings
def get_embeddings(texts):
    inputs = tokenizer(texts, padding=True, truncation=True,
return_tensors="pt")
    with torch.no_grad():
        embeddings = model(**inputs).last_hidden_state.mean(dim=1).squeeze()
    return embeddings.numpy()

# Compute t-SNE and plot
all_texts = df['gloss_sequence'].tolist() + results_df['BART-
base_output'].tolist() + results_df['mBART-50_output'].tolist()
all_embeddings = get_embeddings(all_texts)

tsne = TSNE(n_components=2, perplexity=5, random_state=42)
reduced = tsne.fit_transform(all_embeddings)

import pandas as pd
plot_df = pd.DataFrame(reduced, columns=['tsne_dim_1', 'tsne_dim_2'])
plot_df['text'] = all_texts
plot_df['type'] = ['Gloss'] * 5 + ['BART-base Output'] * 5 + ['mBART-50
Output'] * 5

sns.scatterplot(data=plot_df, x='tsne_dim_1', y='tsne_dim_2', hue='type',
s=100)
plt.title("t-SNE visualization of Embeddings")
plt.grid(True)
plt.show()
```

Output: Sample shown here for five data points

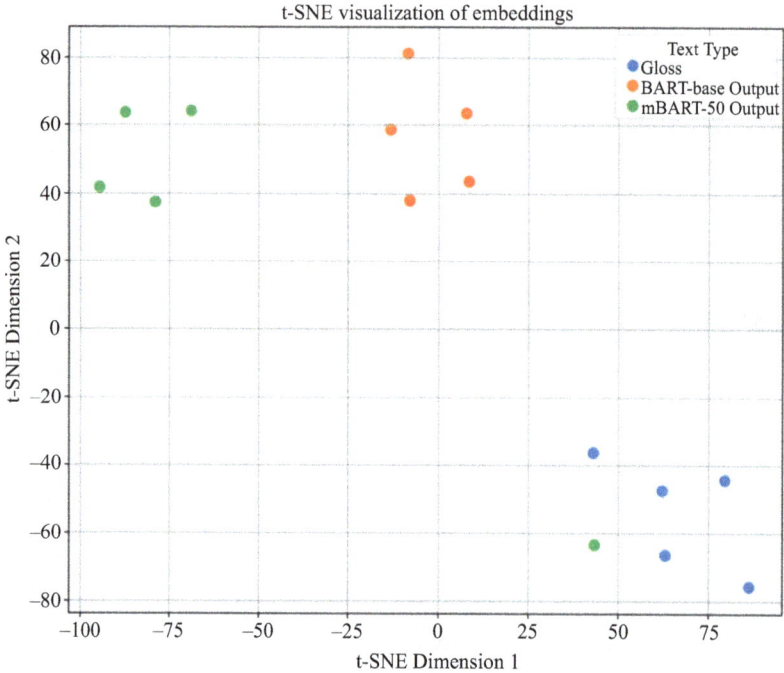

t-SNE visualization of embeddings

(b) **Section 6.2: Simulated diffusion-based denoising on sign keypoints**
This section simulates the effect of adding different types of noise (Gaussian, salt-and-pepper, impulse, occlusion, jitter) to real signer keypoint sequences and demonstrates how a simple iterative denoising strategy can recover cleaner representations. This approximates how generative diffusion models learn to reconstruct data from noise—adapted here to run efficiently in Colab using numpy and matplotlib.

Notebook File: 2_diffusion_demo_simulated.ipynb

Key Dataset: IETGenAI-SLT/Chapter 3/Keypoints/bring_water_for_ me_keypoints.npy

Code Snippet:

```python
# Load and inspect keypoints
from google.colab import drive
import numpy as np
import matplotlib.pyplot as plt

# Mount Google Drive and load keypoints
drive.mount('/content/drive')
keypoint_path = "/content/drive/MyDrive/IETGenAI-SLT/Chapter
3/Keypoints/bring_water_for_me_keypoints.npy"
keypoints = np.load(keypoint_path)
print("Keypoints shape:", keypoints.shape)

# Simulate diffusion process using occlusion noise
def simulate_diffusion(...):
    # See full notebook for implementation
    return noisy_kp, intermediates

noisy_kp, intermediates = simulate_diffusion(
    keypoints,
    noise_type='occlusion',
    noise_probability=0.05,
    alpha=0.2,
    num_denoising_steps=5
)

# Plot original, noisy, and denoised landmark trajectory
landmark_idx = 16
x_idx, y_idx = landmark_idx * 3, landmark_idx * 3 + 1
plt.plot(keypoints[:, x_idx], keypoints[:, y_idx], label="Original")
plt.plot(noisy_kp[:, x_idx], noisy_kp[:, y_idx], label="Noisy", linestyle='--
')
for i, step in enumerate(intermediates):
    plt.plot(step[:, x_idx], step[:, y_idx], label=f"Denoised {i+1}")
plt.legend()
plt.title("Trajectory Denoising: Landmark 16")
plt.show()
```

Output:

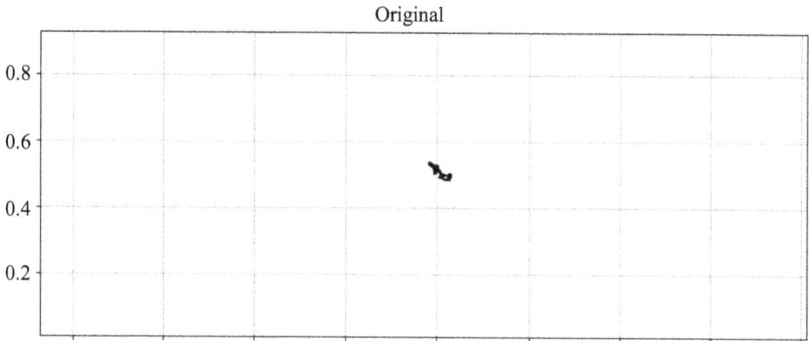

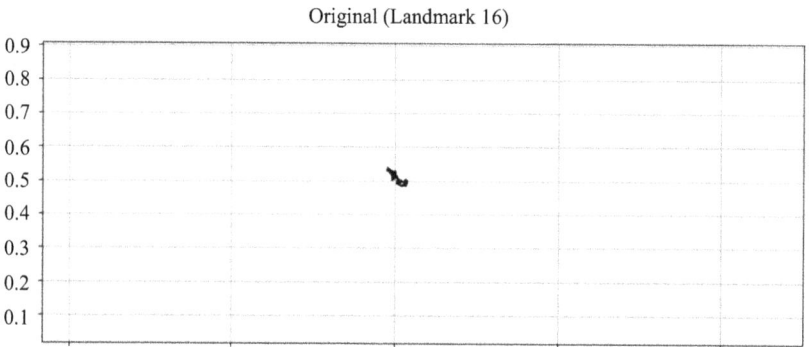

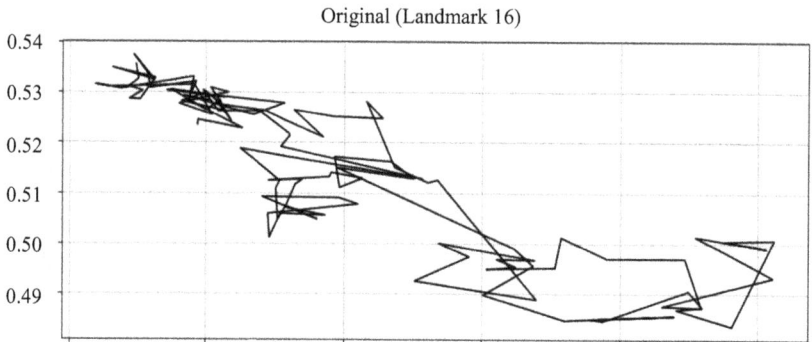

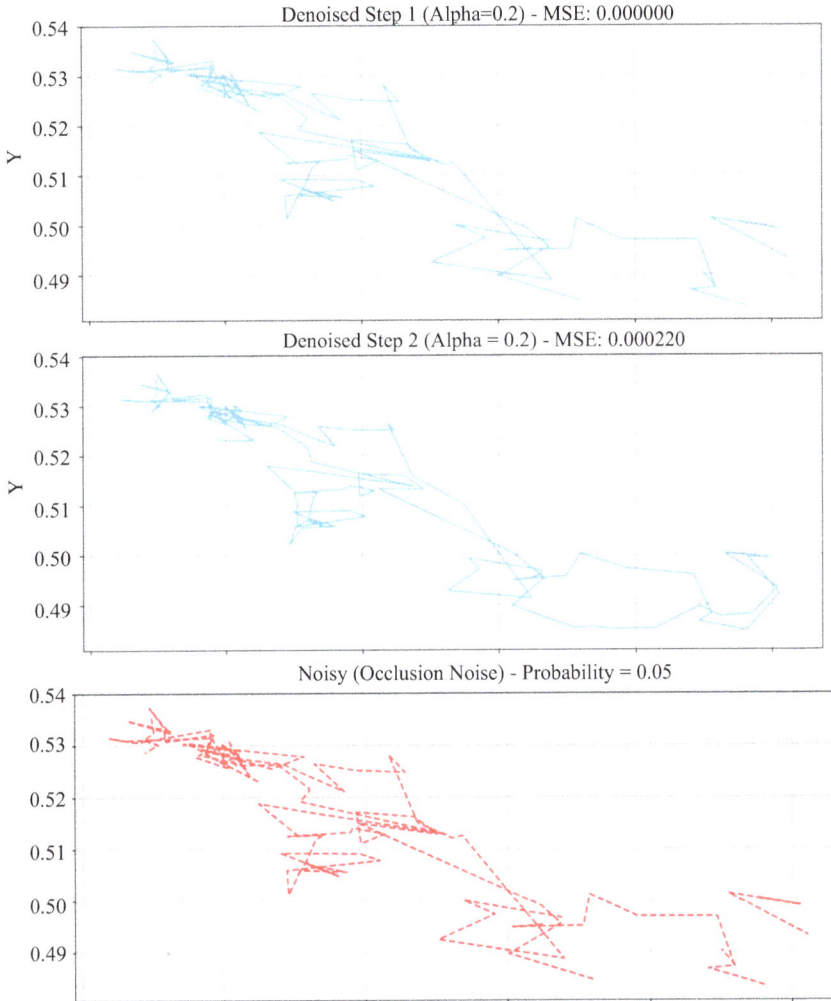

Denoised Step 1 (Alpha=0.2) - MSE: 0.000000

Denoised Step 2 (Alpha = 0.2) - MSE: 0.000220

Noisy (Occlusion Noise) - Probability = 0.05

(c) **Multimodal prompting with BLIP-2 on sign frames**

This section demonstrates how a middle frame from a sign video can be interpreted using the BLIP-2 vision-language model. A signer video is sampled, a frame is extracted, and a text prompt is used to elicit a caption from BLIP-2. This is useful for multimodal SLT setups or cross-modal zero-shot evaluations.

Notebook File: 3_multimodal_llm_flanblip_demo.ipynb

Key Input Video: /content/drive/MyDrive/IETGenAI-SLT/Chapter 3/ Sample Videos/bring water for me (1).MP4

Code Snippet:

```python
from google.colab import drive
import cv2
import torch
from PIL import Image
from transformers import Blip2Processor, Blip2ForConditionalGeneration

drive.mount('/content/drive')

# Extract middle frame from video
video_path = "/content/drive/MyDrive/IETGenAI-SLT/Chapter 3/Sample
Videos/bring water for me (1).MP4"
cap = cv2.VideoCapture(video_path)
frame_count = int(cap.get(cv2.CAP_PROP_FRAME_COUNT))
mid_frame_idx = frame_count // 2
cap.set(cv2.CAP_PROP_POS_FRAMES, mid_frame_idx)
ret, frame = cap.read()
cap.release()

if ret:
    image = Image.fromarray(cv2.cvtColor(frame, cv2.COLOR_BGR2RGB))
    image.save("extracted_frame.jpg")
    display(image)

# Generate caption using BLIP-2
processor = Blip2Processor.from_pretrained("Salesforce/blip2-opt-2.7b")
model = Blip2ForConditionalGeneration.from_pretrained('Salesforce/blip2-opt-
2.7b")
device = "cuda" if torch.cuda.is_available() else "cpu"

prompt = "What is the signer doing?"
inputs = processor(images=image, text=prompt, return_tensors="pt").to(device,
torch.float16)
output = model.generate(**inputs, max_new_tokens=50)
caption = processor.tokenizer.decode(output[0], skip_special_tokens=True)
print("Prompt:", prompt)
print("Model Output:", caption)
```

Output:

Note: The predicted gloss from BLIP-2 may not be accurate or domain-specific. Better quality outputs are possible by applying fine-tuning strategies as demonstrated in Section 5.3.

```
# Run prediction
prompt = "What is the signer doing?"
inputs = processor(images=image, text=prompt, return_tensors="pt").to(device, torch.float16)
output = model.generate(**inputs, max_new_tokens=50)
generated_text = processor.decode(output[0], skip_special_tokens=True)

print("↖ Prompt:", prompt)
print(" ↗ Model Output:", generated_text)

↖ Prompt: What is the signer doing?
↗ Model Output: What is the signer doing?
```

(d) **Model comparison dashboard and visual analysis**

This section provides a comparative overview of different SLT-related generative models using charts and radar plots. The notebook extracts features like parameter size, multilinguality, gloss-to-text/text-to-gloss capability, and hardware compatibility. The analysis is visualized using horizontal bar charts, heatmaps, and polar radar plots.

Notebook File: 4_model_comparison_visual.ipynb
Capabilities Compared:

- Parameter size (in millions)
- Gloss-to-text / text-to-gloss support
- Multilingual vs. monolingual
- Image or sign-motion input support
- Fine-tuning requirement
- Colab-friendliness

Models Included:

- T5, mT5, FLAN-T5, UL2, BART, mBART-50
- BLIP-2 (vision-text)
- SignDiff (motion-aware diffusion model)

Code Snippets:

```python
import pandas as pd
import matplotlib.pyplot as plt
import seaborn as sns
import plotly.graph_objects as go

# Load model data
data = {
    "Model": [...],   # See notebook for full values
    "Parameters (M)": [...],
    "Gloss-to-Text": [...],
    ...
}
df = pd.DataFrame(data)

# Bar chart for parameter size with Colab color flag
colors = [ 'green' if x else 'red' for x in df ["Colab Friendly"]]
plt.barh(df["Model"], df["Parameters (M)"], color=colors)
plt.title("Model Size Comparison")
plt.show()

# Heatmap for binary capability matrix
capability_df = df.set_index("Model").iloc[:, 1:8]
sns.heatmap(capability_df, annot=True, camp="YlGnBu")
plt.title("Model Capability Matrix")
plt.show()

# Radar chart for visual comparison
radar_df = pd.DataFrame({
    "Metric": [...],
    "T5": [...],
    "mBART-50": [...],
    "FLAN-T5": [...],
    "BLIP-2": [...]
})
...
fig.show()
```

Output:

Out[2]:

	Model	Parameters (M)	Gloss-to-Text	Text-to-Gloss	Multilingual	Image Input	Sign Motion	Fine-tuning Required	Colab Friendly
0	T5	220	1	1	0	0	0	1	1
1	mT5	300	1	1	1	0	0	1	1
2	FLAN-T5	250	1	1	0	0	0	0	1
3	UL2	2500	1	0	1	0	0	0	0
4	BART	140	1	0	0	0	0	0	1
5	mBART-50	610	1	1	1	0	0	0	1
6	BLIP-2	1000	0	0	0	1	0	0	0
7	SignDiff	150	0	0	0	0	1	1	0

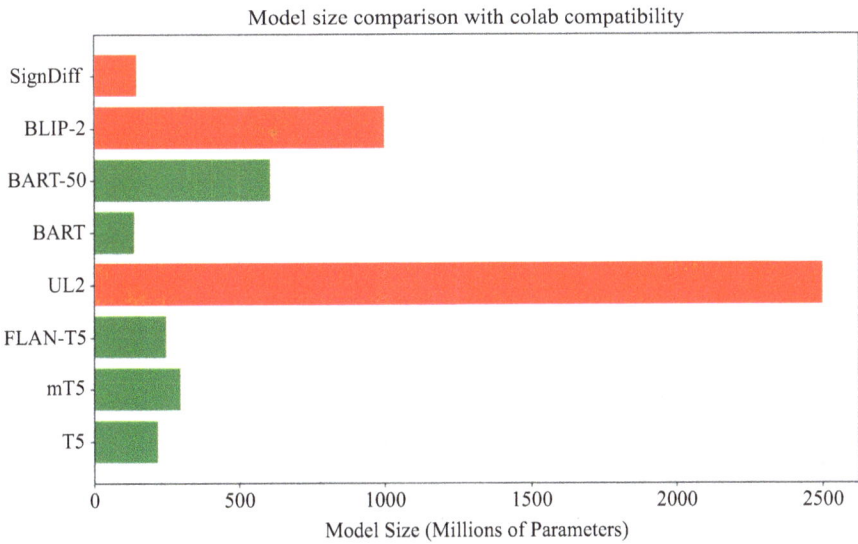

Model size comparison with colab compatibility

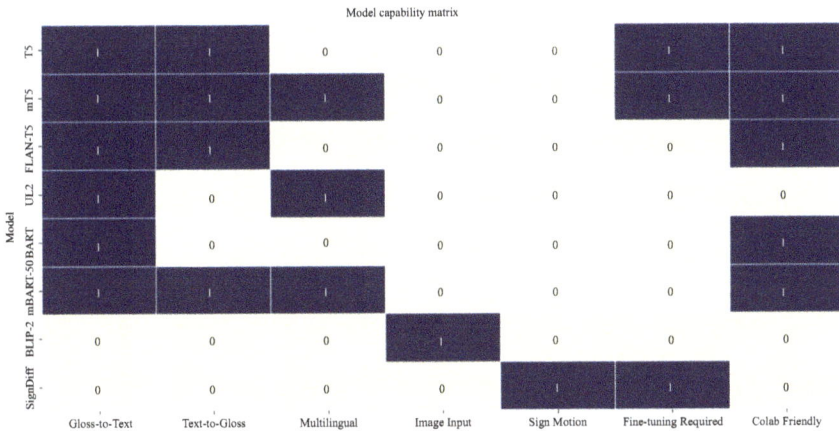

Model capability matrix

Chapter 7: Vision-based sign recognition and pose-based modeling

This section provides complete implementation support for Chapter 7, which explores pose estimation, skeleton-based gesture modeling, and temporal sequence modeling in SLT. The code examples demonstrate how real keypoints extracted from signer videos can be processed using lightweight spatial encoders, graph-based models, and temporal architectures. The section also simulates generative denoising using a simplified diffusion-style loop, allowing readers to visualize the impact of noise and the effectiveness of denoising strategies.

The supplementary notebooks include:

- Keypoint loading and temporal sequence preparation
- GCN/TCN/transformer-based pose encoders
- LSTM vs. TCN vs. transformer for sequential modeling
- Diffusion-driven keypoint denoising and trajectory recovery

🗁 **Chapter 7 GitHub Folder:** https://github.com/Elakkiya16/IETGenAI-SLT/tree/main/Chapter%207

(a) **Visualization of 2D and 3D skeletal poses**
This section demonstrates how 2D and 3D keypoints extracted from signer videos are visualized frame-by-frame. The visualization allows for inspection of pose extraction quality and helps correlate temporal structure in skeletal articulation. The 2D poses are overlaid on original video frames, and the 3D poses are shown using matplotlib's 3D plotting tools.

Notebook File: 1_pose_visualization_skeleton.ipynb

Key Input: - 2D and 3D Keypoints extracted from Chapter 3 - Sample signer video frames

Code Snippet:

```python
# Determine the minimum number of frames for iteration
min_frames_viz_comparison = min (
      len(image_files_viz_comparison),
      extracted_2d_keypoints_comparison.shape[0],
      extracted_3d_keypoints_comparison.shape[0]
)

print(f"Visualizing 2D and 3D skeletal poses for the first
{min_frames_viz_comparison} frames.")

# Iterate through frames to display both 2D and 3D poses
for i in range(min_frames_viz_comparison):
      image_path = image_files_viz_comparison[i]
      frame = cv2.imread(image_path)
      if frame is None:
            print(f"Warning: Could not read image file for visualization:
{image_path}")
            continue

      # Extract 2D keypoints and draw on image
      keypoints_2d_for_frame = extracted_2d_keypoints_comparison[i]
      annotated_image = draw_keypoints_on_image(frame, keypoints_2d_for_frame)

      # Extract 3D keypoints and render with 3D skeleton plot
      keypoints_3d_for_frame = extracted_3d_keypoints_comparison[i]
      fig_3d, ax_3d = draw_3d_skeletal_pose(keypoints_3d_for_frame)

      # Display 2D annotated frame
      annotated_image_rgb = cv2.cvtColor(annotated_image, cv2.COLOR_BGR2RGB)
      plt.figure(figsize=(8, 6))
      plt.imshow(annotated_image_rgb)
      plt.title(f"2D Skeletal Pose - Frame {i+1}")
      plt.axis('off')
      plt.show()

      # Display 3D pose
      fig_3d.suptitle(f"3D Skeletal Pose - Frame {i+1}")
      plt.show()
      plt.close(fig_3d)

print("Finished visualizing 2D and 3D skeletal poses for all frames.")
```

Output:

Sample Frame   2D Skeletal Pose - Frame 10

(b) **Pose-based temporal encoders (GCN, TCN, Transformer)**

This section explores and compares three lightweight temporal encoding strategies—Graph Convolutional Network (GCN), Temporal Convolutional Network (TCN), and transformer—for modeling signer skeletal keypoint sequences over time. Using extracted keypoints from Chapter 3, the notebook creates synthetic gesture sequences and simulates a training setup to measure how each architecture captures spatiotemporal dynamics in sign language motion. The training loss over a demo epoch is visualized for comparison.

Notebook File: 2_pose_temporal_model_comparison.ipynb
Key Input:

- extracted_bring_water_for_me_keypoints.npy keypoint file
- Synthetic sequences and labels for training

Code Snippet:

```python
# Define dummy temporal encoders
class DummyGCN(nn.Module):
    def __init__(self, in_channels, out_channels):
        super().__init__()
        self.linear = nn.Linear(in_channels, out_channels)
    def forward(self, x):
        B, T, J, C = x.shape
        x = x.view(B * T, J, C)
        return self.linear(x).mean(dim=1)

class DummyTCN(nn.Module):
    def __init__(self, in_channels, out_channels):
        super().__init__()
        self.conv = nn.Conv1d(in_channels, out_channels, kernel_size=3,
padding=1)
    def forward(self, x):
        B, T, J, C = x.shape
        x = x.view(B, T, J * C).permute(0, 2, 1)
        return self.conv(x).mean(dim=2)

class DummyTransformer(nn.Module):
    def __init__(self, embed_dim=64, num_heads=4):
        super().__init__()
        self.embed = nn.Linear(33 * 3, embed_dim)
        self.trans = nn.TransformerEncoder(
            nn.TransformerEncoderLayer(d_model=embed_dim, nhead=num_heads),
num_layers=2)
        self.cls = nn.Linear(embed_dim, 32)
    def forward(self, x):
        B, T, J, C = x.shape
        x = self.embed(x.view(B, T, J * C))
        x = self.trans(x.permute(1, 0, 2))
        return self.cls(x.mean(dim=0))

# Simulate data
synthetic_data = torch.randn(10, 50, 33, 3)
synthetic_labels = torch.randint(0, 32, (10,))

# Instantiate models
models = {
    'GCN': DummyGCN(3, 32),
    'TCN': DummyTCN(33 * 3, 32),
    'Transformer': DummyTransformer()
}

# Dummy training loop (1 epoch)
loss_fn = nn.CrossEntropyLoss()
losses = {'GCN': [], 'TCN': [], 'Transformer': []}
for name, model in models.items():
    optimizer = torch.optim.Adam(model.parameters(), lr=0.001)
    total_loss = 0
```

```
for i in range(10):
    x = synthetic_data[i].unsqueeze(0)
    y = synthetic_labels[i].unsqueeze(0)
    optimizer.zero_grad()
    out = model(x)
    loss = loss_fn(out, y)
    loss.backward()
    optimizer.step()
    total_loss += loss.item()
losses[name].append(total_loss / 10)

# Plot comparison
plt.figure(figsize=(10, 6))
for name, loss_list in losses.items():
    plt.plot(loss_list, label=f'{name} Loss')
plt.xlabel('Epoch')
plt.ylabel('Loss')
plt.title('Training Loss Comparison (1 Epoch Demo)')
plt.legend()
plt.grid(True)
plt.show()
```

Output:

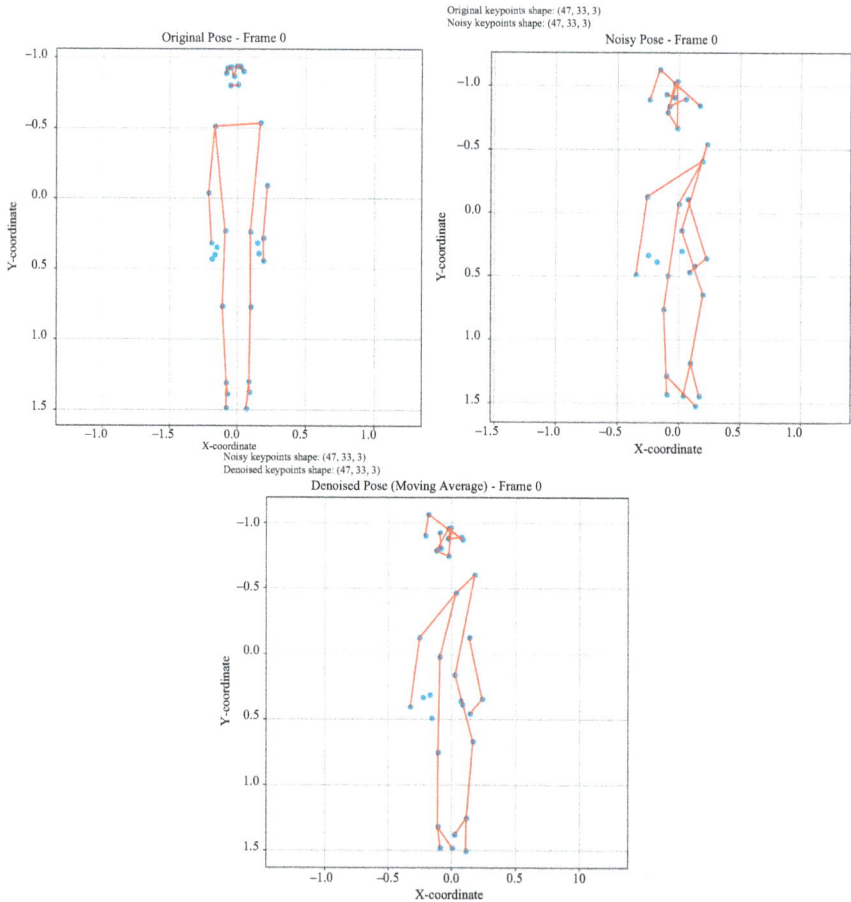

(c) **Section 7.3: Advanced Temporal Models with Evaluation (LSTM, TCN, Transformer)**

This section expands the temporal modeling comparison using more sophisticated sequence encoders: LSTM, TCN, and transformer. Unlike Section 7.2, which employed synthetic sequences and toy architectures, this notebook uses real skeletal pose sequences extracted from Chapter 3, splits them into training/validation/test sets, and compares model performance over multiple epochs. The loss curves and feature dynamics are visualized, and a final t-SNE analysis highlights the learned feature spaces.

Notebook File: 3_temporal_modeling_comparison.ipynb
Key Inputs:

- extracted_bring_water_for_me_keypoints.npy
- Real-time training, validation, and test splits

Code Snippet:

```python
# Instantiate Models
lstm = LSTMModel(input_dim=J*3, hidden_dim=64, output_dim=32)
tcn = TCNModel(input_dim=J*3, output_dim=32)
transformer = TransformerModel(input_dim=J*3)

# Define Loss & Optimizers
criterion = nn.MSELoss()
lstm_optimizer = optim.Adam(lstm.parameters(), lr=0.001)
tcn_optimizer = optim.Adam(tcn.parameters(), lr=0.001)
transformer_optimizer = optim.Adam(transformer.parameters(), lr=0.001)

# Training Loop (abbreviated)
for epoch in range(10):
    lstm_train_loss = train_epoch(lstm, train_dataloader, criterion,
lstm_optimizer)
    tcn_train_loss = train_epoch(tcn, train_dataloader, criterion,
tcn_optimizer)
    transformer_train_loss = train_epoch(transformer, train_dataloader,
criterion, transformer_optimizer)

# Visualization: Loss Curves
plt.figure(figsize=(18, 5))
plt.subplot(1, 3, 1)
plt.plot(lstm_losses['train'], label='Train')
plt.plot(lstm_losses['val'], label='Val')
plt.title("LSTM Loss")
plt.grid(True)
plt.legend()

plt.subplot(1, 3, 2)
plt.plot(tcn_losses['train'], label='Train')
plt.plot(tcn_losses['val'], label='Val')
plt.title("TCN Loss")
plt.grid(True)
plt.legend()
```

```
plt.subplot(1, 3, 3)
plt.plot(transformer_losses['train'], label='Train')
plt.plot(transformer_losses['val'], label='Val')
plt.title("Transformer Loss")
plt.grid(True)
plt.legend()
plt.tight_layout()
plt.show()

# t-SNE Visualization of Classification Outputs
all_outputs = torch.cat((lstm_outputs_cls, tcn_outputs,
transformer_outputs_cls), dim=0).detach().numpy()
tsne = TSNE(n_components=2, random_state=42, perplexity=1)
all_outputs_tsne = tsne.fit_transform(all_outputs)

labels = ['LSTM']*len(lstm_outputs_cls) + ['TCN']*len(tcn_outputs) +
['Transformer']*len(transformer_outputs_cls)
plt.figure(figsize=(8, 6))
for label in set(labels):
    idxs = [i for i, l in enumerate(labels) if l == label]
    plt.scatter(all_outputs_tsne[idxs, 0], all_outputs_tsne[idxs, 1],
label=label)
plt.title("t-SNE of Learned Representations")
plt.legend()
plt.grid(True)
plt.show()
```

Output:

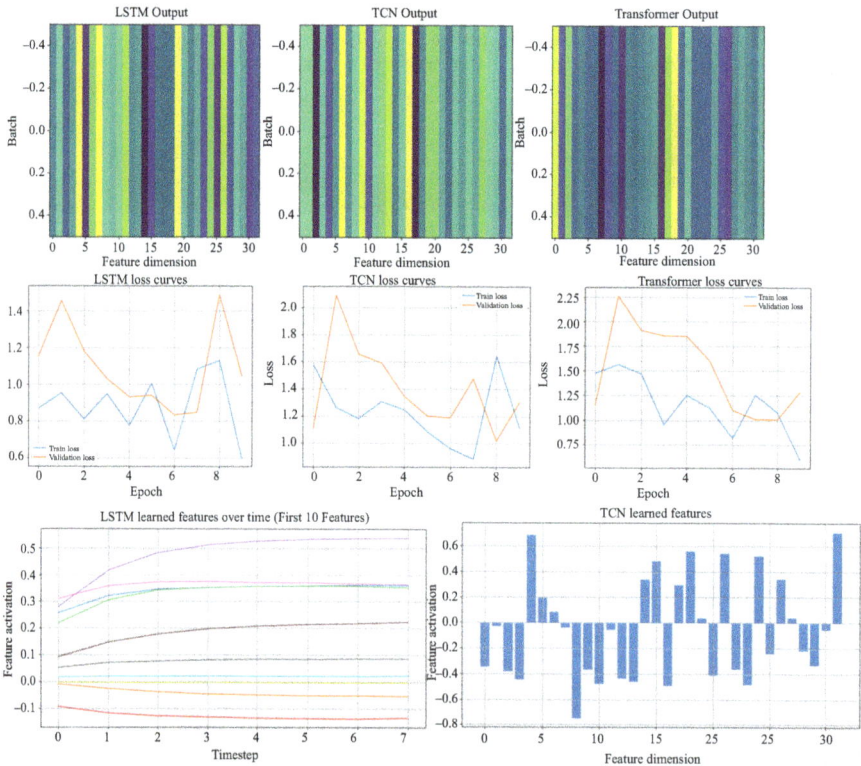

d) **Pose denoising and visualization**

This section demonstrates a complete pipeline for simulating and mitigating temporal noise in 3D signer pose sequences using controlled jitter and iterative denoising. Beginning with real keypoint data extracted in Chapter 3, the notebook introduces temporal jitter through a correlated noise injection function to simulate realistic motion artifacts. A custom denoising function is then applied iteratively across the sequence, progressively refining the temporal consistency of the pose. The notebook also defines anatomical keypoint connections and uses frame-level 2D plots to visualize the original, noisy, and each stage of denoised poses side-by-side—highlighting the impact of each smoothing step.

Notebook File: 4_diffusion_temporal_denoising.ipynb
Key Input:

- extracted_bring_water_for_me_keypoints.npy

Code Snippet:

```python
# Add temporal jitter to simulate motion noise
def add_temporal_jitter(data, noise_level=0.1, correlation=0.5):
    noise = np.random.normal(0, noise_level, data.shape)
    correlated_noise = np.zeros_like(noise)
    correlated_noise[0] = noise[0]
    for t in range(1, len(data)):
        correlated_noise[t] = (1 - correlation) * noise[t] + correlation *
correlated_noise[t - 1]
    return data + correlated_noise

# Apply denoising via temporal smoothing
def denoise(data, alpha=0.2):
    smoothed = data.copy()
    for i in range(1, len(data)-1):
        smoothed[i] = (1 - alpha) * smoothed[i] + alpha * 0.5 * (smoothed[i-
1] + smoothed[i+1])
    return smoothed

# Visualize poses: original, noisy, and multiple denoised frames
fig, axes = plt.subplots(1, len(intermediates)+2,
figsize=(5*(len(intermediates)+2), 6))
plot_pose_2d(original_pose, title='Original', ax=axes[0], line_color='blue')
plot_pose_2d(noisy_pose, title='Noisy', ax=axes[1], line_color='red')
for i, pose in enumerate(intermediates):
    plot_pose_2d(pose, title=f'Denoised Step {i+1}', ax=axes[i+2],
line_color='green')
```

Output:

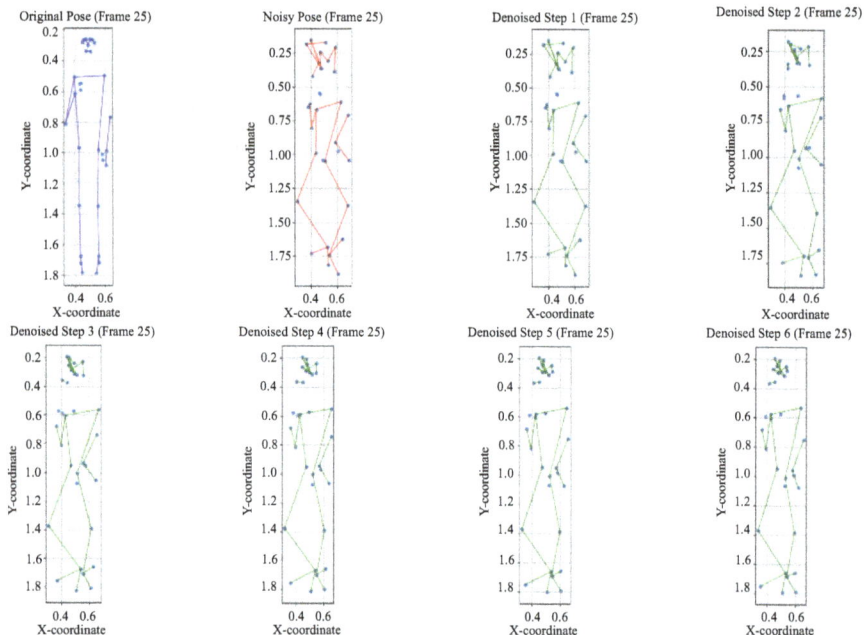

Chapter 8: Sign language generation and video synthesis

This section explores the generation of sign language videos from intermediate representations such as gloss-aligned frame sequences and pose keypoints. It comprises three main synthesis streams:

1. **Sentence-level video synthesis**: Constructing videos directly from sentence-aligned frame folders.
2. **Gloss-level sequence synthesis**: Stitching gloss-wise frames together using gloss-to-frame mappings.
3. **Pose-based video synthesis**: Rendering synthetic sign videos from extracted keypoints (e.g., MediaPipe output).

Each stream supports different stages of the sign language generation pipeline—ranging from visual augmentation and model evaluation to realistic video production from symbolic or spatial data.

GitHub Repository:　https://github.com/Elakkiya16/IETGenAI-SLT/tree/main/Chapter%208

(a) **Video synthesis from pose/gloss frames**

This section demonstrates the synthesis of sign language videos from individual image frames corresponding to glosses or full pose sequences. The video synthesis process involves stitching together static images (frames) to generate fluent sign video clips and evaluating their quality using visual similarity metrics.

Notebook Link: 8_1_video_synthesis.ipynb
Key Inputs and Setup

- Source Frames Directory: /content/drive/MyDrive/IETGenAI-SLT/Chapter 8/ SynthFrames
- Output Video Directory: /content/drive/MyDrive/IETGenAI-SLT/Chapter 8/ Video_Synthesis
- Gloss Mapping File: gloss_mapping.json
- Ground Truth Videos (for evaluation): /content/drive/MyDrive/IETGenAI-SLT/Chapter 3/Sample Videos

Code Snippets:

1. **Frame display for gloss/sentence folders**

```
def display_sample_gloss_frames(gloss_name, num_frames=5):
    ...
    display(Image(data=png.tobytes()))
```

2. Video Synthesis from Frames (Sentencedevel)

```
def synthesize_video_from_frames(folder_name, output_filename):
    ...
    out.write(img)
    out.release()
    display(Video(video_path, embed=True))
```

3. Video Synthesis from Gloss Sequence

```
def synthesize_video_from_gloss_sequence(sentence_id, output_filename):
    ...
    out.write(img)
    out.release()
    display(Video(video_path, embed=True))
```

4. SSIM and PSNR Evaluation Functions

```
def calculate_ssim(ground_truth_video_path, synthesized_video_path):
    ...
    return np.mean(ssim_scores)

def calculate_psnr(ground_truth_video_path, synthesized_video_path):
    ...
    return np.mean(psnr_scores)
```

5. Evaluation Loop Comparing Ground Truth Synthesized Videos

```
for gt_video_path in ground_truth_video_paths_to_evaluate:
    ...
    evaluation_results[sentence_id]["sentence"] = {
        "ssim": ssim_score_sentence,
        "psnr": psnr_score_sentence
    }
```

6. Visualization of Evaluation Results

```
plt.bar(valid_methods, valid_scores, width, label=metric.upper())
plt.title(f'{metric.upper()} Scores for "{sentence_id}"')
```

7. Frame Stitching for Visual Comparison

```
stitched_image_strip =
create_stitched_frames_image(generated_sentence_video_path, ...)
display(Image(data=png.tobytes()))
```

Outputs:

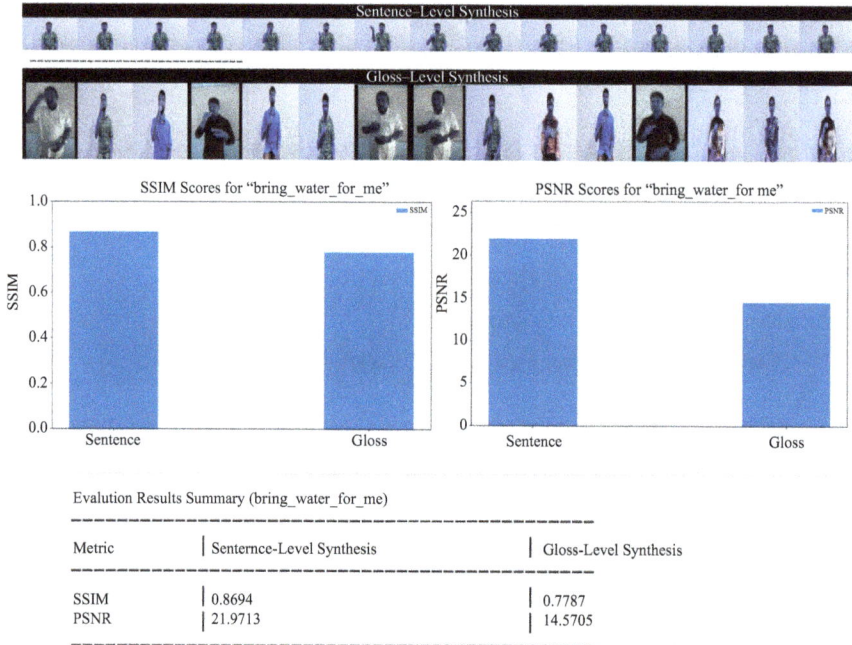

Metric	Sentence-Level Synthesis	Gloss-Level Synthesis
SSIM	0.8694	0.7787
PSNR	21.9713	14.5705

Evalution Results Summary (bring_water_for_me)

(b) Pose-based video synthesis from keypoints

This section demonstrates the process of generating synthetic sign language videos from 3D keypoint data extracted using pose estimation methods (e.g., MediaPipe). The visual output mimics signer motion by rendering poses frame-by-frame and compiling them into a playable video format. Key evaluation is performed through trajectory analysis and temporal smoothness assessment.

Notebook Link: 8_2_pose_sequence_synthesis.ipynb
Key inputs and setup

- Keypoint File: /content/drive/MyDrive/IETGenAI-SLT/Chapter 7/extracted_bring_water_for_me_keypoints.npy
- Output Directory: /content/drive/MyDrive/IETGenAI-SLT/Chapter 8/Pose_Synthesis_Output

Code Snippets
0. Mount drive and import dependencies

```python
from google.colab import drive
import numpy as np
import os
import cv2
import matplotlib.pyplot as plt
from IPython.display import HTML
from base64 import b64encode

drive.mount('/content/drive')
```

1. Load Keypoints and Setup

```python
keypoints = np.load(keypoint_path)
T, D = keypoints.shape
keypoints = keypoints.reshape(T, D // 3, 3)
```

2. Draw Pose on Canvas

```python
def draw_pose(frame, keypoints_frame, connections):
    ...
    return canvas
```

3. Video Generation from Poses

```python
video_writer = cv2.VideoWriter(video_path, fourcc, 10, (640, 480))
for t in range(T):
    frame = draw_pose(t, keypoints[t], pose_connections)
    video_writer.write(frame)
```

4. Display Generated Frames

```python
for i, frame_idx in enumerate(frame_indices_to_display):
    ...
    plt.imshow(img)
```

5. Temporal Smoothness Evaluation

```python
def calculate_temporal_smoothness(keypoints_array):
    ...
    return np.mean(distances)
```

6. Trajectory Plot of Selected Keypoints

```python
plt.plot(keypoints[:, kp_idx, 0], label=f'{name} X')
plt.plot(keypoints[:, kp_idx, 1], '--', label=f'{name} Y')
```

7. Temporal Smoothness Score Interpretation

```python
temporal_smoothness_score = 0.06094
print(f"Temporal Smoothness Score: {temporal_smoothness_score}")
# Interpretation based on expected fluidity of motion
```

8. Keypoint Range Check

```
min_coord = np.min(keypoints)
max_coord = np.max(keypoints)
print(f"Keypoint coordinate range: [{min_coord}, {max_coord}]")
```

9. Moving Average Filter for Smoothing

```
for t in range(T):
    smoothed_keypoints[t] = np.mean(padded_keypoints[start:end], axis=0)
```

Output:

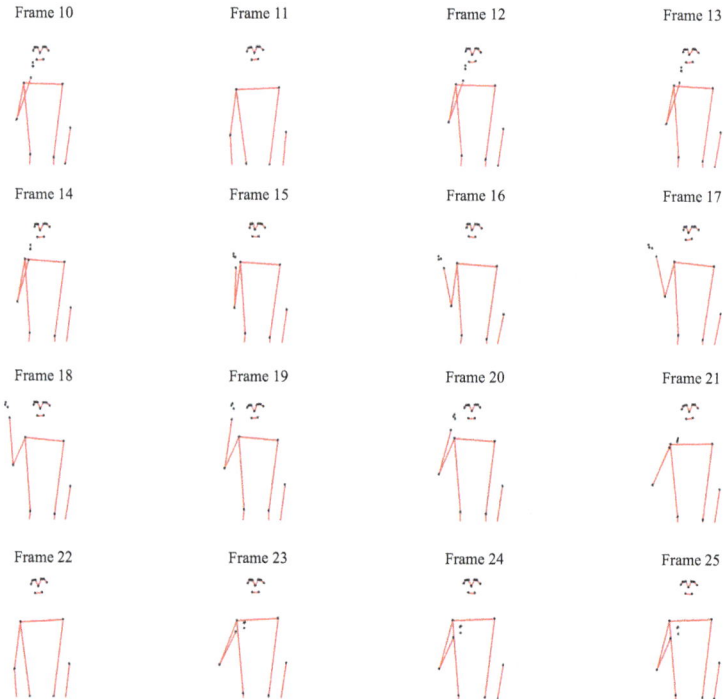

Keypoint coordinate range: [−1.041466474533081, 1.828991413116455]

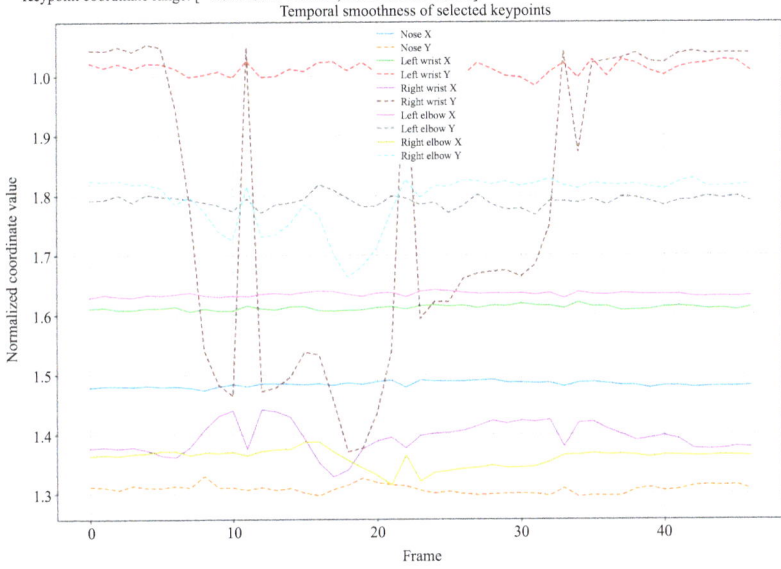

Temporal smoothness of selected keypoints

Generative AI for sign language: recognition, translation, and generation

B.1 Open-source model packages

This document provides a curated list of publicly available pretrained neural network models for sign language processing. These models serve as valuable resources for researchers, developers, and practitioners working on **generative AI for sign language**, spanning three key tasks:

- **Recognition:** Identifying and classifying sign gestures from video or pose data
- **Translation:** Converting signs or glosses to natural language and vice versa
- **Generation:** Producing synthetic sign language videos from symbolic or linguistic inputs

Each entry includes a brief description and a direct link to the GitHub or Hugging Face repository containing downloadable weights and implementation details. These software packages complement the supplementary material presented in the book and offer foundational tools for reproducing, extending, or benchmarking sign language systems.

🧠 Recognition models

Model/library	Task	Link
OpenHands	Pose-based sign recognition across multiple sign languages. Pretrained checkpoints available	GitHub
Gesture-recognition (MediaPipe)	ASL alphabet recognition using MediaPipe landmarks + pretrained TFLite	GitHub
Simba	Mamba augmented U-ShiftGCN for skeletal action recognition	GitHub
CVT-SLR	Contrastive visual-textual transformation for sign language recognition with variational alignment	GitHub
PoseConv3D	3D CNN-based isolated sign recognition using landmark sequences	GitHub
AGMS-GCN	Attention-guided multi-scale graph convolutional networks for skeletal-based action recognition	Github

(Continues)

(*Continued*)

Model/library	Task	Link
SAM-SLR-v2	Skeleton aware multi-modal sign language recognition	Github
MMSkeleton	Pretrained ST-GCN model for action recognition adaptable to sign language gestures	Github
CorrNet_CSLR	Continuous sign language recognition with correlation network	Github

⟳ Translation models

Model/library	Task	Link
SLTUNET	End-to-end sign-to-text transformer model with pretrained weights	GitHub
leakybucket/ SLT-ASL	Gloss-free ASL translation via visio-linguistic pretraining	Hugging Face
rrrr66254/BART_- SIGN2ENG_ finetuned	BART-base fine-tuned on ASL gloss-to-text	Hugging Face
neccam/nslt	Neural sign language translation setup for PHOENIX-Weather 2014T	GitHub
FangyunWei/SLRT	Online continuous recognition and translation; includes pretrained checkpoints	GitHub
DFKI Sign Language gloss-to-text	Gloss-to-text translation tool with training scripts (supports PHOENIX & DGS)	GitHub (GitHub)
TSPNet	Continuous sign-to-text translation with temporal feature pyramid (Phoenix dataset)	GitHub
Frozen pretrained transformers (FPT4SLT)	Gloss-based SLT using frozen pretrained transformers on PHOENIX	GitHub (GitHub, arXiv)
MSKA-SLR/SLT	Multi-stream keypoint attention network for recognition and translation	GitHub (arXiv)
SignSense	Joins video embeddings with T5 to translate ASL to English	Link (UC Berkeley School of Information)
SSVP-SLT	Self-supervised video pretraining for improved translation (ASL)	GitHub
GFSLT-VLP	Gloss-free translation via visual-language pretraining (ICCV 2023)	GitHub

📽 Generation models

Model/library	Task	Link
SignGen (latent diffusion)	End-to-end sign-language video generation from gloss sequences using latent diffusion	GitHub
SignStitchingDemos	Text-to-sign pipeline using SignGAN-based stitching for smooth and natural sign sequences	GitHub
DCGAN-Sign-Language (Arda Mavi)	DCGAN-based sign image generation – suitable for character-level sign visuals	GitHub
SignAvatars	A Large-scale 3D Sign Language Holistic Motion Dataset and Benchmark	GitHub
Advanced SignViP (Sign Video Diffusion)	Multi-condition tokenized video diffusion model for sign generation – includes pretrained weights	GitHub
lang2sign	Pipeline converting English text to ASL video via gloss and pose assembly	GitHub
ShaymaEssghaier/ Sign_language	Gloss-to-video generation from Mediapipe landmarks with Docker packaging	GitHub
sign-language-processing/ spoken-to-signed- translation	End-to-end text → gloss → pose → signed video pipeline supporting multilingual Sg	GitHub
Awesome-Sign-Language (SignLLM)	SignLLM introduces pose generation with Prompt2Sign for multilingual sign production	Github

Glossary of terms

AI (Artificial Intelligence): The field of computer science focused on creating systems capable of performing tasks that typically require human intelligence, such as learning, reasoning, and perception.

ASL (American Sign Language): The primary sign language used in the United States and parts of Canada with its own unique grammar and lexicon.

ASR (Automatic Speech Recognition): A technology that converts spoken language into text; forms the first step in speech-to-sign translation pipelines

Back-Translation: A text data augmentation technique where sentences are translated to another language and back, introducing natural paraphrasing variability.

BCI (Brain–Computer Interface): A technology enabling direct communication between the brain and external devices, explored in hands-free sign language generation.

BERT (Bidirectional Encoder Representations from Transformers): A Transformer-based model providing contextualized word embeddings, useful for sentence representation in text-to-sign tasks.

Bias Mitigation: Techniques to reduce or eliminate demographic or representational biases in AI datasets and models, crucial for equitable sign language systems.

BiLSTM (Bidirectional Long Short-Term Memory): A recurrent neural network that processes input in both forward and backward directions, capturing full sequence context.

BLEU (Bilingual Evaluation Understudy): An *n*-gram overlap metric for evaluating text translation quality, commonly used in sign language translation tasks.

BSL (British Sign Language): The dominant sign language in the United Kingdom, characterized by a two-handed fingerspelling system.

Chereme:	The smallest meaningful unit in sign languages, equivalent to phonemes in spoken languages, composed of handshape, movement, location, orientation, and non-manual signals.
ChrF (Character F-score):	A character-level metric combining precision and recall, suitable for evaluating translations in low-resource languages.
COMET:	A learned metric based on multilingual encoders predicting human judgment scores in translation quality.
Community Co-Creation:	A development approach that involves Deaf community members as collaborators throughout the AI system lifecycle.
Computer Vision (CV):	A field of AI focused on interpreting and processing visual data such as images and videos, widely used in sign language recognition.
Connectionist Temporal Classification (CTC):	A neural network output layer used in ASR to align sequences without explicit timing information.
Consent-Aware AI:	AI systems designed with mechanisms to respect and uphold user consent, especially in data collection and deployment phases.
Cross-Lingual Sign Translation:	AI systems capable of translating between different sign languages (e.g., ASL to BSL) considering cultural and morphological differences.
Dataset:	A structured collection of sign language data (images, videos, multimodal recordings) used to train AI models.
Deaf-Led Research:	Research initiatives where Deaf researchers lead or co-lead the design, execution, and dissemination of sign language AI studies.
Deep Learning (DL):	A subfield of machine learning that uses multi-layer neural networks to automatically learn high-level features from data, essential in video-based sign recognition.
DHH (Deaf and Hard-of-Hearing):	Refers to individuals who are either Deaf or experience varying degrees of hearing loss.

Dialect Representation:	Inclusion of diverse regional and cultural variants of sign languages in datasets and models.
Differential Privacy:	A mathematical framework to ensure individual data privacy by introducing statistical noise, applied in privacy-preserving sign language model training.
Diffusion Model:	A generative AI method that converts noise into structured outputs through iterative denoising; used for high-fidelity sign language video synthesis.
Diffusion Models:	A class of generative models that progressively transform noise into structured data, widely used for pose and video generation.
Dynamic GAN:	A GAN variant optimized for smooth temporal transitions between sign frames, reducing robotic movements.
Encoder–Decoder Architecture:	A deep learning framework where one network (encoder) compresses input into a latent vector, and another (decoder) generates the output; central in translation models.
Ethics by Design:	A framework where ethical principles such as fairness, transparency, and accountability are embedded at every stage of AI development.
Explainable AI (XAI):	Techniques enabling interpretation of AI model decisions, promoting transparency and trust in sign language translation systems.
Face Action Coding System (FACS):	A system to annotate facial expressions using action units, critical for capturing non-manual cues in sign language.
Facial Expression Synthesis:	AI methods to generate realistic facial expressions, ensuring expressive and natural sign language avatars.
Fairness Audit:	The process of evaluating AI systems for demographic and cultural biases, ensuring equitable performance across groups.
Federated Learning:	A decentralized AI training approach where models are trained across multiple devices without transferring raw data, enhancing privacy in sign language systems.

Fingerspelling: A method in sign languages where individual letters are signed using specific handshapes, commonly used for names or technical terms.

(FED) Frechet Expression Distance: A metric measuring the perceptual similarity of facial expressions in generated sign language outputs.

FVD (Fréchet Video Distance): A perceptual metric measuring similarity between real and generated video sequences using pre-trained feature extractors.

G2P-DDM (Gloss-to-Pose Discrete Diffusion Model): A discrete denoising diffusion model generating pose sequences from gloss annotations in sign language generation.

GAN (Generative Adversarial Network): A class of AI models used for generating realistic images or video frames, widely applied in sign synthesis.

GANimation: A GAN-based framework for controlling facial expressions via action units in generated images or videos.

Gloss: The written representation of individual signs, often used as intermediate labels in datasets and translation pipelines.

Gloss Alignment: The process of aligning gloss sequences with pose or text representations, commonly used in translation pipelines.

Gloss-to-Sign Video Generation: The two-stage process converting glosses into pose sequences and subsequently into sign language videos.

HiFiFace: A high-fidelity face synthesis model ensuring expressive and natural facial renderings in sign language avatars.

Homomorphic Encryption: An encryption method enabling computations on encrypted data without decryption, proposed for privacy-preserving inference in sign language AI.

Human-in-the-Loop (HITL): AI systems designed with mechanisms for human oversight, especially critical in high-stakes sign language applications.

Informed Consent: A principle ensuring users understand and agree to data collection and usage, particularly relevant in sign language datasets involving biometric data.

ISL (Indian Sign Language):	The sign language predominantly used in India, exhibiting regional dialects and variations.
Linguistic Parameters:	Components of a sign, including hand-shape, location, movement, orientation, and non-manual features.
LLM (Large Language Model):	Transformer-based AI models trained on large text corpora; increasingly used in cross-modal sign translation.
Log-Mel Spectrogram:	A frequency-domain representation of speech audio on a mel scale with logarithmic compression, used in ASR models.
LPIPS (Learned Perceptual Image Patch Similarity):	A metric comparing deep neural network features between images to quantify perceptual similarity.
METEOR:	A metric incorporating synonym and paraphrase matching for evaluating translation quality with better alignment to human judgment than BLEU.
MFCC (Mel-Frequency Cepstral Coefficients):	A set of audio features representing the short-term power spectrum, mimicking human hearing perception.
MoCoGAN (Motion-Content GAN):	A GAN architecture that separately models motion and content streams for realistic video generation.
Model Cards:	Documentation outlining an AI model's intended use, limitations, and training data characteristics, promoting responsible AI deployment.
MPJPE (Mean Per Joint Position Error):	Measures average Euclidean distance between predicted and ground truth joint coordinates, used in pose estimation.
MSS-GCN (Multi-Scale Skeleton Graph Convolution Network):	A model combining multiple spatial and temporal scales for more expressive gesture representations.
Multimodal Model:	AI models that simultaneously process different types of input (e.g., video, audio, text), crucial for holistic sign language translation.
Natural Language Processing (NLP):	A subfield of AI that enables computers to understand, interpret, and generate human language.

NeRF (Neural Radiance Fields): A volumetric neural rendering technique used for animating photorealistic avatars with view consistency.

Neuroprivacy: The protection of brain-signal data, particularly relevant for BCI-based sign language systems.

NMT (Neural Machine Translation): A method for translating sequences (e.g., text to sign) using deep learning, often involving attention mechanisms.

Non-Manual Signals: Facial expressions, body posture, and head movements that accompany manual signs, conveying grammatical and emotional cues.

On-Device Inference: AI models optimized to run locally on edge devices (e.g., smartphones), improving privacy and reducing latency in sign language translation.

OpenPose: A tool for extracting 2D human pose keypoints (hands, face, body), frequently used in skeleton-based sign language pipelines.

Participatory Design: Design methodologies where end-users, such as Deaf individuals, actively shape AI system development.

PCK (Percentage of Correct Keypoints): Evaluates the proportion of keypoints within a threshold distance from ground truth in pose estimation.

PGMM (Pose-Guided Fine-Grained Sign Language Model): A pose-conditioned generative model incorporating coarse and fine modules for smooth sign video generation.

Pose Estimation: The process of detecting and tracking human body keypoints (e.g., joints, hands) from visual input.

Pose Sequence: A time-ordered set of body, hand, and facial keypoints representing sign language motions.

PoseGAN: A pose-conditioned GAN architecture for generating realistic video frames from pose sequences.

Pretraining: The process of training an AI model on large generic datasets before fine-tuning on task-specific datasets, commonly used in sign language AI.

Prompt Tuning:	A lightweight method to adapt LLMs using task-specific prompts without full retraining, useful for low-resource sign language tasks.
PSNR (Peak Signal-to-Noise Ratio):	A simple pixel-level metric quantifying the reconstruction quality of generated images or videos.
Real-Time Sign Translation:	Systems capable of performing sign language translation with minimal latency, enabling fluid communication.
Responsible AI:	The practice of developing AI technologies in a manner aligned with ethical, legal, and societal values.
RWTH-PHOENIX-Weather 2014T:	A widely used German sign language video dataset annotated with glosses and translations.
SCS (Sign Comprehensibility Score):	A human evaluation score reflecting how understandable generated sign sequences are.
Seq2Seq (Sequence-to-Sequence Model):	A deep learning architecture mapping input sequences to output sequences.
Sign Language Recognition (SLR):	AI systems focused on recognizing sign language from visual input.
Sign Language Synthesis (SLS):	The AI task of generating sign language output, either as gloss-to-sign video or text-to-sign animation.
Sign Language Translation (SLT):	The broader field involving both recognition and generation, converting between spoken/written language and sign language.
SignCLIP:	A contrastive learning model aligning sign videos and text embeddings in a common latent space for retrieval and translation tasks.
SignEdgeLVM:	A quantized low-rank adaptation transformer enabling efficient sign language translation on edge devices.
Signer Adaptation:	Techniques to adjust models to account for signer-specific variations in style, speed, and appearance.
SignGAN:	A GAN-based architecture for generating sign language video frames from pose sequences with temporal consistency.

SignGemma:	A low-latency ASL translation model developed for smartphones focusing on privacy-preserving, on-device translation.
SignGen:	A diffusion-based latent model generating sign videos directly from sentence embeddings without intermediate glosses.
SignLLM:	A large language model architecture fine-tuned for gloss-free sign language translation tasks.
SignMT:	A machine translation framework for spoken-to-sign translation with avatar-based outputs.
SignON Project:	A European research project focusing on inclusive sign language translation incorporating Deaf-led methodologies.
SMPL (Skinned Multi-Person Linear Model):	A parametric 3D human body model used in avatar-based sign language synthesis.
Speech-to-Sign Translation:	The direct conversion of spoken language to sign language gestures, bypassing intermediate text representations.
Spreadthesign:	A multilingual sign language dictionary dataset featuring video-annotation pairs in 44 sign languages, used in zero-shot learning.
SSIM (Structural Similarity Index):	A perceptual metric comparing image structural features, luminance, and contrast.
ST-GCN (Spatio-Temporal Graph Convolutional Networks):	Graph-based neural networks modeling spatial and temporal relationships in pose sequences for sign understanding.
Synthetic Data Augmentation:	The use of AI-generated samples (e.g., via GANs) to expand training datasets and improve model robustness.
TCM (Temporal Consistency Metric):	Measures smoothness of temporal transitions in generated video sequences.
Temporal Dynamics:	The modeling of timing and sequence of signs, crucial for sentence-level sign language translation.
TER (Translation Edit Rate):	Calculates the number of edits needed to convert system outputs to reference translations, considering block shifts.
Topicalization:	A linguistic structure where the topic is highlighted at the start of a sentence, often marked with non-manual signals in sign languages.

Transformer Model:	A deep learning architecture using self-attention mechanisms, core to modern text-to-sign and speech-to-sign translation pipelines.
Transparency Documentation:	The practice of publicly releasing details about datasets and models used in AI systems to promote openness and accountability.
Trustworthy AI:	AI systems that are lawful, ethical, and robust, specifically addressing fairness, privacy, and inclusivity in sign language applications.
Vid2Vid:	A video-to-video translation model synthesizing realistic frames conditioned on pose inputs.
Wav2Vec 2.0:	A self-supervised speech model learning robust audio representations, widely used in speech-to-sign systems.
Whisper:	A multilingual transformer-based ASR model by OpenAI, capable of transcription, translation, and timestamped outputs, suited for real-time sign systems.
Zero-Shot Learning (ZSL):	A method where AI models predict unseen classes (e.g., unknown signs) without explicit training data for them, crucial for low-resource sign languages.

Index

www.ingramcontent.com/pod-product-compliance
Lightning Source LLC
Chambersburg PA
CBHW050512190326
41458CB00005B/1515